D1431923

He Was My Chief

He Was My Chief

The Memoirs of Adolf Hitler's Secretary

Christa Schroeder

Introduction by Roger Moorhouse

Translation by Geoffrey Brooks

Frontline Books, London

He Was My Chief: The Memoirs of Adolf Hitler's Secretary
This edition published in 2009 by Frontline Books, an imprint of Pen &
Swords Books Limited, 47 Church Street, Barnsley, S. Yorkshire, S70 2AS
www.frontline-books.com, email info@frontline-books.com

ISBN: 978-1-84832-536-4

Publishing History
Er war mein Chef: Aus dem Nachlaß der Sekretärin von Adolf Hitler
was first published in German by LangdenMüller in der F.A. Herbig
Verlagsbuchhandlung GmbH, Munich, in 1985. *He Was My Chief* is the first
English language edition of the text and includes a new Introduction by
Roger Moorhouse. Material relating to the author's internment and post-war
relationship with Albert Zoller has been cut from this edition but details of
her trial have been retained. This period in the author's life has also been
summarised in the Introduction by Roger Moorhouse. Additional material has
been abridged due to copyright restrictions.

A CIP data record for this title is available from the British Library.
For more information on our books, please visit
www.frontline-books.com, email info@frontline-books.com
or write to us at the above address.

Typeset by Wordsense Ltd, Edinburgh
Printed in the UK by the MPG Books Group

Contents

Illustrations

Introduction

CHRISTA SCHROEDER WAS AN ordinary woman cast into quite extraordinary times. Born in 1908 in the pretty central German town of Hannoversch Münden, she trained as a stenotypist before moving to Munich in 1930. Whilst there, she replied to an advertisement in the newspaper for a secretarial position at the headquarters of Hitler's stormtroopers – the SA. The association thus forged would be a lasting one. Graduating to a position as Hitler's personal secretary in 1933, Schroeder would be part of the Führer's entourage for the following twelve years, right up the bitter end in 1945.

This memoir, compiled from contemporary notes and letters as well as postwar reminiscences, is Christa Schroeder's own record of those extraordinary times. It gives the reader a fascinating insider's viewpoint on many of the salient events of the Third Reich. She expounds not only on political developments such as the Röhm Purge of 1934 or the attempt on Hitler's life in July 1944, but also on military matters from the Polish campaign through to the final collapse of the Nazi regime, which she experienced from the comparative safety of Berchtesgaden.

Yet it is not primarily for her political insights that Schroeder is of interest. Her experiences certainly ranged widely, but there is a backbone to her book which is not concerned with grand politics

– a subject about which she claimed to have little knowledge or understanding – rather it gives an intimate view of the workings of Hitler's household and of the various characters working therein. In this regard, there is a refreshingly gossipy, chatty flavour to the book, as it illuminates some of the foibles and idiosyncrasies of members of Hitler's entourage, as well as addressing more substantial themes such as Hitler's often difficult and mysterious relationships with women.

Hitler looms large in the book, of course. As secretary to the Führer throughout the Third Reich, Schroeder knew Hitler as well as anyone and was extremely well placed to comment on his behaviour and personality. Indeed, Schroeder was herself no shrinking violet, and often spoke rather too bluntly to her employer. In the winter of 1944, for instance, she asked Hitler to his face if he still believed that the war could be won. Indeed, it seems that her candour almost became her undoing when she was ostracised by Hitler for a number of months after making the mistake of publicly contradicting him once too often. Yet, for all that, Schroeder's is nonetheless a not unaffectionate portrait. Indeed, her presentation of the leader of the Third Reich as a rounded, three-dimensional, human being – with likes and dislikes, hopes and fears – is fascinating. She details his bourgeois manners, his vehement abstemiousness, his mood swings, even his sense of humour. Her description of Hitler is not of the wide-eyed fanatic, so familiar to the modern reader; rather he appears as a generous – even avuncular – benefactor, a kisser of ladies' hands; a man who chatted easily with his secretaries and had a passion for Bavarian apple cake.

For all its gossipy revelations, however, there is a dark side to Schroeder's story. For one thing, the 'tone' of her book is utterly unapologetic; there is nothing, for example, of the sense of perspective or mea culpa that one finds in the memoirs of Hitler's other secretary, Traudl Junge – who famously concluded that 'we should have known' about the horrors of the Third Reich. This lack of remorse is, in part, a consequence of Schroeder's rather cantankerous character: even the editor of this volume, Anton Joachimsthaler, described her as 'tough', 'extremely critical' and even 'wounding' in her ways.

Yet there is more to it than that. Schroeder claimed – convincingly, I think – to have known nothing of the horrors of the Nazi regime and of the crimes being committed in Germany's name. One might legitimately ask how a secretary in the Reich Chancellery could have long remained ignorant of the Holocaust. Yet, for all her closeness to the epicentre of power in Hitler's Germany, Schroeder would have argued that hers was a rather mechanical task largely restricted to the typing up of speeches and mundane daily correspondence, in which such events were rarely mentioned, or else couched in an impenetrable fog of euphemisms and double-speak. The most sensitive of instructions, of course, would always have been transmitted in person, thereby leaving little or no 'paper trail'. Moreover, Schroeder was if anything *too* close to Hitler and the Nazi elite – too close to gain an objective view, too close to question the propaganda, too close perhaps to catch a glimpse of the ugly truth. Confined in the rarefied atmosphere of Hitler's 'court' – in the eye of the Nazi storm – Schroeder was effectively insulated from the grim realities of the world outside.

As the logical corollary to this ignorance, Schroeder found it difficult to imagine that she personally had done anything reprehensible. Nonetheless, classified by the Americans as a war criminal of the first order, she was interned for three years after 1945. This treatment evidently rankled. As she complains in this book: 'Whether my guilt was as great as my expiation is something I do not know to this day.'

There were further grounds for her bitterness. After the war, she was interrogated at length by Frenchman Albert Zoller, who was serving as a liaison officer with the US Seventh Army. Zoller typed up and embellished his interrogation notes and published them under his own name as *Hitler Privat*, in 1949, describing the work as the memoir of Hitler's 'secret secretary', but with Schroeder receiving no credit and, of course, no royalty. She would later complain that Zoller had also taken many of the material mementoes – Hitler's sketches etc. – that she had been given or had rescued from the ruins of the Third Reich. But, what rankled most perhaps, was that she claimed that he had also appended her name to various comments, opinions and anecdotes that she had never given.

Christa Schroeder's memoir was published, in German, soon after her death, aged seventy-six, in 1985. Understandably perhaps, given the injustice that she clearly felt, the book had a hint of obsession about it. She waxed bitterly lyrical about Zoller's perfidy, and appended lists of errors and statements that, she said, had been falsely attributed to her. As a self-confessed 'fanatic for truth', it seems, she was desperate to set the record straight, to put an end to what she perceived as her exploitation and misrepresentation by a generation of historians and writers.

Despite being a critical and commercial success, however, Schroeder's book did not find an English language edition until the present volume, over two decades later. This is peculiar; especially if one bears in mind the reception accorded to the memoir of Hitler's other secretary – Traudl Junge's *Until the Final Hour* – which was published to great acclaim in 2002. It may have something to do with Schroeder's rather prickly and unrepentant nature, and with the precise instructions that she left regarding how the memoir was to be prepared and published. It may also be that such personal testimony was simply out of favour in the mid 1980s. History, at that time, was at the height of its postmodernist spasm and was perhaps too busy finding obscure new perspectives and spurious grand narratives to bother too much with the simple memoirs of a simple secretary.

But there may be another reason why Schroeder's memoir was overlooked by British publishers in the 1980s. Two years before its original publication, the world had been stunned by the grand hoax of 'The Hitler Diaries', supposedly discovered in the GDR, but quickly demonstrated to have been crude forgeries. In the process, of course, a number of historians, publishers and newspapers were embarrassed. And, in the aftermath, many of those same publishers recoiled when they were presented with any work that they considered to be even vaguely similar.

Thankfully, such once-pressing concerns are now history themselves. And, moreover, historical tastes have shifted once again and memoirs and first-hand accounts are once more seen as being of particular value. Though Christa Schroeder was perhaps not as insightful or perspicacious as the modern reader might have hoped, her memoir will certainly not disappoint, not least because so few memoirists stood as close as she did to the very heart of the Third Reich. Her book is engagingly written and contains much of interest: from thumbnail sketches of the characters of Hitler's entourage to an insider's view of the great events of the day, and an illuminating, highly personal portrait of Hitler himself. It fully deserves its place in the canon of first-hand accounts of the rise and fall of the Third Reich.

Roger Moorhouse, 2009

Editor's Introduction

A FEW YEARS AGO I was asked by Walter Frentz, a former Luftwaffe newsreel correspondent attached to Führer-HQ, if I would escort a lady to meet him in Munich. In this way I chanced to know Frau[1] Emilie Christine Schroeder. As her first name, uncommon in Germany, suggests, she was no ordinary person and did not resort to cliché. Educated, musically gifted, always on the quest for truth and the meaning behind matters, she was also tough and extremely critical of people, the modern environment, of herself and her own past. Sometimes she could be direct and wounding in her own way, but the rough exterior hid a nervous, often insecure and sensitive being within.

I was the author of many technical and historical works and was working at that time on a book about Hitler's planned broad-gauge railway for Europe. Thus Frau Schroeder found in me somebody with whom she could converse about her life, her past and Hitler himself. Frau Schroeder was a fanatic for truth. In a newspaper cutting which I found later in her papers she had underscored twice

---

1 Christa Schroeder never married. The practice of addressing women as 'Fräulein' or 'Frau' depending on their marital status was current into the 1970s but has become discontinued in modern Germany as part of the process of female emancipation, and all women out of their teens are now accorded the prefix 'Frau' irrespective of their civil status.

in red the following passage, adding a marginal note: 'This is the correct definition of Truth.'

> The truth is an amazing thing. You can bend it, hide it, trim it, pluck the feathers from it and shake it to pieces. But you can't kill it. Eventually it always resurfaces, one day somewhere it breaks through. There are times when the truth – frequently in the interests of a State – grows dim, when it becomes a target for destruction. But some day it reappears. The same may be said for our private and business lives.
>
> 'Lies and deceit plough the soil of the world' is an old German proverb. The lie will always be with us, but we should never lose patience in waiting for Truth's hour. 'The truth may sink, but it never loses its breath,' reads an inscription over the portals of a patrician's house: and we should remember the old saying, 'The truth must have a thick skull, for how many times is it stood on its head?'

Christa Schroeder wanted to get to the very roots of a thing; she hated distortions, but basically could never come to terms with her own past. Whether that would actually be possible after twelve years close to Hitler is another matter.

Her relationship with the Nazi party

She was not a National Socialist in the true sense. She often said: 'If the job offer had been made to me in 1930 by the KPD and not the NSDAP, perhaps I would have become a Communist.' She was a woman who looked at things critically, observed them, pronounced on them, could analyze them, and so found herself tossed back and forth between Hitler, the friends and events of yesteryear, the Nazi system, the consequences of the war and the cruelty of the extermination programme for the Jews. In her notes she stated:

After three months I was told that I had to join the Party since only NSDAP members could be employees. Since I knew nothing of politics and did not want to lose my job I signed the application form and all was well. It changed nothing in my life. As I was a member of the Reich Leadership Section I never came into contact with the small centres and was only asked once or twice to take part in gatherings and suchlike. I suppose I went a few times to the big assemblies in the Zirkus Krone, but I felt nothing in common with the speakers or the masses and I must have appeared terribly stupid.

An alternative view of her appears in the US Army intelligence report of 22 May 1945[2] in which it is reported that: 'Mr Albrecht . . . interrogated her. She was rather stupid, dumpy and an ardent Nazi.'

In her shorthand notes, Frau Schroeder wrote of this event: 'After the interrogation was over, Lt Albrecht brought me back to Hintersee and had a very friendly conversation with me. When I expressed regret that my whole life, all the years, had been for nothing, he replied, "No, everything has a purpose, nothing is wasted." He added that his wife had assured him so.'

Her letters and postwar notes

In her note of 18 February 1979, Frau Schroeder perhaps admits her inner turmoil, the sporadic progress of her self-set task and her quest for truth:

For years everybody has urged me to write down everything I know about Adolf Hitler. Some time ago I began transcribing my shorthand notes from 1945. But instead of devoting myself to the task, and working industriously at it for two to three hours daily,

2 Univ. Pennsylvania, Charles Patterson Van Pelt Library, microfilm 46M-11FU US Army 101st Airborne Division, Counter-Intelligence Corps, 22.5.1945.

I became aware repeatedly of the many layers of Hitler's character. It plunged me into depression.

I was in that psychic condition which the Russian author Ivan Goncharov described in his 1859 novel about Ilya Ilyich Oblomov, who constantly planned great things for tomorrow or the day after, but then proceeded with his life 'in a certain capricious torpor', preferably spending his time in bed, always exhausted and drunk thinking over his fine plans, intentions and prospects.

It was my mistake to assume that I could unveil the 'true face' of Adolf Hitler. It is simply impossible, because he had so many.

She considered that in Hitler's personality of many layers and pluralities the spectrum extended from extreme kindness and concerned attentiveness to ice-cold brutality. In her copy of the disputed Zoller book mentioned at greater length below she corrected her copy of the text at pages 10–12 and left the following passage standing:

For a long period he was the only string-puller behind all events which occurred in the Reich. Everything to him was calculation and subtlety. To his death he played the role of the theatrical director. Hitler had the gift of a strange magnetic radiance. He had a sixth sense and a clairvoyance which was often decisive for him. He weathered all dangers which threatened him, observed in some mysterious way the secret reactions of the masses, and fascinated his conversation partners in a manner which defies description. He had the sensitivity of a medium and the magnetism of a hypnotist. If one reflects on the series of extraordinary strokes of luck which kept him safe during all the many attempts on his life, and from which he concluded that Providence had selected him for his mission, then one can perceive the significance which the imponderables assumed in his life. These were, I believe, the most prominent characteristics of the peculiar person who almost undermined the basic foundations of the world. There was not just one Hitler, but several Hitlers in one person. He was a mixture of lies and truth, of faithfulness and violence, of simplicity and luxury, of kindliness and brutality, of mysticism and reality, of the artist and the barbarian.

She asked her friend Anni Brandt for her impression:

This morning Anni Brandt[3] confirmed it to me. At the beginning of March 1945 she – Anni – was invited by Eva Braun to tea at the Reich Chancellery, which she took with Adolf Hitler. When a servant appeared and whispered to her that her husband had arrived and was waiting for her downstairs, Hitler wanted to know what had been said. He was always inquisitive when something was whispered, and if one wanted to arouse his interest in anything, the simplest way was to whisper about the matter to a neighbour and one could rest assured that Hitler would enquire.

Shortly after the attempt on Hitler's life in July 1944, Dr Karl Brandt was sent packing. He was obliged to leave the Rastenburg FHQ and had not seen Hitler subsequently. Now Hitler sent for him. Hitler was unsure and at first could not look Dr Brandt in the eye, but then began to converse with him as they used to do in the past. All the more incomprehensible for me was it therefore when only weeks later Hitler sentenced him to death.[4] Thus it is

---

3 Anni Brandt née Rehborn (b. Langenberg 25.8.1904). German Ladies' national swimming champion (crawl and backstroke) during 1923–9 period; 1928 Olympic Games Amsterdam; introduced to Hitler 1925 and from then until 1945 part of his intimate circle at the Berghof. Married surgeon Dr Karl Brandt 17.3.1945, one child: taken into US custody April 1945.

4 SS-Gruppenführer Dr (med.) Karl Brandt (b. 8.1.1904 Mühlhausen, Alsace, d. 2.6.1948 Landsberg Prison, executed as war criminal). Dr Brandt was arrested by the SS on 16 April 1945 for defeatism after sending Hitler a letter on 1 April 1945 expressing doubt in final victory, and sending his wife and child to Bad Liebenstein so that they would fall next day into American and not Russian hands. On 17 April 1945 he was condemned to death by court martial but was still at Kiel awaiting execution when Hitler's death was announced, and Speer had him freed.

understandable that at Ludwigsburg, while amongst the doctors being transported to Belgium for war crimes trials, Professor Brandt, in reply to my question, 'What was the boss, a good or evil man?' should answer spontaneously, 'He was a devil!

Frau Schroeder concluded:

> Thirty-three years have now passed since then. I was never a person interested in politics. It was only Hitler as a man who interested me then: what I experienced of him under dictation; in his personal presence at the evening tea sessions in the 'staircase room' of the Radziwill Palace; in the larger circle at the Berghof at mealtimes or at midnight around the fireplace: and later during the war in the Führer-HQs at tea after the nightly military situation conferences. How I saw everything then – that is what I want to write about.

Frau Schroeder worked only sporadically at her notes. She had a hackneyed book marked 'Shorthand Exercises' on the cover and a lever arch file for manuscripts. The old book contained her shorthand notes made during the period of her internment postwar. The last entries are dated August 1948. They were taken down in Stolze-Schrey shorthand and not, as *Quick* magazine (Issue 19, 15 May 1983, p.156) alleged, 'in a secret script which only Frau Schroeder could read'. At this juncture I would like to thank the shorthand historian Herr Georg Schmidpeter who transcribed those stenographic notes not already typed up by Frau Schroeder. Besides these she had many other notes, observations and slips of paper with jottings noted down as items were remembered or on which she was working currently. By the year of her death, 1984, she had cast 95 per cent of her shorthand notes into typed folios of 162 pages for a manuscript. Some of these pages date from the 1976–84 period and do not appear in the shorthand notes.

The genesis of the Zoller Book

In the first days of her confinement at the US Army Internment Camp Augsburg in May 1945, Frau Schroeder was interrogated by Albert Zoller, a French liaison officer to the US 7th Army. He asked her to write down everything she knew about Hitler, the circumstances of Hitler's life and events during the Nazi period. In 1949 after her release Zoller informed Frau Schroeder that he intended to publish her notes under her name. She was supplied with some limited manuscript material to the book but when Zoller failed to produce the entire manuscript despite repeated requests she refused him permission to use her name as author.

In 1949 the book was published using Zoller's name as author. The original language was French with a translation into German, the result being published by Droste Verlag, Düsseldorf, under the title *Hitler privat – Erlebnisbericht seiner Geheimsekretärin*. The Foreword depicted the person and activity of the 'Secret Secretary' in such a manner as to make it seem that Frau Schroeder was author of the book, but had allowed Zoller to appear as author with her full agreement.

Parts of the text foreign to her notes had been interpolated. The German version was a re-translation from French of the original German draft, this resulting in frequent shifts of meaning. Statements were attributed to Frau Schroeder regarding military-technical matters of which she had no knowledge, or of conversations at military situation conferences which she never attended, and so on. She recognized at once that the falsely attributed statements must have been made by prominent arrestees at the Augsburg Internment Camp, such as photographer Heinrich Hoffmann or adjutant Julius Schaub or others whom Zoller had also interrogated. She did not dispute the veracity of what was alleged in these statements, only that she disputed having spoken or written them herself.

Frau Schroeder worked through a copy of Zoller's book striking out all passages which did not originate from herself. She claimed 160 to 170 pages as her own work and 68 to 78 pages as from other sources, or as being individual passages re-worded or given a different slant by Zoller. In a letter dated 21.11.1972 to Frau Christian she explained:

> It is interesting how Zoller put words in my mouth which are mythical and in reality must have originated from his confidential conversations with General Staff officers which he obtained in his capacity as an interrogation officer. It was quite improper for him to have used these as material for a private publication.
>
> His crafty solution was to put these statements into the mouth of 'the Secret Secretary' where to the outsider and uninformed they appear credible. Here is an example. He writes – puts into my mouth – 'If in military situation conferences the conversation turned to rumours about the mass murders and torture in the concentration camps, Hitler would refuse to speak, or brusquely halt the talk. Only seldom would he respond, and then to deny it. In front of witnesses he would never have admitted the inhuman harshness of the orders he had given. One day some generals asked Himmler about the atrocities in Poland. To my surprise he defended himself with the assurance that he was only carrying out Hitler's orders. But he added immediately: 'The person of the Führer must under no circumstances be mentioned in that connection. I assume full responsibility.' It was moreover self-evident that no Party member, no SS-Führer no matter how influential, would have dared to have undertaken such far-reaching measures without Hitler's agreement . . .

'The foregoing', Frau Schroeder concluded, 'seems absolutely credible, and it originates, and can only have originated, from somebody present at the military situation conferences who did not want to be named, and so the "Secret Secretary" said it. I do not think you could get more crafty than that.'

My own involvement begins

In 1982 Frau Schroeder asked me if I wanted to publish her notes with my own commentaries. This surprised me. I knew of her bad experience with the Zoller book and that she did not want the notes published in her lifetime. Another of her reasons for having delayed publication was that no sooner were memoirs published than they would be pulled to pieces by contemporaries, a sin of which she was of course guilty herself with respect to the books of Linge, von Below, Hoffmann, Krause, Henriette von Schirach and so on. Frau Schroeder wanted no remuneration for the notes. She declined money or reward in kind, emphasizing repeatedly that her pension was sufficient, she had no special wants and was content with what she had. She had no interest in selling the notes. That remained the position until her death although there was no shortage of offers.

When I failed to reply promptly to her enquiry the matter was dropped for a considerable period. As far as she was concerned that was an end to it. Once Frau Schroeder returned from hospital after the removal of a carcinoma, however, she raised the matter of the notes again, and of my compiling them together with a commentary. At the time she could not flex her fingers and had difficulty in typing. She also tired very quickly. The day before she left for the Schlossberg Clinic at Oberstaufen she invited me to call and we spoke in detail about the publication of her notes in the presence of the female friend with whom she was to travel on the morrow. On her return by ambulance she was clearly seriously ill. A few days later she telephoned and asked me to drop by. After explaining that she was to be re-admitted to hospital she gave me a large, old black trunk containing her literary bequest. She was anxious that under no circumstances 'should her entire literary estate fall into the hands of journalists, or no matter who,' and I should remember what she had always said and wanted.

Complying with her wish that her notes should be published after her death, and recognizing that they contained much interesting material, I arranged them in order and supplied the commentary. If the book does not always appear to flow smoothly, the reason is that it was necessary to use incomplete pages of manuscript and single detail notes just as Christa Schroeder prepared them and wanted them published.

Who was Christa Schroeder?

Emilie Christine Schroeder was born on 19 March 1908 in Hannoversch Münden. Her relationship with her mother was not close. The mother was a single parent with a very strong personality who failed to provide her daughter with the warmth and affection she probably craved. The mother died in 1926 when Christa was 18, leaving her orphaned and alone.

After completing secondary education on 11 April 1922 she began a three-year commercial training course at a firm owned by distant relatives, C.F. Schroeder Schmiergelwerke KG, in her home town. Meanwhile she also attended the Commercial Career and Business School, completing her training on 1 April 1925, and continued working thereafter for the Schroeder firm as a shorthand typist until 19 July 1929. She had a great talent for shorthand writing which she continued to develop by intensive continuation training and courses. She often took part in shorthand competitions and not infrequently would emerge with first prize.

In October 1929 she left Hannoversch Münden for Nagold, Württemberg, where she was employed as the sole legal secretary to an attorney. She remained there until 20 February 1930 when she left for Munich in search of a better position and to advance her career. In this period of the Great Depression, Germany had almost 7 million unemployed, and in Munich it was not easy to find a position. She applied to many companies, and responded to newspaper advertisements including one inserted by the NSDAP (Nazi Party) Reich Leadership at Schellingstrasse 50.[5] She was selected from amongst 87 applicants for her outstanding skill and ability. She took up her post in March 1930 and worked in various departments there until 1933. After the election to power of Adolf Hitler on 30 January 1933, various NSDAP Staffs removed to Berlin on 4 March 1933. Frau Schroeder went to Berlin with them at her own request because she was feeling the heat from the Gestapo over her alleged friendship with a Jew the previous year. A short while later while helping out at the Reich Chancellery she came to the attention of Hitler and was transferred into the 'Personal Adjutancy of the Führer'. Early on the Adjutancy consisted of eight or so persons and served as a liaison and communications centre for journeys, the setting of agendas, arranging receptions and so forth, later it expanded to accommodate the military. Frau Schroeder worked at the Reich Chancellery until the outbreak of war in 1939 and was then more mobile as one of Hitler's secretaries. She was in the entourage on all journeys and active at all Führer-HQs (FHQs). Wilhelm Brückner,[6] then Hitler's chief adjutant, described her as follows:

---

5 Following Hitler's release from Landsberg Prison, the NSDAP was reconstituted on 17 February 1925 in a single room at the premises of a publisher at Thierschstrasse 15. As this room was soon inadequate for the membership, on 4 June 1925 several rooms were rented in a building at the rear of Schellingstrasse 50. Although further parts of the premises front and back continued to be rented, the needs of the Party administration soon outgrew them.

6 Oberst Wilhelm Brückner (b. 11.12.1884 Baden-Baden, d. 18.8.1954 Herbstdorf, Traunstein). First World War military service France and Romania, 1918 oberleutnant. 1919 Reichswehr and Freikorps Epp, Munich. 1922 SA-Führer (Munich Regt): involved in failed putsch 1924. 1925–8 active as sports trainer. 1.8.1930 Hitler's adjutant. 1.7.1932 SA-Oberführer. 1.3.1933 SA-Gruppenführer, 1.9.1934 SA-Obergruppenführer, chief adjutant. 18.10.1940 dismissed by Hitler, rejoined army in rank of major, served in France: 1.12.1944 oberst: 4.5.1945 while hospitalised for a wound at Traunstein interned by US Army: released 22.9.1948.

I have known Fräulein Schroeder since 1930. From then until about 1933 she was a secretary in the Reich Directorate of the Supreme SA Command (OSAF), then worked for the head of the Economics Division. In 1933 she transferred from Munich to Berlin with the Liaison Staff. Recommended for her great ability and social graces she arrived eventually in the Führer's Adjutancy as my secretary.

For her typing and shorthand abilities, and her talent for independent working, she was appointed secretary to Adolf Hitler. In all these positions absolute confidentiality – particularly in the latter – was essential. Fräulein Schroeder fulfilled completely all expectations made of her through her unfaltering devotion to duty, her abilities linked to fast comprehension and her independent collaboration when taking dictation. Through her tact, social graces and circumspection she proved herself particularly on journeys and in the various FHQs.

Dr Karl Brandt described Frau Schroeder during his interrogation at the Nuremberg War Crimes Tribunal:

She is a woman who speaks her mind; Christa Schroeder was a different kind of person from Fräulein Wolf.[7] At the beginning of the war this pair alone handled all Hitler's secretarial business. Clever, critical and intelligent, Schroeder had a turnover of work which no other secretary ever matched. She could often spend several days and nights almost without a break taking dictation. She would

---

7 Johanna Wolf (b. 1.6.1900 Munich, d. 5.6.1985 Munich). 1923 private secretary to Hitler's mentor Dietrich Eckart; 1922–8 secretary to Landtag 'Völkischer Block' deputy Dr Alexander Glaser; 5.1928 secretary to Gregor Strasser; 1929 employed by Hitler's private chancellery; 1.11.1929 joined NSDAP, secretary to Rudolf Hess; from 1930 secretary to Hitler's adjutant Wilhelm Brückner; 1933 transferred to Berlin with Hitler's Chancellery and attached to Personal Adjutancy as Hitler's personal secretary. Was often unwell and did not stand flights and road journeys well. Hitler always protected her against efforts to have her replaced. Left Berlin on Hitler's order 21.4.1945; arrested by US forces at Bad Tölz, 23.5.1945; interned; opposed to Frau Schroeder's negotiations with Zoller; released 14.1.1948.

always express her opinion openly and with conviction, and this led on occasion to serious altercations. She held herself apart from the private circle, or Hitler kept her out of it deliberately because he could not tolerate her criticisms. As Fräulein Schroeder's intentions were completely honest this hurt her to the quick and as time went on she became sharply critical of Hitler himself. By doing so her boldness undoubtedly put her life in grave danger.

The war guilt of the shorthand typist

After the collapse of the Third Reich Frau Schroeder was arrested by the US Army Counter-Intelligence Corps (CIC) on 28 May 1945 at Hintersee near Berchtesgaden and interned at various camps and prisons by the occupying Powers. On 13 February 1947 the judicial tribunal of Internment Camp 77 at Ludwigsburg served an arrest order on Frau Schroeder and she was brought before the tribunal for a preliminary hearing next day.

On 24 October 1947 she was accused of being a Group 1 *Hauptschuldige*, a war criminal of the principal group. The indictment specified that Frau Schroeder had been Hitler's shorthand typist and had received from him a gold badge for efficient service. Nothing else was alleged. At the full hearing on 8 December 1947 she was convicted of being a Group 1 major war criminal on the facts cited in the specification and was sentenced to three years' labour camp, to the forfeiture of all her goods and possessions (5,000 marks) and that 'the consequences of Article 15 are to apply for the next ten years.'

On 20 April 1948 the Ministry for Political Freedom of Württemberg-Baden overturned this verdict on the grounds that 'the classification of the accused as a major war criminal is based upon an error in law', and referred the matter back to the tribunal. On 7 May 1948 after the review hearing it was held that:

. . . the accused can under no circumstances be considered a Group 1 war criminal . . . from the beginning to the end she was employed as a shorthand typist. Her work was wholly mechanical, she lacked any kind of independent organized authority and at best can only have exercised the least possible influence on the direction of events. She was highly paid only for her outstanding talent and great competence as a shorthand typist. As regards her obligation to expiate her activity, it is taken into consideration that she was bombed out of her home and is penniless, has already spent a long period in custody and has thus expiated sufficiently.

Frau Schroeder was reclassified as a Group IV *Mitläuferin* (collaborator) and released from detention at Ludwigsburg on 12 May 1948. She concluded: 'Whether my guilt was as great as my expiation is something I do not know to this day.'

In civilian life from 1 August 1948 until 1 November 1958 she worked as a private secretary to Herr Schenk, the owner of a light metal works at Schwäbisch Gmünd and then at its Maulbrunn main plant until 31 October 1959 after which, as in 1930, she returned to Munich. There she accepted employment on 1 November 1959 with a property insurer in a managerial capacity. On 26 June 1967 at age 59 and in ailing health she retired and lived a secluded life in Munich until her death on 28 June 1984.

About herself

It is interesting to observe how Frau Schroeder saw herself in the last years of her life. In a memorandum 'About Myself' she wrote:

> I am attentive, judgmental, critical, willing to help. I have the ability to rapidly size up a situation, and the gift of intuition. From a person's face and mannerisms I am able to read much about his character. I seldom find a person to be nice. If I do, however, then I

jump across all barriers. Unfortunately! My capacity for criticism is coupled to an irresistible urge for truth and independence. I despise people who are self-important, who need to dominate others, who have no opinions of their own but adopt the views of others. I despise people who are materialist, who are conventional, who lie, who prejudge and are never prepared to reflect upon everything which has led to this point.

During her time as Hitler's secretary Christa Schroeder never knew a private life – the life a young woman imagines for herself. After a less than enjoyable youth, she never was to find the tranquillity of existence a woman would wish for. This tragic aspect of her life probably left its mark on her.

In 1938, Frau Schroeder became engaged to Yugoslav diplomat Lav Alkonic although she knew that this could have consequences with Hitler who would never have given his blessing to such a liaison. At the beginning of 1939 she asked Hitler: 'Mein Führer, how would you feel if one of your secretaries wanted to marry a Yugoslav?' Hitler answered: 'There would be no question of it.' Frau Schroeder then suggested that the secretary could leave the employment to which Hitler replied: 'I would know how to prevent that.'

Alkonic had contacts within Yugoslav officers' circles and was later involved in shady business dealings in Belgrade. After references to his 'contact in the Reich Chancellery in Berlin' the Gestapo took an interest and interrogated Frau Schroeder. She described the situation in a letter from the Berghof to her friend Johanna Nusser[8] on 22 February 1941. Frau Schroeder stated that the 'suspicion' had arisen following the interception by the Vienna censor of a letter

---

8 Johanna Nusser was a long-term friend of Frau Schroeder with whom she maintained an intimate correspondence during the war. She spoke on her behalf at the war crimes tribunal hearing and helped Frau Schroeder after her release in 1948. In the 1950s Frau Nusser returned a batch of letters written to her by Schroeder during the war and allowed her to pass another batch to the historian David Irving. The latter are now at the Institut für Zeitgeschichte.

from a certain Djuksic, and she had seen no alternative but to tell the Gestapo the truth.

As a result of the foregoing we cannot write to him again – at least not until the war is over. Consul-General von Neuhausen of Belgrade, whom I met in the former Rothschild Palace at the invitation of General Hanesse, gave me this advice. Neuhausen did not think much of Lav, he had been involved in some dubious business affairs which had not been very fair. He also believed that Lav was working with the Yugoslav General Staff. 'You understand what I mean by that, don't you?' he said. The Gestapo man then interposed that Lav was mentioning his 'contact in the Reich Chancellery' when calling on German firms. How much truth there is in that is hard to tell. In any case, I said, one shouldn't take it too seriously, everybody does it. I hope the OKW is satisfied with my statement, I wouldn't want them to go delving any further into the matter.

The engagement was broken off in 1941.

It may be interjected here that there was also no fulfilment in life for the 55 million or so victims of the Second World War, for the people in the prisons and concentrations camps of the Nazi system: and that these people suffered more than a secretary of Hitler. As an individual human fate, however, one cannot avoid seeing that for Frau Schroeder the years alongside Hitler were years lost, that in her heart she was never happy to be there, and her health was seriously affected by living in damp and musty bunker rooms at FHQ and later in Allied internment. But certainly it was just one fate amongst millions of others.

Life for Christa Schroeder in proximity to Hitler was marked by the need for her constant presence and compliance with the regulations for State protocol laid down by Hitler. Only limited areas of free movement existed in the Reich Chancellery, at the Berghof or in the various FHQs. She saw continuously the same people and the same faces of the entourage with whom she was obliged to co-exist day in, day out, within the enclosure of the FHQ – described by Generaloberst Jodl[9] at Nuremberg postwar as 'a cross between a monastery and a concentration camp'.

Lacking regulated duties or a service schedule she formed part of Hitler's most intimate circle which served him as a kind of substitute family. Depending on his mood when the evening 'tea hour' began, he would deliver to his captive audience his endless monologues into the early hours. Christa Schroeder summarized her unhappy existence:

> 15 years of service, three of them with the Supreme SA leadership (OSAF) and its Economics Department, in between a couple of weeks break with the Reich Leadership of the Hitler Youth, and twelve years in the personal adjutant of the Führer and Reich Chancellor; these were for me 15 years cloistered away from a normal, everyday, civilized existence. A life behind defences and guarded barbed wire fences, especially during the war years in the various FHQs.

On 30 August 1941 she wrote to her friend Johanna Nusser from FHQ Wolfsschanze, Rastenburg in East Prussia:

> Here in the compound we come up eternally against sentries, eternally have to show our identity papers, which makes one feel trapped. I believe that after this campaign I should make the effort to make contacts with life-affirming people beyond our circle, for otherwise I shall become withdrawn and lose contact with real life. Some time ago this sense of being hemmed in, this being shut away from the rest of the world, became etched in my consciousness. Walking inside the

---

9 Generaloberst der Artillerie Alfred Jodl (b. 10.5.1890 Würzburg, d. 16.10.1946 executed Spandau). From 23.8.1939 Chief of Wehrmacht Policy Office (later Wehrmacht Policy Staff) at FHQ. As Hitler's chief of staff advised him on tactical and strategic matters; 7.5.1945 Wehrmacht signatory to partial capitulation to Western Allies, Rheims; interned 23.5.1945 Mürwik; 30.9.1946 sentenced to death as war criminal.

fence, passing sentry after sentry, I realized that it is really always the same whether we are in Berlin, on the Berg[10] or travelling: always the same old circle of faces, always the same round. In that there lies a great danger and a powerful dilemma from which one longs to be free but then, once beyond it, one knows not where to begin because one has to concentrate so utterly and totally on this life, precisely because there is no possibility of a life beyond this circle.

After the war she concluded:

Belonging to Hitler's intimate Staff, always treated as *persona grata*, all the instincts of struggle in one's personality remained underdeveloped. And how they were needed in the situation at the war's end, at the disintegration of the Third Reich and during my three-year internment in Allied camps and prisons. It was in such a condition, rather like an egg without a shell, that on the night of 20 April 1945 in company with my old colleague Johanna Wolf, Adolf Hitler took his leave of us and told me to get away from Berlin for a dark, uncertain future, of which I had no foreboding that the 15 years past and the three years of internment ahead would leave an indelible physical and psychic mark on me which I still have to this day. My past has demanded much of me, both now and when the past was still the present. It does so today to a much harsher degree!'

Anton Joachimsthaler
Munich, June 1985

---

10 From 1936 Hitler's house on the Obersalzberg was given the name 'Berghof'. Hitler's Staff and the inner circle always referred to it as 'the Berg'. On 2.2.1942 at FHQ Wolfsschanze, Hitler stated that the Berghof was also 'Gralsburg' (The Grail Fortress). Heinrich Heim: Adolf Hitler, *Monologe im FHQ*, 1941–1944.

Chapter 1

How I Became Hitler's Secretary

A S A YOUNG GIRL I wanted to see Bavaria. I was told it was very different there from central Germany where I had grown up and spent all 22 years of my life. So, in the spring of 1930, I arrived in Munich and started to look for work. I had not studied the economic situation in Munich beforehand and I was therefore surprised to find how few job opportunities there were and that Munich had the worst national rates of pay. I turned down some work offers hoping to find something better, but soon things began to get difficult, for my few savings were quickly melting away. As I had resigned of my own accord from the Nagold attorney whom I had used as a springboard to Bavaria, I was unable to claim unemployment benefit.

When replying to an extremely tiny advertisement written in shorthand cipher in the *Münchner Neuesten Nachrichten*, I had no premonition that it was to open the doors to the greatest adventure, and determine the future course of my life, whose effects even today I am still unable to shake off. I was invited by an unknown organisation, the 'Supreme SA leadership (OSAF)' to present myself in the Schellingstrasse. In this almost unpopulated street with its few businesses the Reich leadership of the NSDAP, the Nazi Party, was located at No. 50 in the fourth floor of a building at the rear. In the past, the man who would later become Adolf Hitler's official photographer, Heinrich Hoffmann, had made his scurrilous films in these rooms. The former photographic studio with its giant oblique

1

window was now occupied by the Supreme SA-Führer, Franz Pfeffer von Salomon and his chief of staff, Dr Otto Wagener.

Later I learned that I had been the last of eighty-seven applicants to keep the appointment. That the choice fell on me, a person being neither a member of the NSDAP nor interested in politics nor aware of who Adolf Hitler might be, must have resulted purely from my being a twenty-two year old with proven shorthand-typing experience who could furnish good references. I also had a number of diplomas proving that I had often won first prize in stenographic competitions.

Below the roof at No. 50 was a very military-looking concern, an eternal coming and going by tall, slim men in whom one perceived the former officer. There were few Bavarians amongst them, in contrast to the majority of men on the lower floors where other service centres of the NSDAP were located. These were predominantly strong Bavarian types. The OSAF men appeared to be a military elite. I guessed right: most had been Baltic *Freikorps* fighters.[1] The smartest and most elegant of them was the Supreme SA-Führer himself, retired Hauptmann Franz Pfeffer von Salomon. After the First World War he had been a *Freikorps* fighter in the Baltic region, in Lithuania, Upper Silesia and the Ruhr. In 1924 he was NSDAP Gauleiter (head of a provincial district) in Westphalia, and afterwards the Ruhr. His brother Fritz, who had lost a leg and was prematurely grey, functioned as his IIa (Chief of Personnel).

In 1926 Hitler had given Franz Pfeffer von Salomon the task of centralising the SA men of all NSDAP districts. Originally, every Gauleiter 'had his own SA ' and his own way of doing things. Many were 'little Hitlers', which certainly did not serve the interests of unity in the Movement. As Hitler took upon himself the decision

---

1 'Baltic fighters' were members of the various German *Freikorps* who united with Baltic nationals in 1918–19 to resist the advance of the Red Army and secure the German eastern border. In the autumn of 1919, Germany had about 420,000 Freikorps men under arms. Many of these militants went later to the NSDAP.

in all matters of 'degrees of usefulness', he considered it opportune to suppress the Gauleiters by centralising the SA. This was a clever chess move, for he envisaged the SA as the sword by which he proposed to force through the political will of the Party. Since this struggle did not go his own way, Hitler delegated this unpleasant job to Hauptmann Salomon. This 'keeping myself out of it' was a crafty move to which Hitler often resorted later. The Gauleiters were incensed by the reduction in their power, went all out for Salomon and constantly reported their worst suspicions about him to Hitler. Hitler had of course expected this, which was the main reason for his having delegated the job, and no doubt he gave an inward smile of satisfaction at his own foresight.

In August 1930 Hitler was obliged to give in to the pressure of the trouble-makers and sacrificed Pfeffer von Salomon, something which to all appearances he regretted having to do, although he did not much like the man. After making it clear that Salomon had outlived his usefulness, the latter resigned in August 1930, and Hitler took the opportunity to appoint himself Supreme SA-Führer in his place. Franz Pfeffer von Salomon was a critical sort of man. I often had cause to confirm this. One day for example I saw a copy of the Party newspaper *Völkischer Beobachter* lying on his table. It showed a photograph of Hitler. Salomon had doodled Hitler's filthy, unkempt uniform jacket into a slim, tailored shape. The debonair Salomon seemed to find Hitler's figure and manner of dressing apparently not to his taste, as probably others did too.

The OSAF chief of staff was retired Hauptmann Dr Otto Wagener, a former general staff officer and *Freikorps* street fighter, like Salomon from comfortable origins and full of vigour for putting Germany back on her feet. He had given up a directorship in industry and, relying on his comrade-in-arms Salomon, had followed Hitler's call for collaborators. Dr Wagener lectured at Würzburg University. That he was a man of wide education with far-reaching contacts to politicians, industrialists and the nobility was obvious from the very comprehensive correspondence which I had to transcribe for him. Whilst he held the post of OSAF chief of staff, Dr Wagener drafted the 'Economic-Political Letters' whose length and multiplicity of subjects caused me much toil. My work for Dr Wagener was interrupted for a few weeks towards the end of 1930 when on Hitler's orders he took over the leadership of the SA in September to fill the gap before the arrival of Hauptmann Ernst Röhm, recalled from Bolivia.

Ernst Röhm was the son of a senior railway inspector in Munich. He was commissioned in 1908 and in the First World War fought at Flaival on the Western Front. He was seriously wounded three times and lost the upper part of his nose to a shell splinter. He met Hitler in 1919 as a *Reichswehr* Hauptmann in Munich. As a liaison officer to the *Reichswehr*, Röhm was an important member of the Nazi Movement and was on familiar terms with Hitler. He was discharged from the *Reichswehr* for his involvement in the 1923 putsch, but a year later was active in the *Deutsch-Völkische Freiheitspartei* as a Reichstag Deputy and organised the National Socialist armed group *Frontbann*, although he gave up leadership of it once Hitler was released from Landsberg prison. At the end of 1928 he was reinstated in the rank of Oberstleutnant in the *Reichswehr* and as a general staff officer was sent to La Paz as a military instructor. In 1930 Hitler recalled him to lead the SA.

I then spent a couple of weeks with the Reich leadership of the Hitler Youth which at the time was housed in a private apartment. After the lively workload at OSAF I found this to be almost a punishment. When Dr Otto Wagener was appointed leader of the NSDAP Economics Office (WPA) on 1 January 1931, he asked for me as his secretary. The WPA offices with their various departments for Trade, Industry and Farming were located in the Braunes Haus at Brienner-Strasse 54, the former Barlow Palace opposite the Catholic seminary.[2] Dr Wagener used to dictate long reports about discussions he had had without mentioning the name of the other party. He also made long trips away from the office, and on his return would dictate long memoranda which when complete would then disappear into his desk. I would often get annoyed about this unnecessary production of paperwork, or so it then seemed, and all too much cloak-and-dagger. It was not until 1978 when I read the book by H.A. Turner jr, *Aufzeichnungen eines Vertrauten Dr h.c. Wagener 1929–1932*[3] that I saw immediately that Wagener's mysterious partner on his trips and discussions had been Adolf Hitler. His other conversation partners were Franz Pfeffer von Salomon and Gregor Strasser.

In my opinion these three saw in Hitler a singular visionary genius. They also recognised the danger of such genius which, strengthened by the suggestive power of his oratory, drew almost everybody under his spell. These three well-above-average men were probably agreed in taking the opportunity of the frequent and long conversations to test Hitler's infallibility by queries and objections, which he would have not found pleasant. As his intuition could not be faulted with logic because it has a visionary origin and lacked any basis of logic, he considered them to be fault-finders and pedants and eventually he cast them aside.

OSAF Franz Pfeffer von Salomon was relieved of the post of OSAF and left out in the cold.[4] At the end of 1932 secret negotiations

---

2 When the rented premises at Schellingstrasse 50 were no longer adequate for the NSDAP Reich leadership, on 5 July 1930 Hitler bought for RM 1.5 million the former Barlow Palace at Briennerstrasse 45. Built in 1928 it was converted by Professor Troost and Hitler, and was enlarged. Renamed 'Braunes Haus' on 1 January 1931, it housed the NSDAP Reich leadership on three floors. Later other buildings were purchased including two during the reconstruction of the Königsplatz on Arcisstrasse which remain standing today.

3 The title means 'Notes by a Confidante'.

4 Franz Felix Pfeffer von Salomon (b. 19.2.1888 Düsseldorf, d.12.4.1968 Munich). Pfeffer remained in Munich without an office after his withdrawal but lived with Party associates until elected to the Reichstag on 6.11.1932. In 1933 police commissioner in Kassel; 1938 president, provincial government at Wiesbaden; 1944 briefly under arrest in connection with July Plot; interned by Allies; released 1946.

between Gregor Strasser[5] and Schleicher regarding his being offered the vice-chancellorship led to the total break with Hitler. In 1934 he was killed 'by mistake' during the Röhm putsch. Dr Otto Wagener moved to Berlin in 1932 and was relieved of all offices in the summer of 1933. Apparently his closest colleagues favoured him for finance minister. I never heard of him again.[6] It is no wonder that hardly anybody knows the name after he withdrew and was apparently no longer required after 1933. No doubt Dr Wagener, Pfeffer von Salomon and Strasser were personalities with too much independence for Hitler's liking. In any case, after Hitler took power I never heard them spoken of again.

A person then active in the OSAF who did achieve a meteoric rise was Martin Bormann, still of interest today to authors and historians. The worst character traits were attributed to him, and all decisions he imposed were blamed 'entirely on him' postwar, not only by journalists and historians but above all by the surviving NSDAP bosses, Gauleiters, Ministers and also people of Hitler's entourage, who should have known better.

Martin Bormann was simply one of the most devoted and loyal of Hitler's vassals who would often force through ruthlessly and

---

5 Gregor Strasser (b. 31.5.1892 Geisenfeld, d. 30.6.1934 Berlin). 9.6.1932 head NSDAP Reich Organisational Directorate; 8.9.1932 resigned from Party activities after accusation of disloyalty by Hitler in the Schleicher affair; expelled from the Party, returned to industry in Berlin; murdered by Gestapo by shooting at their Prinz-Albrecht-Strasse prison.

6 Otto William Heinrich Wagener (b. 29.4.1888 Durlach/Baden, d. 9. 8.1971 Chieming-Stöttham/Bavaria). Took over position of acting OSAF from Salomon until 31.12.1930; from 1.1.1931 head of Economic-Political Office (WPA) at Braunes Haus; 4.9.1932 resigned office, attached to Führer-Staff for special purposes, Berlin; 20.4.1933 resumed former WPA post; 3.5.1933 Reich commissioner for trade and industry; 12.6.1933 relieved of all posts after Hitler and Göring suspected him of lobbying for post of minister for industry; following USCHLA hearing cleared of all involvement; end 1933 Reichstag deputy Koblenz-Trier; 30.6.1934 arrested in Röhm purge, released and returned to Erzgebirge to farm, but remained Reichstag deputy until 1938 and SA-Gruppenführer; fought in the Second World War; PoW (British) 1944 in rank of major general; 1947 convicted in Italy of war crimes; 1952 released.

sometimes brutally the orders and directives given him by Hitler. Seen in this way, Bormann 'followed the same kind of path as did Franz Pfeffer von Salomon, running battles with Gauleiters, ministers, Party bosses and the rest being the rule. In the spring of 1930 at OSAF, Bormann was as yet unburdened by the far-reaching and unpleasant tasks which Hitler gave him later. Bormann could never be called an attractive man. He had married Gerda Buch, the beautiful daughter of Party judge, retired Major Walter Buch, who as the Reich USCHLA judge in the NSDAP was highly respected and enjoyed Hitler's confidence.[7] Buch had been an active officer and subsequently an instructor at an NCO training school. In the First World War he was regimental adjutant and later commander of a machine-gun sharpshooter unit. In 1918 he took over an officer-candidate battalion at Döberitz. After the war he left the army in the rank of major and joined the NSDAP. In 1925 he was appointed USCHLA chairman, a position which required a lot of understanding for human inadequacies, much tact, energy and authority. He was predestined for the office, for his father had been president of the Senate at the Oberland tribunals in Baden. With his long face and tall, slim figure he always looked very elegant. He had been present at the marriage of his daughter to Martin Bormann, which was naturally very beneficial for Bormann's prospects.

At OSAF, Martin Bormann headed the SA personal injury insurance plan designed by Dr Wagener, later known as the NSDAP *Hilfskasse*.[8] All SA men were covered by it. At their gatherings there

---

7 USHLA = *Untersuchungs-und Schlichtungsaussschuss*, NSDAP Reich Leadership Committee of Investigation and Reconciliation, renamed 'The Supreme Party Court' by Hitler on 31.3.1933. Its purpose was to 'protect the collective honour of the Party and its individual members, and where necessary to settle differences between individual members in an amicable way'.

8 The SA personal injury insurance scheme started with the Giesinger SA in Munich and at the beginning of 1927 was extended to cover the entire SA under the administration of OSAF in a special sub-division *Versicherungswesen*. By 1 January 1928 it was so well capitalised that only death and invalidity was reinsured out.

tended to be a lot of brawling which tended to result in bodily injuries. The insurance was useful and necessary. It was created to serve the single primitive purpose which the genius of Martin Bormann could not cover. Only after beginning work on the staff of the Führer's deputy did Bormann succeed later in proving his extraordinary qualities. His career took off in the course of the 1930s. From chief of staff to Rudolf Hess he became NSDAP Reichsleiter and then Hitler's secretary. He expected from his staff that same enormous industriousness which distinguished himself, and this did not help to make him loved. 'Hurry, hurry' was his celebrated phrase. Hitler, always full of praise for Martin Bormann, once said:

> Where others need all day, Bormann does it for me in two hours, and he never forgets anything! . . . Bormann's reports are so precisely formulated that I only need to say Yes or No . With him I get through a pile of files in ten minutes for which other men would need hours. If I tell him, remind me of this or that in six months, I can rest assured that he will do so. He is the exact opposite of his brother[9] who forgets every task I give him.

Bormann came to Hitler not only well prepared with his files but was also so in tune with Hitler's way of thinking that he could spare him long-winded explanations. Anyone who knew how Hitler did things will realise that this was decisive for him!

When the reinsurer demanded a hefty rise in premiums at the end of 1928 for increased risk, OSAF abandoned reinsurance altogether and under the direction of Martin Bormann from 1 January 1929 the insurance was turned into a giant Party enterprise with no private involvement, being known as the NSDAP *Hilfskasse* from 1 September 1930.

9 Albert Bormann (b. 2.9.1902 Halberstadt, d. 8.4.1989 Munich). Brother of Martin Bormann; joined NSDAP 27.4.1927; NSDAP *Hilfskasse* 12.5.1931; head of 'Private Chancellery Adolf Hitler' February 1933; from 1938 Reichstag deputy, 1934–29.4;1945 personal adjutant to Hitler; in Bavaria then assumed the name Roth and worked as a farm labourer until 5.4.1949 when he surrendered to the authorities; interned; released 4.10.1949.

Many of the rumours still current about Bormann have in my opinion no basis in fact. He was neither hungry for power nor the 'grey eminence' in Hitler's entourage. To my mind he was one of the few National Socialists with clean hands,[10] if one may put it that way, for he was incorruptible and came down hard on all corruption he discovered. For his oppressive attitude in this regard he increasingly antagonised corrupt Party members and many others.

I am of the opinion today that nobody in Hitler's entourage save Bormann would have had the presence to run this difficult office. For sheer lack of time Hitler could not attend to all day-to-day affairs, and perhaps whenever possible he avoided doing so to prevent himself becoming unloved! Accordingly all the unpleasant business was left to Martin Bormann, and he was also the scapegoat. Ministers, Gauleiters and others believed that Bormann acted from his own lust for power. I remember for example that at FHQ Wolfsschanze Hitler would often say: 'Bormann, do me a favour and keep the Gauleiters away from me.' Bormann did this and protected Hitler. The Gauleiters were as a rule old street fighters who had known Hitler longer than Bormann and felt senior to him. If a Gauleiter then happened to cross Hitler's path while strolling, Hitler would play the innocent and gasp: 'What? You are here?' When the Gauleiter then held forth on Bormann's shortcomings, Hitler would put on his surprised face. 'I know that Bormann is brutal,' Hitler said once, 'but whatever he takes on is given hands and feet, and I can rely on him absolutely and unconditionally to carry out my orders immediately and irrespective of whatever obstructions

---

10 Although Schroeder may have thought him to be Herr Incorruptible, the 'clean hands' of Martin Bormann were the result of his personal devotion to the Nazi cause. In a letter to Hess on 5 October 1932 he summed up his attitude thus: 'For me and all true National Socialists the only thing that matters is the Movement, nothing else. Whatever or whoever is useful to the Movement is good, whoever damages it is a parasite and my enemy.' Bormann executed all Hitler's orders faithfully and without question, never asking if they were right, humane or serving some useful purpose.

may be in the way.' For Hitler, Martin Bormann was a better and more acceptable colleague than Rudolf Hess had been, and of whom Hitler once said: 'I only hope that he never becomes my successor, for I do not know whom I would pity more, Hess or the Party.'

Rudolf Hess was born in Alexandria, Egypt, the son of a wholesaler. His father came from Franconia and his mother was of Swiss descent. He was brought up in Egypt until aged fourteen, when he attended a special school at Godesberg on the Rhine, took the one-year examination and then a course in business practice which took him to the French-speaking region of Switzerland and then Hamburg. At the outbreak of the First World War he volunteered for military service and in 1918 was an airman with *Jagdstaffel 35* on the Western Front with the rank of lieutenant. After the 1919 revolution he joined the Thule Society* in Munich and took part in the overthrow of the revolutionary councils in Munich, receiving a leg wound. Next he entered commerce and studied economics and history. One evening in 1920 he happened upon an NSDAP meeting and joined the Party immediately as an SA-man. In November 1923 Hess led the SA Student's Group and was at Hitler's side for the putsch attempt of 9 November 1923, being involved in the detention of the ministers at the Bürgerbräukeller. Following the failure of the putsch he spent an adventurous six months in the

---

* The Thule Society was a cornerstone of the Nazi Movement. The three co-founders were mystics. Guido von List (1865–1919) was the first popular writer to combine racial ideology with occultism. He advocated the racist State with a self-elected Führer, and saw international Jewry as the enemy of Germanism. His friend and pupil Lanz von Liebenfels (1874–1954), a former Cistercian monk, propagated racial purity in his first book in 1905. He wrote a magazine Ostara in Vienna in 1907–8. Hitler collected all issues, which von Liebenfels gave him free of charge. The third co-founder was Rudolf von Sebottendorf (1875–1945?), who had studied sufism, rosicrucianism and astrology in Turkey.

Dr Wilfred Dahms, Viennese psychologist and biographer of Lanz von Liebenfels whom he knew well, stated in the biography *Der Mann, der Hitler die Ideen gab* that the primary aim of the Thule Society was to create a Nordic-Aryan race of Atlanteans. All inferior races were to be exterminated.

Bavarian mountains. Two days before the abolition of the Bavarian peoples' court he surrendered to the police, was tried and sentenced immediately, and taken to Landsberg prison where he remained with Hitler until New Year's Eve 1924. Later he became an assistant to the professor for geopolitics, General Haushofer, at the German Academy at Munich University. From 1925 he was Hitler's secretary. Martin Bormann was certainly not dismayed by Rudolf Hess's flight to Britain in 1941. I remember that on the evening of 10 May 1941, after Hitler and Eva Braun had gone upstairs, he invited a few guests sympathetic to him to his country house for a celebration. That evening everybody reported on how relieved he seemed!

The NSDAP economics department at Munich went on, but suffered changes of leader after the departure of Dr Wagener. For a short while Walter Funk, later the Reich economics minister, held the seat, and at the end of my spell in Munich it passed to Bernhard Köhler, known for his thesis *Arbeit und Brot* (Work and Bread). Köhler remains in my mind for his advice to me: 'The person who defends herself, accuses herself!' and dissuaded me from instigating an USCHLA hearing. My idea was to throw light on a slander circulating about me which was making my life in Munich hell.

The whole affair began with a telephonist hearing a surname incorrectly. The male telephonist at the Braunes Haus had misunderstood the name of a friend who had called me. Instead

---

The original Thule Society was founded in 1910 by Felix Niedner, translator of the old Norse Eddas: the 1919 Thule Society was an amalgamation of the original society with the Germanen Order, a secret anti-Jewish lodge founded in 1912. The emblem of the Thule Society was a circular swastika superimposed upon a broadsword within a wreath. Amongst the members were Karl Haushofer, Rudolf Hess and Hitler's mentor Dietrich Eckart. The Nazi swastika was designed by Dr Krohn, a Thule Society member.

Hitler was not a member of the Thule Society but the link was the DAP founded on 5 January 1919 by Anton Drexler which was useful for contacts, members and the interchange of information. The DAP was the forerunner of the NSDAP. The Thule Society was still in existence in 1933 when it was probably absorbed into the SS. (Translator's Note)

of Vierthaler, a pure Bavarian name, he misheard Fürtheimer, a Jewish name. Shortly before, in October 1932, I had gone on a coach excursion through the Dolomites to Venice with an older female colleague. The excursion had been arranged by a Herr Kroiss and his wife from Rosenheim. He drove the coach himself and had apparently taken a liking to me. As soon as we made a stop anywhere, Herr Kroiss and his wife would invite me to their table, ignoring my travelling companion. Herr Kroiss, who knew the route very well, was asked twice by three gentlemen in a large Mercedes where the best place was to spend the night. As fate would have it, these three gentlemen booked into the same Venice hotel as ourselves and even invited themselves to sit at our table. One of them invited me to take a trip with him in a gondola that afternoon, which I was pleased to accept, never suspecting what was in store for me as a result of my companion's envy and feelings of being abandoned, and the telephonist's later error at NSDAP HQ.

Back in Munich a friend, the niece of the NSDAP Reich treasury minister Franz Xaver Schwarz, surprised me with the question: 'Christa, are you really having a relationship with a Jew?' When I asked who had said so, she replied: 'An SS-Führer!' I asked her to have him present himself so that I could clear up the matter, and a couple of days later he turned up – I have forgotten his name – and asked me: 'Do you perhaps wish to deny that you are having a relationship with the Jew Fürtheimer, and were together with him in Italy?' My assurances and explanations availed me nothing, not even when my friend Vierthaler provided an affidavit swearing to his pure Aryan origins. A statement by Herr Kroiss that he organised his tours in such a manner that nobody could absent themselves overnight was similarly unsuccessful in putting an end to the accusations.

Bernhard Köhler, then my boss in the economics department, with whom I lodged the various affidavits told me: 'Whoever defends herself, accuses herself!' I did not understand the sense of this, but realised that he opposed an USCHLA hearing. Despite this proof of my manager's confidence in me, the suspicions of the Party members smouldered and I suffered very much as a result of it.

One evening a male friend came to collect me from my small hotel. Next day the owner's son advised me: 'Fräulein Schroeder, be cautious!' He said nothing else. Apparently the SS had asked the hotelier to look at my friends closely. The gentleman caller had invited me to a recital. He was a dark-eyed, black-haired attorney and apparently looked Jewish; whether he was or not I have no idea, I never asked him. In order to sweep aside all suspicions I decided to reject all future invitations, and instead took every course going at the Berlitz School and local college.

If the dyed-in-the-wool Bavarian of the early 1930s was filled with the proverbial hatred of the Prussians,[11] they also avoided me with a hurtful distrust. It was precisely this hatred of the Prussians which now changed the course my life was to take.

Once Hitler had become Reich Chancellor, NSDAP Reich treasurer Franz Xaver Schwarz, chief personnel officer at the Braunes Haus, called for stenotyists to volunteer for the NSDAP Liaison Staff in Berlin. The Munich girls held back; they were not keen on Berlin. All the greater was my own readiness. I informed the Reich treasurer, and next day he told me that it had been arranged. In March 1933 I arrived in the capital.

The office block in which the NSDAP Liaison Staff was housed in Berlin was at Wilhelm-Strasse 64, diagonally opposite the Reich Chancellery. Headed by Rudolf Hess, its function was to act as the contact office between Party centres and the Reich ministers.[12] Upon my arrival I was acquainted with my duties by the elegant and robust Consul Rolf Reiner, Röhm's adjutant in Bolivia. I would spend most

---

11 Prussians were all those who came from northern Germany or, by extension, those people who spoke High German.

12 The liaison staff at Wilhelm-Strasse 64 in Berlin was a service office of Hitler's deputy Hess, the actual head office was in the Führer-building on Arcis-Strasse in Munich.

of my time with the Liaison Staff although from time to time I might be required to make myself available to Hitler's chief adjutant, SA-Gruppenführer Wilhelm Brückner in the Reich Chancellery.[13] In 1933, all Hitler had was one office and a room for his adjutants. This left him with nowhere to install a female secretary.

Whether it was the proverbially good Berlin air or the atmosphere with my more united Berlin colleagues I felt I had shed the suspicions which had weighed down so heavily on me in Munich, although I was never able to shake off completely the effects of the slander. The experience of how readily believed were those who pointed the finger of suspicion, and how easy it was to become their victim, became deeply engraved within me. After this nasty experience, I think I looked at things rather more critically and became less trusting.

Work with the Liaison Staff was for the most part very easy. Nearly all incoming mail was passed to the competent SA centre. Working for Hitler's chief adjutant Wilhelm Brückner was far more interesting. At least every two days he would summon me by telephone to the Reich Chancellery for dictation. I would then type up his letters in the Liaison Staff and bring them back in the post-portfolio for him to sign.

Wilhelm Brückner came from Baden-Baden, his father was Silesian and his mother from the Thuringian aristocracy. He was an engineer by trade but studied economics later. After the First World War he remained in the *Reichswehr* as an Oberleutnant then joined Freikorps Epp, helping to put down the revolutionary council in Munich. After more study, this time as a film engineer for three

---

13 The palace at Wilhelm-Strasse 77 built by Graf von der Schulenburg between 1738 and 1739 was bought by the Radziwill family in 1796. The Reich bought it from them in 1875. Bismarck, the first Reich Chancellor, moved in after rebuilding, and renovation work was completed in 1878. During the Weimar Republic the palace was the seat of the Reich government, and from then until 1939 further building and expansion work was always in progress, particularly after the compulsory purchase of all buildings in the Voss-Strasse in 1938. At the end of the war only ruins and rubble remained.

years he joined the NSDAP in 1922 and the following year led the proscribed SA Regiment Munich. That earned him four and a half months in jail, and at the end of 1924 another two months for membership of a banned organisation. Subsequently he took office as the third general secretary of the *Verein für das Deutschtum im Ausland* (Association of Germans Abroad) in Munich. At the end of 1930 he was appointed SA adjutant to Hitler although in this role he was more a personal aide in constant attendance.

Brückner was not only one of the best-looking men in Hitler's circle, very tall, blond and blue-eyed, but he also had charm. Very reasonable and practical, even when he gave someone a ticking off nobody could get mad at him. Once a letter came from a schoolboy which said: 'So long as he – Brückner – is close to Hitler, one need never worry about Hitler's safety.' After Hitler took power in 1933, Brückner was given a whole new set of duties in addition to those he already exercised as Hitler's chief adjutant. One of his most important jobs was to receive members of the public who wanted to make a request, complaint or suggestion, or give encouragement, to Hitler in person. They came to the Reich Chancellery in the hope of talking to Hitler. Brückner had a ready ear for everybody and, so far as possible, would help out financially in needy cases, immediately and in an unbureaucratic manner. He would note the request, complaint etc. on a small white card which he used to tuck into the sleeve turn-up of his SA uniform.

Over the years Brückner gradually fell into disfavour with Hitler. After a car accident in 1933 at Reit im Winkl when he lost an eye and suffered various fractures, he was on sick leave for a long period. His fiancée Sophie Stork,[14] a frequent guest at Obersalzberg, who

---

14 Sophie 'Charly' Stork (b. 5.5.1903 Munich, d. 21.10.1981 Seeshaupt) was introduced to Hitler at Obersalzberg in the spring of 1932. She was a frequent guest at the Berghof and received commissions from Hitler for her hand-crafted ceramics etc. After Brückner broke off the engagement in 1936, according to Schroeder she received from Hitler compensation in the sum of RM 40,000 which caused her many problems with Allied investigators after the war.

had been a passenger in the car, also suffered serious injuries. Her father owned a noted sporting business in Munich. Sophie was a very talented artist. She painted a coffee service for Eva Braun, made personalised tiles for the pastry area of the new Berghof dining hall and the large hand-crafted ceramic oven in the lounge. Particularly after the accident Hitler took a dim view of Brückner not marrying Sophie Stork and made her a large ex-gratia payment from his own pocket. Brückner, a good-looking man and always the optimist, liked happy, carefree people and had an eye for a pretty woman. Sophie Stork was the jealous type and often let it show, which apparently used to annoy Brückner. When he fell in love with the daughter of the 'other woman' cited as a co-respondent in the Magda Quandt divorce – before Magda met and married Goebbels – Hitler's displeasure with Brückner grew.

When Brückner brought his Gisela to the Berghof one evening to meet Hitler, the latter gave her a frosty welcome. After dinner, Hitler stopped at the dining room door and said to Brückner: 'I expect you will be escorting Fräulein Gisela back down into Berchtesgaden tonight?', which was a serious snub. For more than a decade Brückner had stood at Hitler's side even in the difficult times, and served him loyally. It came therefore as a severe blow when Hitler dismissed him without ceremony in October 1940 after an intrigue by Kannenberg, the house manager. In occupied France he had the post of city commandant. After a long period of internment after the war he lived for some years after his release at Traunstein where his sergeant from the First World War let him have two small rooms. Possibly Brückner made too light of many things in life but he was a gentleman and his charm created a good atmosphere in Hitler's entourage. After his dismissal in 1940 Julius Schaub became chief adjutant, but he was no substitute for Brückner.

The demands made of Brückner in the Reich Chancellery were of great importance for those involved, and there was always urgency about the work. Therefore I came under pressure all the time and shuttled assiduously between the NSDAP Liaison Staff and the Reich Chancellery. One day when I was giving Brückner his outgoing mail to sign Hitler came into the room. He stopped, gave me a questioning look and said: 'Do we know each other?' I replied, 'Yes, Herr Hitler, I did some work for you in Munich.' That had happened one Sunday in 1930. Hitler, coming back from the mountains, had something he wanted to dictate urgently, but Fräulein Frey, who was then his stenotyist, could not be contacted. Herr Hölsken, who worked in Rudolf Hess's secretarial office, was asked to find an experienced substitute. Remembering my fast typing speed at OSAF he came to my flat and said: 'Herr Hitler has returned from the mountains and has something he must dictate. His secretary cannot be contacted and I would like you to come with me.'

At the Braunes Haus, Rudolf Hess received me in an ante room and led me to Hitler's study. It was my first direct meeting with Hitler. He came to me in a friendly manner and said: 'I am very pleased that you will write for me. It is only a draft and so it will not be important if you make a few typographical errors.' At that time I did not realise Hitler's importance and was used to typing dictation directly into the machine so I went ahead without any inhibitions. I must have done the job to his satisfaction for he gave me a box of chocolates as I left. Whenever he met me afterwards in the Braunes Haus he would always acknowledge me in a very friendly way. He had an above-average memory for faces and events, and as a result he remembered me so that soon I was working not only for Brückner but also for Hitler personally whenever he requested it.

On 23 December 1933 upon completing a task for Hitler I requested a signed photograph. I was surprised when he wanted to know my name. Rather taken aback I said, 'Schroeder!' 'No, I know that,' he replied, 'I mean your first name.' When I said in embarrassment that I had an ugly name, Emilie, (Christine is my middle name) he contradicted me: 'You ought not to say it is an ugly

name, it is very beautiful, it was the name of my first sweetheart.'
Naïvely, I happened to mention this to Henriette von Schirach,
not suspecting that she would use it without permission in her
book *Anekdoten um Hitler*.[15] She inflated this little aside out of all
proportion. I record it here not to put matters straight but because
Hitler's remark had the simple interpretation for me that as a young
man he had led a normal love life.

Officially as Reich Chancellor, Adolf Hitler had two civil servants
at the Chancellery available to him as personal secretaries. These
were Fräulein Bügge and Fräulein Frobenius. Perhaps he was put
out by the fact that they had done work previously for several of
his predecessors and had been employed as secretaries by them. In
any case he ignored them completely. In 1930 at the Braunes Haus
Hitler had used as his secretary Fräulein Herta Frey (later married
as Oldenburg) from Hess's Chancellery, and from 1931 or 1932
Johanna Wolf who had been in the NSDAP Gau of Lower Bavaria
and worked for Hitler's mentor Dietrich Eckart in 1923 until his
death that year. The two private secretaries Fräulein Wolf and
Fräulein Wittmann whom he employed in 1933 had no office space
in the Reich Chancellery and worked a roster between themselves of
four weeks in Munich with Rudolf Hess and four weeks in Berlin
at Hitler's private chancellery run by Albert Bormann from outside
the Reich Chancellery.

Albert Bormann had been introduced by his brother Martin into
the *SA-Hilfskasse* insurance scheme in 1931, from where he graduated
into Hitler's private chancellery under Rudolf Hess, and took over
running it from 1933. That same year he married a woman of whom
brother Martin disapproved because she was not Nordic, and the
two brothers became estranged. If they were standing together, each
would ignore the other. If for example Hitler gave one of them a job
to pass to the other, that brother would send for an orderly officer to

---

15 Türmer Verlag, 1980.

convey the instruction to his brother standing a few feet away. If one of the brothers told a funny story everybody present would laugh except the other brother who would keep a straight face. When Albert Bormann divorced after a few years and married his ex-wife's cousin, he wanted to inform his brother of the fact. Martin Bormann refused to receive him with the remark: 'I don't care if he marries his grandmother.'

Since I was resident in Berlin and always on call – I had only to walk across the Wilhelm-Strasse – I was summoned to Hitler's Reich Chancellery more frequently than Johanna Wolf. Before Hitler could move into his flat in the Radziwill Palace as Reich Chancellor, the old walls had to be renovated. This was especially necessary in the historic Congress Hall where Bismarck had celebrated the now-famous Berlin Congress of 1878. It was also in this hall that Hindenburg had received Hitler and appointed him Reich Chancellor. 'The old gentleman', Hitler said, speaking of Hindenburg, had told him on that occasion: 'Keep to the walls if you can, Herr Hitler, the floor won't last much longer.' Accordingly, after his appointment to Reich Chancellor, Hitler had given orders to renovate the old palace. Until the work was completed Secretary of State Lammers made available to him the service flat under the roof of the old Reich Chancellery on the corner of Wilhelm- and Voss-Strasse. I spent a long period shuttling back and forth between the old Reich Chancellery and the Liaison Staff. After the Radziwill Palace was ready the 'Personal Adjutancy of the Führer and Reich Chancellor' was housed in a large room next to the so-called Bismarck room, and I moved in as Brückner's secretary. Most of the time I sat alone looking out on the old park.

The Personal Adjutancy now underwent expansion. Julius Schaub's[16] desk was there. He was Hitler's factotum and had followed

---

16 Julius Gregor Schaub (b. 20.8.1898 Munich, d. 27.12.1967 Munich). 31.1.1917 conscripted; spent most of the First World War in military hospitals either as an attendant or patient; 10.10.1920 joined NSDAP; 1923 active role in putsch, fled

him like a shadow since 1925. A typical Bavarian, he was probably the only person who knew all Hitler's intimate and personal secrets. Schaub was not very prepossessing. He had rather bulging eyes and limped because he was missing some toes from frostbite in the First World War. This handicap was perhaps the reason why he was so irritable. He was ever suspicious and additionally very inquisitive, and since he boycotted anybody not to his liking affection for him in Hitler's circle was very limited. Schaub had trained in pharmacy and after the First World War worked at the main supply office in Munich. He joined the NSDAP early on and came to Hitler's attention as he limped around the NSDAP meetings. He was involved in the 1923 putsch. This earned him some jail time which he spent with Hitler at Landsberg am Lech. After early release he became Hitler's constant companion from January 1925. He was so loyal to Hitler that at his request he gave up smoking, but not alcohol. Hitler knew that Schaub liked his tipple, and finally abandoned the struggle to make Schaub teetotal. When told that Schaub had been hitting the bottle at a reception Hitler made a despairing gesture with his hand and sighed: 'Yes, I know, it is sad. But what can I do, I have no other adjutant.'

After taking power Hitler needed a qualified valet, and Schaub was retained to handle all his confidential affairs. He kept all Hitler's secret files in an armoured safe, scheduled the important birthdays and made lists of presents.[17] Since Hitler never carried a pen or pencil on his person, in the early years of power it was always: 'Schaub, write this down!' Before Martin Bormann ascended into Hitler's close circle, Schaub was always Hitler's mobile notebook. Schaub

to Austria; 20.4.1924 arrested on border at Salzburg, sentenced to 18 months at Landsberg; released 31.12.1924, next day appointed Hitler's private valet; SS-Obergruppenführer and Reichstag deputy; at war's end released by Hitler; fled to Kitzbühl using alias 'Josef Huber'; 8.5.1945 detained by US forces; 17.2.1949 released.

17 The list of presents was arranged by donor, article and year. For the 1935 and 1936 lists see BA Koblenz R43 II 967b, sh. 27–31.

also handled some of Hitler's financial affairs, settling invoices and so on. He carried Hitler's loose change, since the latter did not like money on his person.

One day a pretty young girl brought a letter to the Braunes Haus for Hitler's personal attention. In it she described her poverty-stricken circumstances. I think it was December 1936. Her fiancé, an Austrian, had done much for the Nazi Movement and was on the run to avoid arrest. She begged Hitler to find him work, for she earned very little herself and the couple was keen to marry. Hitler checked the details and finding them true found the man a position. Naturally without their knowledge Schaub had to rent the couple a two-room flat and furnish it (carpets, bedding, curtains, furniture). Then a Christmas tree was set up with the usual adornments and the candles lit while Schaub fetched the young couple in the car. That they were overjoyed goes without saying.

It was also one of Schaub's duties to visit variety performances and theatres at change of programme in order to keep Hitler informed whether a visit might prove rewarding. Schaub often recalled with pride that his mother, who died in the 1908 Messina earthquake, had been a dancer. That was probably the reason why he was so fond of dancers and cabaret artists. When he had to ring up actresses and dancers inviting them to the Führer's flat for an evening chat[18] he could even be charming. He was an enemy of the gutter press, which was a big plus point with Hitler.

After Wilhelm Brückner was sacked by Hitler in 1940, Schaub received the title 'personal adjutant' with the rank of SS-Gruppenführer, as from 1943 SS-Obergruppenführer. This position

---

18 Schroeder explained that since there was no dancing at Hitler's banquets in the Reich Chancellery, he invited singers from the Berlin Opera and dancers from the theatrical operas and the Charlottenberg Opera. Every year he threw a banquet for artists and another for industrialists, the main purpose of these being to raise money for Winter Relief Work. During the Berlin Olympics a great banquet was held at the Reich Chancellery for all competitors. A large reception was arranged for the Party at NSDAP HQ in Munich every year.

often brought him into situations which he was not competent to handle. It made no difference to Hitler. When in April 1945 he told Schaub to destroy all personal property at the Berghof which might suggest to people a female presence, and all files and papers there and at the Munich flat, Schaub obeyed without question.

From the SS bodyguard stationed around the Führer apartment a mature SS-Führer[19] trained in commerce was selected for service in the Personal Adjutancy and to handle our telephone exchange. SS-Obersturmbannführer Paul Wernicke had good office experience, was capable and tidy and soon made himself indispensable to Brückner and Schaub, neither of whom had a clue how to run an office. As the pair of them had plenty to do elsewhere they gave Wernicke and me a free hand and so we kept the office work in the Personal Adjutancy flexible and fairly unbureaucratic. Wernicke soon proved himself an important and reliable colleague.

Things changed when Hauptmann Wiedemann[20] was appointed Hitler's adjutant. As regimental adjutant with 16. Bavarian reserve infantry regiment, Regiment List, in which Hitler had served as despatch runner, Wiedemann had been Hitler's immediate superior. Released from the *Reichswehr* in 1919, Wiedemann studied political economics in Munich. In the 1920s he met Hitler again at a regimental reunion, where he was offered the opportunity to lead the SA, which Wiedemann turned down. He next met Hitler by chance in December 1933 when he was in financial difficulties

19 Paul Wernicke (b. 14.1.1899 Ribbeck/Templin, d. 6.8.1967). 1930 joined SS; attached to Sonderkommando Der Führer at the Reich Chancellery, February 1933; entered Personal Adjutancy 2.5.1934; dismissed along with Brückner by Hitler 18.10.1940 with the observation: 'I am sick of the problems in the Adjutancy'; to LSSAH 2.7.1941; Cdr, Div-Staff HQ, Eastern Front, rank of SS-Obersturmbannführer.

20 Fritz Wiedemann (b.16.8.1891 Augsburg, d. 24.1.1970 Fuchsgrub). 1.1.1935 adjutant at Personal Adjutancy as NSKK Brigade-Führer; 1938 Reichstag deputy; March 1939 consul-general at San Francisco; July 1941 expelled from United States with all German diplomats; November 1941 consul-general Tientsin (China); 18.9.1945 brought to Washington; 5.8.1948 released from internment.

after the failure of a dairy enterprise in which he had invested. When Hitler asked how things were going, he replied: 'grim'. Hitler offered him the post of adjutant, which he accepted at once. After an eleven-month training period with the staff of Rudolf Hess at the Braunes Haus in Munich, Wiedemann took up his post as Hitler's Adjutancy on 1.1.1935 at the Reich Chancellery in Berlin, where he was in principle Brückner's office replacement. As Brückner was not an office person, and tended to put things off for tomorrow, the adjutancy correspondence and filing was in something of a mess. Wiedemann combined his work as adjutant with a re-organisation of the day-to-day office procedures in the Personal Adjutancy and increased the staffing level.

Wiedemann made several trips abroad. He flew to the United States a few times and frequently to England. The impressions he got there led to his becoming ever more downbeat when speaking to Hitler. In contrast to the positive Brückner, whom Hitler called 'my ultra-optimist', his replacement was soon labouring under the designation 'my ultra-pessimist'. In January 1939 Hitler could stand no more and told Wiedemann that in his closest circle he could not use a person not in agreement with his policies. For this reason Wiedemann was sent as consul-general to San Francisco. In late 1941 he returned to Germany, from where he was next sent in the same role to Tientsin in China. In 1945 the Americans fetched him home as a witness for the Nuremberg trials.

As already mentioned, after taking power Hitler required a properly trained manservant whom he found initially in Karl Krause.[21] When dismissed, Krause was replaced by Hans Junge[22]

21 Karl Krause (b. 5.3.1911 Michelau). 1.4.1931 Reichsmarine; 1.8.1934 selected as manservant for Hitler; September 1934 at Obersalzberg with rank of SS-Obersturmführer; 10.9.1939 dismissed by Hitler for lying; 1.3.1940 returned to Kriegsmarine; 2.11.1940 to LSSAH Waffen-SS as Oberscharführer; December 1943 to 12.SS-Panzer Div. Hitler Jugend; 1945 SS-Untersturmführer and highly decorated; June 1946 released from Allied internment.

22 Hans Hermann Junge (b.11.2.1914 Wilster/Holstein, fell 13.8.1944). 1.11.1933

and Heinz Linge,[23] although these men were known as orderlies. After Krause, Hitler's servants and orderlies were drawn from the *SS-Leibstandarte Adolf Hitler* (LSSAH)[24] having been selected by Sepp Dietrich, LAH commander, for service with Hitler. They had to look good, be tall if possible, blond and blue-eyed, capable and intelligent. From the men selected by Dietrich, Hitler would then choose the ones he wanted. A few months at the Munich-Pasing servant training school made them into perfect servants.

A valet's duties consisted of attending to Hitler's personal requirements. In the morning at the agreed time Hitler would be awoken by a knock on the bedroom door. The servant would then place newspapers and reports before the door and retire. While Hitler was reading, the servant would prepare his bath and set out his clothing for the day. Hitler would never have a manservant help him dress. In the evening the servant would report to Hitler once all his guests had assembled for dinner. At the Berghof he would always be told: 'Mein Führer, it is arranged that you will lead in Frau Such-and-Such . . .' During the war the servants in the FHQs would invite the participants by telephone to the nightly tea session after the military situation conference. The servants had a very important role to play for the invitees – informing them of Hitler's mood!

joined SS; 1.8.1934 volunteered for LSSAH; 1.7.1936 with *SS-Begleitkommando Der Führer*; from 1940 orderly to Hitler; 19.6.1943 married Hitler's secretary Gertraud Humps; 14.7.1943 drafted into Waffen-SS; 1.12.1943 12 SS-Panzer Div. Hitler Jugend, SS-Obersturmbannführer; killed in action.

23 Heinz Linge (b. 23.3.1913 Bremen, d. 1980 Bremen). 17.3.1933 entered LSSAH; 24.1.1935 manservant to Hitler, remained at FHQ to the end; 2.5.1945 Soviet PoW; released 1955.

24 On 17 February 1933 a private bodyguard for Hitler consisting of 117 selected SS-Führer and SS men was formed into the *SS-Sonderkommando Berlin* under SS-Gruppenführer Dietrich. Accommodated initially in the Friesen Barracks in Berlin, the SS-Sonderkommando moved to the cadet academy at Lichtenfelde in April 1933. The on-duty guard was stationed in the Inner Court at the Reich Chancellery. On 3 September 1933 the *SS-Sonderkommandos* were consolidated into the Adolf Hitler Standarte, renamed LAH on 9 November 1933 with 835 men, and from 13 April 1934 LSSAH, although in general conversation the 'SS2' was dropped.

From my work space in the Adjutancy I looked down on the fine old trees in the Reich Chancellery park where Bismarck used to stroll. On the other side of the room were the tall wing-doors opening to Hitler's room and then beyond that to the Congress Hall made famous by Bismarck. At about ten each morning Hitler came through the high wing-doorway at my back from his flat in the Radziwill Palace. He passed through the Personal Adjutancy to reach his study in the Reich Chancellery. Secretary of State Dr Lammers would have drawn up a schedule the day before for the high-level discussions to be held. On his way to these conferences Hitler would always be in haste but on the way back took his time. Mostly he would stand at the large table and look over the materials there. These might be applications for honorary citizenship, presents from supporters and adoring women, pictures, books, handicrafts, artwork, etc. laid out for him there. Often he would give a short instruction or sign those documents appearing to be urgent.

At this time I saw Hitler daily, except for weekends which he usually spent in Munich. He would always give me a friendly greeting: 'How are you?' He was not an office or desk person and preferred to hold his afternoon conferences in the Winter Garden strolling up and down with his conversation partners. In fine weather the glass doors would be fastened wide open and his great, bright room used only as a corridor to the Reich Chancellery park.

The Personal Adjutancy was only a liaison and communications centre. Sitting at my work position I knew only rarely with whom Hitler would be having a conference, and it was impossible to have a peep. All important correspondence was kept by Hitler personally in his private room while Schaub kept much more in the strongbox. We secretaries only had access to Hitler's study for dictation. All political directives and orders for home and overseas Hitler distributed orally to the Reichsleiters, to Himmler, to the ministers or their representatives and to the foreign ministry. The conferences were not tailored to a particular timetable and would often last into the early hours. The conversation partner would then carry out the directive or order, or have it typed up for his signature later. I never learned anything about the measures being introduced and current events, or at least less than the secretaries to the Reichsleiter, ministers and so on. If Hitler's 'Basic Instruction'[25] was enforced strictly anywhere it was in the Personal Adjutancy. When something of importance had occurred, or was about to, then one would get a certain feeling, and the atmosphere would become ominous, or at least so it seemed to me.

The person absolutely in the know in the Adjutancy was Julius Schaub. He was informed about everything and apparently enjoyed his unique privilege. If by chance I got wind of something and was imprudent enough to even think about asking Schaub, he would give me a warning look from the corner of his eye over the spectacles perched low on his nose. I would feel a nasty tightening of the chest should he then decide to investigate further with a 'What? What's up?' Personally that always made me feel threatened and I would try to extricate myself from the business as quickly as possible, perhaps remarking: 'Oh, I was just wondering.' One was always groping in the dark for information, rarely getting to know something concrete. Even the trips out would only be announced very shortly before departure. While I was living in Wilmersdorf and had to go back there to pack after a trip came up out of the blue, all the secretiveness created a whirlpool which made me quite nervous.

---

25 Hitler issued his 'Basic Order' respecting secrecy on 25 September 1941. This was published to all military and Reich centres by the interior minister on 1 December 1941. Part I prescribed: 'Nobody, no centre, no official, no employee and no worker may know of any secret matter which it is not absolutely necessary for that person to know in the course of his or her duty.'

Chapter 2

The Röhm Putsch 1934

A T THE END OF June 1934 a large number of secret machinations was afoot. Hitler had gone to Essen as witness to the marriage of Gauleiter Terboven.[1] On the evening of 28 June in Berlin I received telephoned instructions to fly by Ju 52 that night from Tempelhof aerodrome to Godesberg. We took off at about 0300. Goebbels was aboard with some of his staff. It was my first flight high above the clouds and I was enchanted by the sight; I seemed to be over a white, foaming sea. I was still in this dreamy state when I arrived at Hotel Dreesen, where I was soon awakened to raw reality. Chief adjutant Brückner gave me the job of making telephone reservations at Hotel Hanselbauer, Bad Wiessee, for some high-ranking SA leaders for the next day. No explanation was given why. There was nothing you could put your finger on, but one could sense something in the wind. Hitler was not visible; he had conferences to attend.

In the early hours of 30 June, without previous warning, we received orders to fly to Munich. Hitler was in the first aircraft to go. He was accompanied by his closest staff: Brückner, Schaub, Reich press chief Dr Dietrich, Goebbels and the officials of the Criminal-

---

1 Hitler attended the wedding ceremony with Göring on 28 June 1934 and afterwards visited the Krupp works at Essen.

Police Division[2] under Rattenhuber. I flew in the second aircraft, the only woman present amongst the *SS-Begleitkommando* (bodyguard) under Gesche, which always took off a little later than Hitler's aircraft. When we arrived in Munich something unexpected occurred. Bruno Gesche had not been informed of where to go from Munich. The adjutants had simply forgotten to tell him. Gesche was scratching his head as to how to proceed and I mentioned to him the SA conference at Wiessee set for that day, intending that to be a clue for him. Gesche had already asked if there were any orders left for him at Hitler's flat in the Prinzregenten-Platz but had drawn a blank.

We were all still in the dark when, after a long drive to Bad Wiessee, we entered the foyer of the Hotel Hanselbauer to find there the same oppressive atmosphere we had sensed in Godesberg. There was something in the wind but impossible to identify what. The Criminal-Police officials looked at me in surprise as I went up to SA chief of staff Röhm, who was sitting in a winged-back armchair, his fine shepherd dog resting alongside him, gave him the friendliest handshake and said: '*Heil* Hitler, *Stabschef*!' What must he and the police have thought? I had no inkling of what had transpired beforehand, that Hitler himself, only half an hour previously, had roused his former friend Röhm for his bed and had him arrested.

We, the occupants of the second aircraft, knew nothing of the main drama which had played out in the Hotel Hanselbauer, being left only with this scene in the reception lounge. After Rattenhuber had briefly updated Gesche on events, we had to almost do an about-face and get back in our cars. Röhm and other arrested SA leaders were driven at once to Munich in Hitler's convoy of vehicles.[3] Hitler,

2 In March or April 1933 Hitler formed a 'Police Commando for Special Purposes' headed by Johann Rattenhuber, a lieutenant in the Bavarian provincial police force and from 10 March 1933 adjutant to Himmler as president of police. The squad, all from Munich, was eight strong and worked alongside Hitler's bodyguard, the *SS-Begleitkommando*. By 1944, designated RSD (Reich Security Service) it had grown in size to 250 men.

3 Hitler's driver Erich Kempka stated postwar that Hitler went to Bad Wiessee

in the leading car, stopped all vehicles coming from the opposite direction (mostly containing SA leaders I had told to proceed to Wiessee), had them get out and personally tore the shoulder straps from their uniforms. I saw this perfectly clearly from where I sat in one of the cars to the rear. Those arrested were slotted into Hitler's column of vehicles in their own car but under guard.

The journey, interrupted by various stops of a similar nature, ended in the courtyard of the Braunes Haus on Brienner Strasse 45, where a *Reichswehr* company had paraded, and saluted Hitler. Hitler, visibly moved, delivered a brief address from which one phrase has stuck in my mind: 'I am pleased – or I am proud, that I have you!' Meanwhile alarming news had filtered through, talk being of shootings at Stadelheim[4] amongst other things. The event of that day which remains imprinted indelibly in my memory was my meeting alone with Hitler in the *SS-Begleitkommando* dining room at the Radziwill Palace. After the return to Berlin I had gone to the dining area at the Reich Chancellery for a snack. I was sitting at a table all alone when the door opened and Hitler came in. He glanced at me, sat himself near me at the oval table and, taking a deep breath, said: 'So, I have bathed and feel as if newly born.'

I was very surprised at Hitler's presence in this area, in the kitchen region, where I had never seen him before. This part of the kitchen was not on the way to his private apartment on the first floor of the palace. What had brought him there? What did he mean when he told me he felt 'as if newly born?' In his own dining room on the park side Goebbels and the other men of his staff were waiting for him, yet he sat with me, rather like a person who, having gone

---

with his staff and the police commando only. The *SS-Begleitkommando* was left in the dark, a fact of which they took a dim view.

4 On 30 June 1934 at Stadelheim prison, Munich, the SA leaders Uhl, von Spretti, Heines, Hayn, Heydebreck, Schneidhuber and Schmidt were shot. Other executions followed next day at Dachau concentration camp and elsewhere. The official list has eighty-three names, but the actual number of victims was greater.

through some dreadful experience, has to say: 'Thank God . . .' This 'feeling as if newly born' was a 'thank God', a sigh of relief from Hitler delivered to somebody who knew nothing of the background particulars to the occurrence.

After 30 June 1934 people puzzled a lot over whether Röhm really had been planning a coup. Purely subjectively, in my opinion he had not, but after Himmler had inveigled his SS people into the police, Röhm probably wanted at least the status of a people's militia for his uneasy and temporarily unemployed SA force. That would have been a breach of the political accord with France. Hitler wished to avoid difficulties in that direction and feared that Röhm had a private political agenda. Judging by the files to which I had access later, and Röhm's order to the SA of 10 June 1934, it cannot be ruled out however that it was his intention. The last paragraph of his order reads:

> I expect that on 1 August the SA will be ready, fully rested and invigorated, to fulfil those honourable and onerous duties which Volk and Fatherland expect of them. If the enemies of the SA are hopeful that the SA will not become involved after their leave, or only partially, then we shall allow them this short, joyful respite. At the time and in the manner which appears necessary afterwards they will receive the appropriate answer. The SA is and remains the destiny of Germany.

This means that chief of staff Röhm had sent his 4.5 million SA men on leave, but as he did so threatened to strike out with a hefty paw. He spoke of 'enemies of the SA'. According to this order by Röhm, the SA 'fully rested' would serve not 'Führer and Reich' as it was then the practice to say, but be at the disposal of 'Volk und Vaterland'. What also struck me in this order was the absence of the usual salute 'Heil Hitler!' with which it was customary to conclude all official correspondence.

Chapter 3

Hitler's Dictation and the Staircase Room

H ITLER GAVE DICTATION MAINLY in the late evening or at night because that was when he had the best ideas, he informed me. So that a secretary (or often two) would be available fresh from rest, Schaub would give early notice of the work that had to be done. Often the dictation would be postponed for days, and Schaub would explain by saying that 'the boss is waiting for a report'. This gave rise to a secretary-on-standby service where one of us would sit in wait in the so-called Staircase Room near Hitler's study. House manager Kannenberg would ensure that we did not go hungry. When I first arrived in Berlin and was 'on call' with the Liaison Staff across the road from the Führer-apartment, the sight of the bowls of fruit alone, with their Williams pears, blue Brussels grapes, apples, oranges and plates with various sandwiches was a delight for the eye.

The Führer's household was run by house manager Arthur Kannenberg and his wife Freda. As guests were always invited for midday and the evenings, one could compare the Führer household to a well-run restaurant. Kannenberg actually came from an old Berlin family of gourmets. His father had owned a licensed restaurant of renown in the capital, and in the 1920s his son became the proprietor of the popular and well-loved eating house on the outskirts of Berlin known as 'Uncle Tom's Cabin'. I never went there myself, but Frau Magdalene Haberstock, a Berliner and widow of art-dealer Karl Haberstock, whom Hitler employed to buy antique paintings, told me once. 'You took tram 76 to Hundekehle and then made a pilgrimage on foot to the beautifully positioned garden restaurant which served not only coffee and pastries but also high-quality meals in the evenings.' Immediately after this restaurant went into liquidation, Kannenberg opened another near the Berlin Anhalter railway station. Goebbels recommended Hitler to visit the establishment, and from then on whenever Hitler arrived at the Anhalter aboard the express from Munich with his entourage he always liked to go to Kannenberg's and tuck into the outstanding vegetable and salad dishes which were a speciality of the house. Kannenberg was not only an outstanding gourmet but an excellent humorist blessed with the legendary Berlin wit. Hitler found his clowning and folksy musical renderings on the accordion so much to his taste that at the beginning of 1932 he appointed Kannenberg to manage the officers' mess at the NSDAP Braunes Haus in Munich.

After taking power in 1933, Hitler brought Kannenberg and his nice, quiet wife Freda, daughter of a German forester, to his apartment in the Radziwill Palace from where the Kannenbergs ran the Führer-household until 1945. Their field of competence included hiring staff, providing uniforms, pay and accommodation, recruiting personnel for house and kitchen, the purchase and control of food and drink, household laundry and preparing the daily menu. Their jurisdiction extended to state receptions and all organisational matters such as the floral decoration of tables, reception and social rooms and the hiring of additional servants and waiters (at major state receptions these were drawn from the *SS-Leibstandarte Adolf Hitler* and the president's Chancellery in livery). The major-domo for the latter would pound the floor with his mace before announcing each guest or couple by name.

Hitler had a great fear of committing a *faux pas* at receptions. He was always plagued by the idea that his staff might err and so lose him prestige. He threatened Kannenberg with disciplinary action should he be guilty of any slip-up of this kind at a reception. Before his guests arrived, Hitler would always cast his eye over the dining table to ensure nothing had been forgotten. In 1939 in conversation with an officer of the close staff who had accompanied Ribbentrop to Moscow, the officer related to Hitler how Stalin had checked the table before dinner to make certain was all in order. I said: 'Stalin seems to have the same concerns as yourself that something might go amiss,' to which Hitler replied: 'My servants are in order.'

Kannenberg had an important function just before every Christmas. It always gave Hitler special pleasure to send presents to people he liked and to whom he felt close. For birthdays and especially at Christmas Hitler never forgot to select his presents for this personal circle comprised not only of Hitler's closest colleagues and their wives, and artists and artistes whom he respected, but also people he knew and friends from the old street-fighting days, especially women with whom he had been friendly before taking power and had formed part of his social circle at that time. Hitler often expressed his regret when taking tea with his female secretaries in the Staircase Room that as Reich Chancellor it was no longer possible for him as it had once been previously to go shopping in Berlin for presents. He said that this had always given him great pleasure in the past. Since Hitler wanted to choose the presents for himself, house manager Kannenberg would select pieces of art from Berlin's most exclusive shops for Hitler to make his choice at the Reich Chancellery. On several occasions he allowed me to assist in the choice.

Before Christmas, Hitler would have Kannenberg set out the presents on tables, chairs and on the floor of the private library and in Hitler's study. I can still picture these presents before me today – paintings, Meissen porcelain, silver trays and bowls, travel necessities, bracelets, dress handbags, opera glasses, hair driers, travel rugs, table lamps, coffee and tea services, silver spoons, gold watches, books and picture frames, articles for the writing desk, leather trunks, car rugs and so on. Hitler would then decide from a long list of recipients who would receive what this year. Julius Schaub kept this list, which also indicated what everybody had received from Hitler in past years.

Kanneberg administered a small empire. Hitler once said of him: 'He controls the kitchen like a Pasha!' Kannenberg was absolutely certain of his power, reigned like a sovereign and was not averse, particularly during the war, to making generous gifts from the Führer-household supplies in order to curry favour with prominent individuals. During the war, every year before Christmas, Hitler received from the Iman of Yemen a couple of sacks of coffee beans as a present. Everybody on his presents list would receive a few pounds of the beans, which at that time were very welcome. Anybody in Kannenberg's good books never went without coffee or other goods then subject to rationing. Frau Magda Haberstock, who stayed during the war as a guest with her friend Kluge on a Silesian property, recalled Kannenberg 'turning up there with a carload of food and things. We stood there gaping, I can tell you. It was all on the side.' To my question whether Kannenberg would have accepted money for it, Haberstock replied: 'No, he wanted to make himself loved!' To my observation: 'He was always a bit of a wheeler and dealer,' Haberstock retorted: 'A bit is putting it mildly!'

Kannenberg's wife was very adept and had a good eye for the placing of table decorations and floral arrangements. Flowers were delivered to the Reich Chancellery by Berlin's leading florist, the Rothe firm in the Hotel Adlon on Unter den Linden. The Kannenbergs were often sent to the Berghof for the visit of prominent guests and to ensure the smooth running of the state dinners. Here Frau Kannenberg would decorate the Great Hall, with its museum-like coolness, with vivid blooms. She was always able to find a blend between the colours of a painting and the flowers she put nearby.

Her arrangements always met with Hitler's full approval. For him she represented the personification of the ideal German housewife. She always styled her hair the same way, the then modern Olympia style; she was well-groomed, circumspect and of quiet demeanour, and without doubt the nicer half of the Kannenberg pair.

Kannenberg himself was small and round, but unusually mobile, even bouncy. He always reminded me of a rubber ball. He had rather protuberant – even hyperthyroidic – eyes and was perhaps unstable emotionally. Unfortunately he liked intrigue and playing on words: house manager-house manipulator was always a phrase that came to my mind when I thought about him. It was Kannenberg who engineered the fall from grace of Hitler's long-serving chief adjutant Wilhelm Brückner and the transfer of orderly officer Max Wünsche[1] to the Front. Both were victims of Kannenberg's intrigues.

In the Führer-apartment and at Obersalzberg the orderlies, or whatever one likes to call them, good-looking young men who wore a white dinner jacket with neck collars, and black trousers, worked as servants, valets and waiters. They were seconded from the *SS-Leibstandarte Adolf Hitler* and after a training course at the Pasing Waiter's School were attached to the serving staff of Hitler's household. This brought them into Kannenberg's empire, although they were not employed by him or to serve under him. This cut both ways, for Kanneberg felt that he ought to be able to regiment them as he did his own people. This was naturally not acceptable to the *SS-Leibstandarte* men and they gave adjutant Max Wünsche plenty of opportunity to intercede on their behalf. He had one particular

---

1 Max Wünsche (b. 20.4.1914 Kittlitz, d. 17.4.1995 Munich). 10.7.1933 joined LSSAH; 25.4.1935–31.3.1936 SS-Junker School at Bad Tölz; 20.4.1936 SS-Untersturmführer; 11.9.1938 SS-Obersturmführer, detached to Hitler as orderly officer and later to adjutant until 24.1.1940, duty at Front; 1.6.1940 returned to FHQ as adjutant; 18.10.1940 dismissed with Brückner by Hitler; as an SS man highly decorated; 24.8.1944 SS-Obersturmbannführer and regimental commander; PoW (British); released 1948.

altercation with Kanneberg on personnel matters which the latter did not forget.

When the Italian princess Mafalda visited in 1940, Kannenberg was ordered to Obersalzberg but did not arrive until after adjutant Wünsche and housekeeper Josefa had got everything arranged. Brückner had not been involved in it at all. Hitler was delighted that everything had gone off so well and he praised Kanneberg for the excellent preparations, which of course had not been his. Kannenberg now seized the opportunity to unleash his grudge against Wünsche. Hitler was convinced and ordered Brückner to his presence. When Brückner took the side of Wünsche against Kanneberg, Hitler dismissed Brückner on the spot and sent Wünsche to the Front.

Hitler probably realised later that he had been sold a dummy by Kannenberg but that did nothing to lower Kannenberg in the Führer's estimation. Since Hitler was so anxious that everything should run perfectly at state banquets and the annual festivals for the arts, and Kannenberg had never let him down, and had always provided the fullest satisfaction, it was not surprising that in time Kannenberg would be allowed some leeway to play the fool. Hitler valued his technical capabilities and enjoyed his clowning, which Kannenberg had brought to a fine art in the 1930s during the picnic outings. On these occasions Kannenberg would delight Hitler and guests with his music and clowning. A pictorial book published by Heinrich Hoffmann in 1937, *Hitler abseits vom Alltag*, has a number of photos (e.g. 'A carefree hour in the Harz') which show Hitler in the completely relaxed type of mood such as he rarely enjoyed later. Kannenberg left the Reich Chancellery in 1945, shortly before the collapse, and fled to the Thumsee in the south. Later in Düsseldorf he opened a hostelry, the Schneider Wibbel Stube, which attracted a lively affluent clientele, perhaps because Kannenberg still had the knack of amusing and entertaining his guests.

But back to the Reich Chancellery. Directly opposite the door to Hitler's study a couple of steps led to a long corridor, beyond which was the so-called adjutancy wing with the rooms for Hitler's aides. The first room was the Staircase Room (*Treppenzimmer*) which will often be mentioned again. Then one came to the rooms of Schaub, Dr Dietrich (Reich press officer), Sepp Dietrich and Brückner (later Alwin-Broder Albrecht). If one went beyond these and descended the staircase one came to the so-called ladies' saloon, actually the reception room, to the left of which wing doors, always pegged open, led into the film room with its hearth. To the right was the Bismarck room, also known as the smoking room. The dining hall was next to it and annexed to the elongated Winter Garden with its chintz-covered armchairs. The far end of the Winter Garden ended in a fine semi-circular path. From the tall glass doors at that end one had a panorama of the trees in the Reich Chancellery park.

Breakfast was taken in the Winter Garden. Wilhelm Brückner used to say that 'breakfast is the nicest time of year' and he would readily accept any excuse to be delayed in the Winter Garden. In the afternoon Hitler held most of his talks strolling its length. He only used his office when Secretary of State Lammers made an appointment for him there expressly. When I was settled into the Personal Adjutancy in the spring of 1934, the regular mealtimes were initially taken with Sepp Dietrich, Dr Dietrich, the SS-Führers and men of the *SS-Begleitkommando*, the adjutants and servants. We ate in the basement of the Department for Economics at the Radziwill Palace. On Hitler's orders guests and staff in the basement dining room received the same fare as was served in the dining room to the Führer-apartment. There was no difference in the menu. In later years we secretaries would eat mostly in the Staircase Room which, as I mentioned previously, was at the entrance to the adjutancy wing. We also took our afternoon tea there.

One day Hitler happened to pass the Staircase Room, saw us sitting there and asked if he might join us. This hour of easy chatter, which developed quite naturally, was so much to his liking that he would often come by at this hour and later came to tea almost daily.

The afternoon tea hour in the Staircase Room became a fairly fixed ritual. Usually we two secretaries would keep Hitler company, later occasionally all three, namely Johanna Wolf, Gerda Daranowski and myself.

Actually the Staircase Room was rather functional. It had a very high ceiling and was only used for visitors in an emergency because it had no bath, only a washstand with mirror. The simple furnishings were a chintz-covered couch, a wardrobe, a safe, the typists' table, lamp standard and octagonal table with wickerwork chairs. From when war broke put in 1939 we secretaries served mostly at the current FHQ then in use, or on an alternating roster. The Staircase Room was our permanent office for when we were in Berlin, although purpose-built work rooms were planned for us in the new Reich Chancellery they proved too far away. There was no fixed eight-hour day. We were on call twenty-four hours and had to be permanently at Hitler's disposal, and since Hitler stayed in his apartment, except when engaged in official conferences, we were closer to him in the Staircase Room than the new Reich Chancellery and within immediate reach. His study, the library, his bedroom and later alongside it Eva Braun's apartment were all on the first floor of the Radziwill Palace.

Despite the simple furnishings of the Staircase Room Hitler liked it very much. It was a place where he could relax and I always had the impression that he felt unburdened there. He used to talk about the experiences of his youth and the past, subjects which he might never mention again, or would touch upon later in the evening tea circle and at table in the FHQ officers' mess. One felt that what he said in the Staircase Room came from a secret memory box which at all other times he kept locked shut.

Hitler regretted very much not being able to wander the city and go shopping. 'How wonderful that used to be with Geli,' he would often say. She would drag him into a hat shop and try them all on only to discover that none suited her. Once when he said: 'You cannot do that and just leave without buying something,' she laughed and replied: 'That's what the salesgirls are there for.'

In the Staircase Room he told us of the pranks he played in late childhood. He said once that his aversion to the clergy stemmed from that time. He mentioned a professor of religious instruction at school who was always unkempt. He would have food stains on his jacket and carried a handkerchief so incredibly filthy and encrusted that he would have to tug it open before use. The professor had admonished the class for not kneeling in the approved manner in church. Hitler replied with a straight face that he did not know how one should kneel and would like the professor to demonstrate. The professor, pleasantly surprised that this boy was so interested in being taught the correct position took out his filthy handkerchief, opened it, spread it on the floor and knelt on it. At that moment the school bell rang for break. The master stood up, laid his handkerchief on a small stool and left the room to converse with colleagues, as was his custom. As his classmates looked on, Hitler picked up the handkerchief by its extreme tip and approached the group of teachers, offering the handkerchief to the teacher with a smile: 'The Herr Professor has forgotten his handkerchief.'

A much-loved activity at his school was reflecting the sun with a hand-mirror. Hitler was so keen on 'mirroring' that a teacher felt compelled to make an entry in the class register. During the break the boys looked at the entry, and to their delight saw that the master had unintentionally made a rhyme of it: '*Hitler ist ein Bösewicht, er spiegelt mit dem Sonnenlicht*' (Hitler is mischievous, mirroring the sunlight). When the master returned, the boys chanted the rhyme in unison.

Hitler recalled that as a twelve year old he wagered his classmates that he could make the girls laugh during a religious service. He won the bet by intently brushing his non-existent moustache whenever they glanced at him. On the subject of drinking and smoking he admitted:

As a boy I did once smoke a cigarette, or part of one. It made me feel terrible, I ran home and was sick repeatedly. My mother was very concerned, and so I told her that I had eaten deadly nightshade. She sent for the doctor, who examined me, checked my mouth and looked at me suspiciously. Then he went through my trouser pockets and found the cigarette butt. Later I bought a long porcelain pipe. I smoked like a chimney even when I was in bed. Once I fell asleep smoking and woke up to find the bed on fire. That was the moment when I swore never to smoke again, and I have kept my promise.

He went on:

After our final exams I went with my classmates to a farmer's barn to celebrate with schnapps. It made me feel sick and I went to the manure heap behind the house to vomit several times. Next morning I looked in vain for my school-leaving certificate which my father wanted to see. All my enquiries met no success, and so I went to the headmaster to request a copy. There I experienced the greatest shame of my youth, for the headmaster produced the original certificate. The farmer had found it in his manure heap and had returned it to my school. I swore to myself then and there that I would never touch another drop.

He also spoke of his mother, to whom he was very attached, and of his father's violence:

I never loved my father, [he used to say,] but feared him. He was prone to rages and would resort to violence. My poor mother would then always be afraid for me. When I read Karl May once that it was a sign of bravery to hide one's pain, I decided that when he beat me the next time I would make no sound. When it happened – I knew my mother was standing anxiously at the door – I counted every stroke out loud. Mother thought I had gone mad when I reported to her with a beaming smile, 'Thirty-two strokes father gave me!' From that day I never needed to repeat the experiment, for my father never beat me again.

Later when he understood how hard life could be, Hitler said that he had the greatest respect for his father for having worked his way up from being an orphan child to a customs official. Hitler also liked to speak of the abilities of his mother as a housewife, who gradually increased the family property.

He often used to speak of his sisters, who were simply 'geese' for him. He would criticise them for their disapproval of his favourite sport, rat-hunting in the churchyard with an air gun. He confided to us that when his half-sister Angela got engaged, he advised the prospective groom, whom he liked, to break off the engagement and 'let the stupid goose go'. Hitler had no sense of family. His sister Paula was quite a few years younger than he was. She was a quiet, shy child and he had no great opinion of her. It may have been for the difference in their ages that he shut her out of his life. Paula lived in Vienna until the end of the Second World War, and then in Berchtesgaden until her death.

In a letter dated 29 August 1956 she wrote: 'I did not grow out of Vienna, in the true sense of the word, until after the war ended.' In another letter dated 7 February 1957 she said:

I always had to give way to my half-sister, who was older and more ebullient than I, although my brother and I had the same parents. It was clear to me that we could not allow everybody to see that we were fighting over him. Therefore I stayed in Vienna and my half-sister became his housekeeper on the Obersalzberg. That era ended in 1935. He wanted to be free and unrestricted in every direction. In every direction in a private sense.

On 5 February, two days earlier, she had explained: 'We sisters were too jealous of him in his eyes; he would rather have strangers around him whom he could pay for their services.'

Alois Hitler, his half-brother senior to him by seven years, never played a role in his life. This half-brother married an Irish girl who gave birth to two sons. The first of these, William Patrick Hitler, came to attention in 1939 when he wrote a book, *Mon Oncle Adolphe*. The other son fell as an officer on the Eastern Front. Alois Hitler had a restaurant on the Wittenberg-Platz [in Berlin] during the Third Reich but his name was never mentioned in Hitler's presence, neither were the relatives at Spittal.

Hitler spoke frequently about the period of struggle and Dietrich Eckart. He once said that 'this friendship was amongst the finest to which I was party in the 1920s!' Dietrich Eckart, born the son of a notary at Neumarkt in the Upper Pfalz, was a journalist and ethnic poet. He had made his name as a theatre critic at Bayreuth and was friendly with Henrik Ibsen. Eckart translated *Peer Gynt* from the Norwegian into German, which brought him much recognition. He had met Hitler at a political meeting in 1920. Eckart was a father figure and would often help Hitler out of his financial plights. Hitler always became very emotional when recounting this to us in detail. Eckart served time with Hitler in 1923 at Landsberg prison, from where he was released at Christmas that year suffering from a terminal illness, spending his last days with a friend, the owner of the Brüggen fief at Berchtesgaden, where he died before the end of 1923. He was buried in the old section of the Berchtesgaden cemetery. His motto *Deutschland erwache!* was turned by Hitler into the battle cry of the Nazi Movement.

Eckart's death was a heavy blow for Hitler. In later life he was never to find a friend with whom he had similar harmony in thought and feeling, he said. Whenever he spoke of Dietrich Eckart his eyes would water. Repeatedly when in power he would rue the death of the 'loyal Ekkehard' and regret that now he had the power to do so he could not repay all the good Eckart had done him. Everything connected with Dietrich Eckart touched Hitler. When I told him one day of a female friend who had inherited some handwritten poems by Dietrich Eckart from the widow of Ernst von Wolzogen, Hitler wanted to buy them at once, and when he identified them as Eckart's earliest work, most of which had been destroyed by his jealous wife, he raised his bid immediately, so great was his joy at having something in his friend's handwriting in his own hands. It was from his loyalty to Dietrich Eckart that he based his attachment to Johanna Wolf, Eckart's former secretary, whom he nicknamed 'Wolferl'.

Hitler spoke a lot of the journeys he made in the years of struggle. In the summer they always drove in the open Mercedes, Hitler seated beside chauffeur Julius Schreck, who died in 1936. Schreck was succeeded by Erich Kempka. They would often stop for a rest at Lambach on the Chiemsee. Hitler was very fond of Lambach;* he had been there when Hindenburg's invitation reached him in 1932, summoning him to Berlin. Hitler related how difficult it was on these journeys to remain anonymous. When Schaub reminded him of the Hotel Elephant at Weimar, Hitler went on:

> I had a permanent room there with running water but no bath, and
> the bathroom was at the other end of the corridor. Every time I was
> forced to run the gauntlet, for whenever I left my room the word got
> round like wildfire through the entire hotel and by the time I left
> the WC, the corridor would have filled with people, and with raised
> arms and an embarrassed smile I would be manhandled hither and
> thither all the way back to my room.

---

* August Kubizek, *Adolf Hitler – Mein Jugendfreund*, Leopold Stocker Verlag, unabridged impression and reprint 2002, pp.55–6; Hitler attended school at Lambach in 1895 and 1896–8, when he also sang as a chorister at Lambach monastery. (TN)

He described the games they played to pass the time on the drives, for example 'Dr Steinschneider'. There were no fixed rules, and one did not realise it was a game until one had lost. Somebody would tell a story so convincingly that the listeners were forced to ask at the end: 'Who was with them?' If the answer was 'Dr Steinschneider', everybody realised it was a hoax and the questioners had been caught out. Another game was 'The Beaver'. A 'beaver' was a man wearing a full beard, and if one was spotted on the journey you had to shout 'Beaver!'', and the first to do so won a point. This kind of game would always put Hitler in the best of humour. Occasionally he would imitate the speech and mannerisms of his old comrades. He was an excellent mimic. A highlight of his repertoire was his imitation of the fast-speaking and repetitive Bavarian publisher Max Amann. From Hitler's impression one could imagine him shrugging his shoulders and gesticulating furiously with his right hand. The tremendous voice of the partially-deaf printer Adolf Müller was also the subject of Hitler's mimicry. He also liked to imitate foreign statesmen. He could copy exactly the sharp laugh of King Victor Emmanuel of Italy, and showed very skilfully how the king, who appeared gigantic when seated, could stand up and appear to be of normal size.

In this prewar period Hitler could be merry and humorous and knew the value of humour: 'A humorous word in a difficult situation has often worked wonders', he said, 'not only in the First World War, but also in the period of struggle.' That would not be the case once the first setbacks began in 1941–2, when Hitler became more reclusive and almost inaccessible. He often spoke of the financial bonds in which the Party invested earlier, and were signed by him. Often somebody had to be found at the last moment to redeem them. He liked to quote this example:

> I had signed a Loan Note for the Party for 40,000 RM. Money I was
> expecting had not been received, the Party coffers were empty and

the redemption date on the note was coming nearer without any hope of my getting the money together. I was considering shooting myself, since there seemed no alternative. Four days before the redemption date I informed Frau Bruckmann of my unfortunate plight. She phoned Emil Kirdorf[2] and sent me to see him. I told Kirdorf of my plans and won him over at once to the cause. He placed the money at my disposal and thus enabled me to liquidate the debt on time.

Hitler also related that at Landsberg prison he either typed parts of the text of *Mein Kampf* himself or dictated it to Hess. His time there was very strictly scheduled, and he confined his reading matter to history, philosophy and biographies. Whilst in Landsberg he worked on plans for the autobahns and to make available to every citizen a four-seater car for 990 RM. The car was to resemble a May beetle, and each should have its own garage. The ideas for the VW car and the autobahn both occurred to Hitler in 1922 and he said that he had drawn up the plans for both at Landsberg. The highway over the Bavarian Alps was also his idea. This would enable people to experience the beauty of the mountains. The Transalp highway from Lindau to Berchtesgaden was the second point of his programme.

There was really no subject he had not dwelt on: architecture, painting, sculpture, theatre, films, artistry: all were an inexhaustible fund for conversation. If there was a pause in the talk and we were stuck for something to discuss, it was only necessary to mention any of the foregoing and Hitler was in his element. The Church was always a favourite topic. Hitler had no affiliation. He considered the Christian religion to be a hypocritical trap which had outlived its time. His religion was the Law of Nature.

---

2 Emil Kirdorf (b. 1847, d. 1938). From 1892 Dir-Gen. Gelsenkirchner Bergwerke AG; 1929 guest of honour Nuremberg rally; from 1931 arranged that for every ton of coal sold by Rhine-Westfalen Coal Syndicate, 5 pfennigs would go to the NSDAP.

Science has not yet decided from which roots the human race sprang forth. We are probably the highest stage of development from some mammal or other which had developed from the reptile, and then perhaps through the apes to the human being. We are a limb of Creation and children of Nature and the same laws apply to us as they do to all living beings. In Nature, the law of the jungle has been in force from the beginning. All those unsuitable to live, and the weak, are trampled underfoot. Man, and above all the Church, have made it precisely their goal to keep alive by artificial means the weak, those unfit for life and the invalids.

Hitler was clever enough to know that he could not destroy the moral high ground which religious belief provided, and he remained to the end a Catholic, although he intended to renounce membership as soon as the war ended. This act would have a symbolic significance: for Germany the end of an historical epoch and for the Third Reich the beginning of a new era. On the subject of the closing ceremonies at the Nuremberg rallies he once said: 'The closing Congress must be as solemn and festive as the Catholic mass. The bringing in of the standards, the whole ceremony should be planned like a ritual of the Catholic Church.' He also planned mass marriages with 50–100 couples. 'The mass service will make it possible to have very festive ceremonies.' Great music bands, flower decorations everywhere.

He also spoke of the motherly, self-sacrificing ladies of high society, in whose salons new contacts would be made. He said that it reinforced in him the impression 'that he was being eyed-up like an ape in a zoo'. One day after the renovation work at the Radziwill Palace, I was called to the Reich Chancellery apartment in the late morning. Hitler was at breakfast with his adjutants in the dining room. I was asked to take a seat at table. Scarcely had I sat than the waiter Karl Krause led in a very young and pretty blonde. This was the baroness Sigrid von Laffert, whose photo at the time was gracing the title page of the *Berlin Illustrierte* under the heading 'A German Girl!' She was the daughter of an officer from Doberan in Mecklenburg, but better known as the niece of Hitler's patroness Viktoria von Dirksen. David Irving related the following anecdote about her in his very superficial analysis *How Sick was Hitler Really?*:[3] 'There was for example Viktoria von Dirksen, an ambitious 150 per cent National Socialist who once managed to inveigle a twenty-one-year old relation, pretty as a picture, naked into Hitler's bed at the Reich Chancellery. Hitler found her there, but did no more than politely request her to dress and leave the room.' This was a fable, however.

Viktoria von Dirksen ran a political saloon in which Hitler was often centre-stage. In later years in the Staircase Room he would make remarks about the invitations and say: 'I felt there like an exotic zoo animal, peered at curiously by everybody as an attraction.' At this time he was probably still enjoying the invitations of Her Excellence. He was pleased by her pretty niece and took a few steps in her direction, saying something like 'Here comes my sunshine' or 'The sun is rising', I cannot be sure any more. In any case, his attraction to Sigrid von Laffert could not be missed, and neither could it be hidden from Eva Braun in Munich.

Hitler's clothing was purely functional. He hated trying things on. Since he made lively hand and arm movements to emphasise points he was making in his speeches, and also liked to extend his body while strolling in conversation, especially when the subject was one which excited him and which he did mainly by raising the right shoulder, he had an aversion to a close fit. His tailor[4] had to shape all uniforms and suits for comfort in this regard. This occasional raising of the right shoulder may have been due to the left shoulder being stiff. During the putsch of 9 November 1923 Hitler fell to

3 Wilhelm Heyne Verlag, Munich 1980, p.27.

4 Hitler's wardrobe came almost exclusively from the Wilhelm Holter's gentleman's outfitters on Wilhelm-Strasse 49, Berlin.

the pavement, dislocating his left shoulder. Dr Walter Schultze, husband of Ada Klein and leader of the SA medical corps, could not convince Hitler to have it X-rayed. Hitler feared being 'bumped off' at the hospital. The shoulder was therefore never properly fixed and remained stiff ever afterwards, which I often had cause to notice.

Although with this slightly lop-sided posture and ample jacket Hitler did not exactly cut an elegant figure, he still commanded respect. As soon as he entered a room everybody present would notice him. Looking back this seems to have been because he never hurried. His manner of walking was always measured, almost ceremonial, when he went to greet somebody. This tended to induce in the other person a feeling of uncertainty, for it contrasted with the free and unforced approach one expected. Hitler had always to be the controller! He mentioned frequently for example: 'how uncertain it made visitors to the new Reich Chancellery to have to cross the long marble hall, polished like a mirror, and then traverse his large study to get to his desk'.

I found his eyes expressive. They looked mostly as if interested and searching, and became increasingly animated during conversation. They could look friendly and warm-hearted, or express indignation, indifference and disgust. In the last months of the war they lost expressiveness and became a more watery, pale light blue, and rather bulging.

One could always tell his mood from his voice. It could be unusually calm, clear, exact and convincing, but also excited increasing in volume and overwhelming in aggression. Often it would be ice-cold. 'Ice-cold', or 'Now I am ice-cold' were much-used phrases of his. 'I am totally indifferent to what the future will think of the methods which I have to use,' I heard frequently. 'Ruthless' (*rücksichtslos*) was common in his vocabulary: 'Force it through ruthlessly, whatever the cost!' Other phrases to crop up a lot were 'with brute force!' and 'with brutal energy!', and in conclusion, 'simply idiotic!'

Hitler's nose was very large and fairly pointed. I do not know whether his teeth were ever very attractive, but by 1945 they were yellow and he had bad breath. He should have grown a beard to hide his mouth. During the years of his friendship with Ada Klein[5] he told her: 'Many people say I should shave off the moustache, but that is impossible. Imagine my face without a moustache!' and at that held his hand below his nose like a plate. 'My nose is much too big. I need the moustache to relieve the effect!'

I liked his hands, either in motion or at rest. They were not manicured, but had a cared-for look with their short nails. Over the years the joints got increasingly thicker. During a flight a photographer, perhaps Heinrich Hoffmann himself, took a very fine photograph showing Hitler's hands on the armrest of his seat. Hitler never wore personal jewellery. Even his gold watch he carried loose in his jacket pocket. It was always a few minutes fast so that he arrived at meetings and conferences punctually. He doubted the reliability of his waiters and adjutants although he was perpetually asking them for the time.

From 1933 Hitler avoided personal contact with money which seemed in some way repugnant to him. His adjutant Schaub would settle everything. Before 1933 he carried a wallet and put loose coins in his jacket pocket. According to Ada Klein, when paying off a taxi he would always give a big tip 'almost equivalent to the fare'. She repeated his often-expressed conviction: 'Rich people are tight, they spare on tips!'

It amused Hitler that there were men always looking for new ties. 'When I saw a tie I liked, I would buy several of the same kind,' he said once. Later he only ever wore black ties, to go with the uniform. He placed no value on having a variety of dress styles. He rarely spoke on fashion, although he could deliver a surprising commentary on a dress and pay compliments to the lady wearing

---

5 See Chapter 10.

it. He would go to town on certain dress crazes, such as shoes with cork soles, but I am convinced it was all done for some purpose or other. I often heard him say in admiration to Eva Braun: 'Ah, you are wearing a new dress!' and she would reply indignantly: 'Oh, come on, you've seen it before, I've worn it often enough.'

Hitler set great store on hygiene. He bathed daily, often several times a day, particularly after meetings and speeches, from which he would return sweating. His skin was very soft. Probably he always shaved himself. A manservant would not have been called upon to do much for him. At the beginning of the 1930s his clothing was sent to a large Berlin laundry which would put pins into the upper part of the shirts to retain their shape. Hitler rarely had occasion to remonstrate with his servants, but when he did he could be very angry, as when Karl Krause forgot to take out the pins from his shirts one day.

Hitler was very strong-willed. During the 1933 Nuremberg rally I was summoned there and ordered to the Deutscher Hof Hotel where Hitler dictated to Johanna Wolf and myself that night the speeches he delivered next day. We watched from the hotel window as Hitler saluted the march past by the SA, SS and RAD (Reich Work Service). I was surprised that he could stand for hours at a stretch with his arm extended. During a tea hour he revealed that he had 'done daily training with an expander', but that 'a strong will' was also needed. Additionally he would always try to look every man in the eye to give him the feeling that the Führer had seen him. Often one actually heard it said: 'The Führer saw me, he looked into my eyes.'

One must mention that Hitler did no sport. He did not like horses and hated snow (especially after the winter of 1941), and sunshine made him feel bad. He did not like the sun and had bought the Berghof precisely because it was situated on the north side of the Obersalzberg. The house was in shadow all day, and the thick walls made sure no warmth got through from outside. Even in summer it was unusually cool, and cold when it rained. Hitler loved this cold, although his guests found it unpleasant. He was afraid of water. I do not believe he could swim.* One day he told me: 'The movements a person makes while at his daily work is enough to keep his body in shape.'

Undoubtedly he knew how to charm a person under his spell during conversation. He could expound even the most complicated subjects clearly and simply. He had the power to relate something so convincingly that he fascinated his listeners. He possessed extraordinary powers of suggestion, and this was no doubt the reason why people who came to him in desperation went away reassured. I remember that in March 1945 Gauleiter Forster came from Danzig totally demoralised. He told me that Danzig was surrounded by 1,100 Russian tanks and the Wehrmacht was opposing this force with four Tiger panzers, and these were short of fuel. Forster was determined to hold nothing back and tell Hitler the whole truth about the situation in Danzig. When I encouraged him to do so, he replied: 'You can rely on it. I am going to tell him everything, even if I run the danger of being ejected.' To my surprise he returned from his talk with Hitler a changed man. 'The Führer has promised me new divisions for Danzig,' he said in relief. He countered my doubting smile: 'I admit I have no idea where he will be getting them from, but he assured me that Danzig will be saved, about that there is no doubt.' Such were Hitler's powers of suggestion.

Harsh and inflexible as Hitler could be with others, he did not exempt himself. He never spared himself. He would reject tiredness and would call upon endless reserves of energy. He was a prisoner to the delusion that an iron will could succeed everywhere. No wonder that the trembling left hand was such an embarrassment to him. The knowledge from 1944 onwards that he was no longer master of his own body was a heavy burden. When surprised visitors saw his trembling hand, he would cover it instinctively with the other. Despite

---

* According to Kubizek, *Adolf Hitler – Mein Jugendfreund*, Leopold Stocker Verlag 2002, p.34, Hitler was a 'tolerably good swimmer' and one day dived into the river Rodel to save Kubizek's mother from drowning after she slipped from a rock. (TN)

51

every effort of will he could do nothing to stop the trembling. Yet to the end he remained master of his emotions. Should bad news arrive during a private conversation the only clue would be a movement of his jaw and he would carry on calmly. I remember him receiving the report about the destruction of the Möhne and Eder dams, which flooded much of the Ruhr. As he read it his face turned to stone, but that was all. Nobody could have gauged how deeply the blow had struck him. It would be hours or days before he would refer to such an event, and then give full vent to his feelings.

With equally astonishing self-mastery he kept his secrets. He was convinced that nobody should know more than what was needed for the discharge of his or her office. He would often say: 'A secret shared is no secret.' He never spoke of his secret intentions and plans nor dropped hints about an impending military operation or suchlike.

From his youth onwards Hitler had a great lust to read. He told me one day that during his youth in Vienna he had read through all 500 volumes at the city reference library. This passion for books, and to assimilate contents of the most diverse kinds, enabled him to extend his knowledge into almost all areas of literature and science. I was always amazed at how precisely he could describe any geographical region or speak about art history or hold forth on very complicated technical matters. In the same way he could describe with amazing detail how theatres, churches, monasteries and castles were built. Even during his incarceration at Landsberg he studied tirelessly the historical buildings of all European countries and would often boast that he 'knew the architectural beauties of those countries better even than the experts who were native to them.'

The Oberbürgermeister of Munich[6] with whom Hitler enjoyed discussing the expansion and beautification of the city related

6 Karl Fiehler (b. 31.8.1895 Braunschweig, d. 8.12.1969 Munich). 5.11.1923 joined NSDAP; active in Hitler's storm troops; 28.4.1924 sentenced to fifteen months' imprisonment for participation in the putsch of 1923; by 1930 NSDAP Reichsleiter; 20.3.1933 Oberbürgermeister of Munich until 1945; 1945–16.1.1949 interned.

how surprised he was when Hitler recalled the minute details of a conversation they had had months previously. Hitler had reproached him: 'Six months ago I told you I wanted to have it done this way!' and then repeated word for word the conversation they had had on the subject, a fact confirmed by architects Speer and Giesler postwar.

Hitler could not only recall very easily names, books and statistics, but faces too. He could remember exactly the time, place and circumstances under which he had met a person. He retained a mental image of all persons whom he had got to know in his life, and on reflection surprising personal details might also occur to him. Equally he could describe the atmosphere and sequence of events at rallies at which he had spoken. The friends of his youth in Vienna, of the First World War, the period of struggle and the seizure of power were all deeply embedded in his memory with all their peculiarities. If he was in a good mood he enjoyed describing the great receptions at the Reich Chancellery. He could see in his mind's eye what dress this or that artiste had worn, and repeat the serious or light-hearted conversations he had had with his guests.

It was no different with his impressions of theatrical presentations or films: he could describe a scene he had watched in Vienna as a young man down to the last detail. He would mention the names of actors and recall how the critics had treated them. I have asked myself very often how a human mind can have retained so many facts and impressions. It is confirmed that from his youth onwards Hitler had the gift of an unusual memory, but his secret was that he trained and expanded it every day. He said that when he was reading he tried to grasp the essence of a thing and fix it in his mind. It was his practice or method during the tea hours and when chatting at the hearth over a subject he had been reading about to repeat it several times in order to anchor it more firmly in his memory.

Hitler seemed able to follow a conversation in English or French if it was not spoken too quickly but explained: 'I have not made the effort to be fluent in a foreign language because in talks with foreigners every word counts. While my interpreter translates, I gain time to think of new, appropriate ways to phrase a thing.'

Despite the effort Hitler made to surprise people with his rich trove of knowledge, and to show them his superiority, he made sure he never let them know the sources of this knowledge. He was expert at convincing his listeners that everything he said was the result of his own deliberations and critical thinking. He could recite pages and pages of books and so give the impression that his ideas had evolved from his own comprehension. Nearly everybody with whom I discussed it was convinced that Hitler was a profound thinker, and a wonderfully sharp, analytical spirit. Once I began working for him, I wanted to get the thing straight. One day Hitler launched into a philosophical dissertation on one of his favourite themes. To my astonishment I realised that he was reciting a page from Schopenhauer which I had just finished reading myself. Summoning all my courage I drew the fact to his attention. Hitler, taken a little aback, threw me a glance and then explained in fatherly tones: 'Do not forget, my child, that all knowledge comes from others and that every person only contributes a minute piece to the whole.'

In the same convincing manner Hitler spoke about famous men, foreign countries, about cities, buildings and theatrical plays without actually knowing or having seen them. The confident and decisive manner of expressing himself, and the clear dialectic with which he formulated his thoughts, must have convinced his listeners that he actually knew all this from his own experience; one was forced to draw the conclusion that everything he described in his narratives with such astonishing precision he had thought through or experienced personally. One day he delivered a damning criticism of a theatrical presentation which I knew he had not seen. I therefore asked him how he could judge the director and performers if he had not been present. He answered: 'You are right, but Fräulein Braun was there and told me everything.'

Back in the Staircase Room I would wait on standby until a valet shouted through the wing door: 'The chief is asking you to come for dictation!' Therefore up and follow the valet. He would open the door to the library and shut it as he withdrew, hanging a notice on the latch: 'Do not disturb.' As a rule Hitler would be standing at or bent over his desk, working on the punch lines for a speech, for example. Often he would appear not to notice my presence. Before the dictation I would not exist for him, and I doubt whether he saw me as a person when I was at my typist's desk.

A while would pass in silence. Then he would close in on the typewriter and begin to dictate calmly and with expansive gestures. Gradually getting into his stride he would speak faster. Without pause one sentence would then follow another while he strolled around the room. Occasionally he would halt, lost in thought, before Lenbach's portrait of Bismarck, gathering himself as it were before resuming his wandering. His word flow would be stemmed again as he paused before the commode, lifting up to admire one of the small bronze figurines. After staring at it for some time, he would replace it.

If he touched upon Bolshevism in his speech, emotion would take possession of him. His voice often skipped over bits. That also happened if he mentioned Churchill or Roosevelt. Then his choice of words would not be so fussy. For my part if he mentioned the 'whisky-guzzler' (Churchill) or the 'bloodhound' (Stalin) too often, I would simply omit some of the references. Interestingly enough, when reading through the draft he would never notice these cuts, a sign of how worked up he had been. In these situations his voice would increase to maximum volume, over-pitch so to speak, and he would make lively gesticulations with his hands. His face would become florid and the anger would shine in his eyes. He would stand rooted to the spot as though confronting the particular enemy he was imagining. During the dictation I often found my heart racing as Hitler's excitement spilled over me. It would certainly have been easier to have taken this dictation in shorthand but Hitler did not want this. Apparently he felt himself as if on wings when he heard the rhythmic chatter of the typewriter keys. Besides, he had before his eyes the written record of what he had just said. During the dictation he spoke no private words.

These dictations were as a rule speeches for the Reichstag, for meetings, Party rallies, at opening ceremonies for car, artistic, farming or technical exhibitions, for foundation-stone laying ceremonies, opening ceremonies for completed stretches of autobahn, for the New Year reception of diplomats and so forth. Also letters to foreign heads of state such as Mussolini, Antonescu (Romania), Horthy (Hungary), Inönü (Turkey) and Mannerheim (Finland) were dictated. He dictated private letters only when protocol demanded it, to thank somebody or offer condolences. He would send birthday greetings to Frau Goebbels, Frau Göring, Frau Ley, Winifred Wagner and others on handwritten white cards bearing his name in gold lettering below the eagle and swastika in the top left corner.

Dictating into the typewriter required extreme concentration. One had to follow his sense, and apply some intuition, for fragments of his sentences were often lost. He would start off by speaking none too clearly and his voice often echoed as he strolled the large room. Additionally the typewriter had its own mechanical noise. In those days of course there were no electronic machines. As Hitler would never be seen wearing spectacles in public, typewriters were later manufactured with 12-mm characters so that he could read the script in public without glasses. The 'Silenta' brand machines had the advantage of typing quietly but the keys tended to tangle if one typed over a certain speed. Since Hitler did not – or did not want to – notice this and kept on dictating, this was naturally very unsettling for the typist and often made her very nervous. One became anxious that while unscrambling the keys a sentence might be missed and the text would not flow. This would result in bated breath while watching Hitler correcting the draft afterwards.

When the dictation was finished, Hitler would occasionally sit at his writing desk, put on his gold-rimmed spectacles, take up the fountain pen from the old-fashioned black penholder and start changing words, striking some out, inserting new ones, and all scrawled in his *Fraktur* style. From time to time he would look up and say: 'Look here, child, see if you can read this!' When I assured him that I could, his voice would sound a little disappointed: 'Yes, you can read it better than I can!'

Correcting the draft was a labour which never ended. After every assault on it the modified version had to be retyped. More than once I had to run to his car to hand over the last pages. At that time there was still the personal contact with him. Once when giving him some pages before he left for the Reichstag I asked him not to speak so loud because the microphone distorted his voice if the volume was too great. In 1937–8 Hitler would receive that kind of advice without demur. Every secretary had 'her time' when she would be favoured by him over a longish period. On one occasion I did not like the way he had phrased something. When I dared mention it, he looked at me, neither angry nor offended, and said: 'You are the only person I allow to correct me!' I was so astonished, perhaps also disbelieving, that I forgot to thank him.

From the outbreak of war Hitler would never deliver a speech without a manuscript. 'I prefer to speak, and I speak best, from the top of my head,' he told me, 'but now we are at war I must weigh carefully every word, for the world is watching and listening. Were I to use the wrong word in a spontaneous moment of passion, that could have severe implications!' Only internally, before Gauleiters, the military or industrialists, did he speak freely and unscripted. Once he had finished the outline of a speech he would seem to have thrown off a burden. If he dictated it during a stay at the Berghof, he would announce the next day at lunch that his speech was ready and he expected it to be well received. Then he would heap praise on the skill of his secretaries or, as he called us at the beginning, 'his writing force'. Often there would be two of us together when one would relieve the other after a couple of hours of dictation, and he would praise us: 'You write faster than I dictate, you are true queens of the typewriter!'

He liked to relate the difficulties he had had in earlier years when he needed to dictate something during a visit to a Gauleiter, for example. 'Mostly the girls would get so excited when they saw me, blushing furiously, and would be unable to do the work as I wanted. When I noticed that I would break off the dictation pretending that I had to wait for some report or other before I could continue.' I found this tactful of Hitler, for it was not easy to work for him. 'Shall I demonstrate my own typing skills?' he joked. 'I do it more or less like this.' And then he would pretend he was seated at a machine ready to type. He would flex his imaginary sheet of paper, straighten it up carefully, adjust the platen with the knob at the side and then, to the laughter of the onlookers, begin typing with his forefingers, not forgetting to use the carriage lever, space bar and upper case keys as the occasion demanded. He aped the movements so accurately that no professional mime artist could have done it better. Undoubtedly he had great talent as an actor and people-impersonator.

Chapter 4

Travelling With Hitler

U P TO 1937 HITLER would only take one secretary with him on his travels, either Fräulein Wolf or myself. Our private life was very curtailed, and existed only when the opportunity for it occurred. Even when officially off duty we had to leave a phone number where we could be reached. Hitler knew that he weighed us down with work but did not care to enlarge the pool of secretaries because he could not stand having new faces around him. For this reason we had almost no personal freedom and were on call day and night. Once in the train to Hamburg I was ordered by radio message to take the next train back; on another occasion sitting in the stands on the Odeon Platz during the October Festival I heard a loudspeaker announcement: 'Fräulein Schroeder should report immediately to the Prinzregenten-Platz' (Hitler's flat). Even when I was taking the cure I was often recalled just to take a single dictation.

Hitler's principle of keeping a plan secret to the last possible moment kept us under constant pressure. The trips and excursions were probably always arranged well ahead but Hitler would only announce the time of departure at the last minute. During the long period of waiting for the announcement we would always be on tenterhooks. If someone ever passed a remark about how little free time he left us, however, Hitler would put on his surprised face and

59

assure them: 'I allow everybody in my circle their freedom,' but in reality he would not tolerate anybody daring to go their own way.

When I was confined for several weeks at the Berlin University Clinic in 1938, Hitler visited me the day before Christmas Eve in company with Dr Brandt and his chief adjutant Brückner. He presented me with a bouquet of long-stemmed pink roses which it was his custom to send, and a book with his dedication written on the fly-leaf. In good humour he told me that as he got out of the car in front of the Women's Clinic in the Ziegel-Strasse a small crowd gathered. 'Everyone who saw me go through the Women's Clinic will definitely think I am visiting a friend I got pregnant,' he smiled. He pressurised the senior surgeon, Dr Stoeckel, into promising to do all he could to get me well again, because he needed me urgently. At that time I was certainly his No. 1 stenotyist. All his secretaries had a time when they were 'in' with Hitler. I was 'in' until 1941–2, a little after the invasion of Russia.

In 1937 a new secretary joined us, and now I shared Hitler's favour with Gerda Daranowski who had previously worked at the Private Chancellery. Sometimes she had been called to the Personal Adjutancy to take down speeches because my colleague Johanna Wolf was often off work sick: now she transferred in permanently. She was a young Berliner, not only very capable but attractive and always well-humoured, and knew how to goad Hitler into talking at tea, in the Staircase Room and when travelling in the Mercedes. From her work with Elizabeth Arden, Dara, as we called her, knew how to give her face just the right look to excite a man. Hitler was delighted by her skill with cosmetics and would pay her the most unfettered compliments. Since I was very economic with make-up he once glanced at me (probably hinting that I should give myself a beauty spot): '. . . and Schroeder has the intelligence of an above-average man.' Receiving the same treatment, we were a good team in those years.

Dara and I accompanied Hitler on his journey to Austria at the annexation in March 1938. After 1945 it was loudly asserted that Hitler had dragged Austria 'home into the Reich' against the will of the people. That was not the impression I received when I saw the enthusiasm with which Hitler and the Wehrmacht were greeted in Austria. The almost hysterical outbursts of joy got on one's nerves. I remember particularly the people of Linz who crowded before the Hotel Weinzinger until the late hours chanting '*Ein Reich, ein Volk, ein Führer!*'[1] and the ending chorus pleading for Hitler to show himself at the hotel window. And Hitler showed himself, again and again. When the enthusiasm had not abated by midnight, the *SS-Begleitkommando* was told to ask for quiet and get the crowd to disperse. After that it gradually grew quieter. It was still quiet next morning. This did not seem right to Hitler. When he left the hotel to no ovation he was clearly annoyed. Schaub whispered to me: 'He needs the shout of jubilation just like the artiste does his applause.'

From Linz we drove back to the Hotel Imperial in Vienna. Hitler did not occupy the VIP suite – he used this only for official purposes – but had instead a small apartment on the first floor decorated in the Schönbrunn baroque and completed with a magnificent floral arrangement. The most glorious bouquets of flowers were handed in at reception for Hitler, typical Viennese sprays of white lilies and pink roses, and the most precious orchids. It was overwhelming. Dara and I took only the rare orchids and put them in the Mercedes for the drive back because they lasted the longest: the car was a sea of blooms. Thousands of Viennese waited outside the hotel, never tiring of calling for Hitler to emerge and speak. Next day Cardinal

---

1 The slogan '*Ein Volk, ein Reich, ein Führer*' (meaning 'One People, one State, one Leader') was one of the most renowned of the Third Reich, yet Schroeder recites it incorrectly here as '*Ein Reich, ein Volk, ein Führer*'. It may be a simple typographical error, of course, but it may also be indicative of Schroeder's lack of political awareness.

Innitzer[2] visited Hitler at the hotel. Hitler was very impressed by this visit and kept referring to it during our conversation at tea.

On our return to Berlin the jubilation of the population was deafening. Hitler Youth had strewn the Wilhelm-Platz with flowers, draping them from the tree tops; they waved flags and applauded loudly as Hitler drove past. It was all rather too much for me. We had to endure similar receptions in 1938 on the return from Italy, in 1939 from Prague and later following the successful military campaigns in Poland and France, when Hitler was at the peak of his power.

Between 2 and 9 May 1938 I was the only secretary in the Führer's special train[3] for the state visit to Italy. My colleague Johanna Wolf was on Rudolf Hess's special train for the trip to Rome. She was attached temporarily to his staff. My younger colleague Gerda Daranowski came by plane. Johanna Wolf and I stayed in the Quirinal in rooms between the ground and first floors apparently meant for staff. I remember the wood-framed bay windows which went almost to

---

2 Theodor Innitzer (b. 25.12.1875 Neugeschrei/Erzgebirge, d. 9.10.1955 Vienna. 13.3.1933 Cardinal.

3 In 1933 as Reich Chancellor, Hitler ordered a special train built. By 1943 it had no less than forty coaches available. From 1937 it was stationed at Berlin Anhalter Bahnhof and had ten coaches initially, from 1938 also a command coach and two flak wagons. Named *Amerika* it was drawn by two steam locomotives (usually BR S 05). The flak wagons were positioned one between the locomotives and the leading coach, and the other at the tail of the train. Armament was a 2-cm quadruple barrelled weapon. Crew of each was twenty-six men.

No. 1 saloon coach (the *Führerwagen*) consisted of a wood-panelled saloon with bed compartment, bathroom and small compartments for the manservant and adjutants. No. 2 coach was the military command coach in which the situation conferences were held. The radio rooms and telex centre were located aboard. No. 3 coach was the diner, coaches Nos 4 to 9 were sleepers for the *SS-Begleitkommando*, Kripo, Hitler's staff, guests and the OKW.

Hitler used the train as his FHQ during the campaigns in Poland and the Balkans, and travelled across France in it on several occasions, including to the Spanish border for his talks with Franco in 1940. During the Russian campaign it was stationed at Görlitz within FHQ Wolfsschanze. It was destroyed on Hitler's orders at Mallnitz on 1 May 1945.

the floor. We were cared for by a round signora dressed in black who curtsied whenever she spoke to us and tended our needs. We were served exquisite vegetable dishes prepared with oil and easily digestible. We saw nothing of the parades in Rome held in Hitler's honour, but once we were driven by the chauffeur of Italian Crown Prince Umberto to Tivoli to see the wonderful gardens of the Villa d'Este. The Vatican was closed probably because of Hitler's visit(?) but there was so much to see in Rome that Dara and I decided not to go to Naples for the naval review and went instead to Florence because the journey home was to begin there. As we strolled the Ponte Vecchio a coach containing the Duce and Hitler and drawn by the finest horses came towards us. We waved, laughed and saluted. Hitler used to say of this encounter later: 'I was just about to say to the Duce what beautiful women there are in Florence when I recognised my secretaries.'

Scarcely had Hitler's special train steamed out of Florence for the journey home than Hitler was dictating telegrams thanking the Italian king and the Duce. Ribbentrop was watching him. Hitler said: 'If you can find a better way of putting it, then change the text.' Ribbentrop then re-dictated the telegrams at least ten times but despite his best endeavours in the end he settled for the text Hitler had had in the first place.

The Italian visit was the main topic in many subsequent conversations, both in the positive and negative sense. Hitler had been inspired by Italian art, the buildings and military parades, less so by the court ceremonial. Hitler found the dryness and arrogance of the nobility a challenge to his self-control. The Duce did not have the same leading role in Italy as Hitler did in Germany and had no influence on the protocol. The demeaning treatment 'those courtesans' handed down to the Duce outraged Hitler. As he said, he had to suppress his instincts to break off the state visit prematurely because of the way in which Mussolini was continually humiliated. During the military parade in Rome seats had been reserved for the members of the royal house and for Hitler while Mussolini was forced to stand the whole time. 'That made me so indignant that I almost made a public fuss. Only for the Duce's sake did I exercise restraint,' he said. The basis for his grudge against the Italians was founded in Rome on this visit and not later by the surprises which they had in store for him in the war.

Shortly before Czechoslovakia was incorporated into the Reich in 1939, the Czech state president, Hacha,[4] came to Berlin for a conference. The talks took place on the night of 14 March 1939 in Hitler's large study at the new Reich Chancellery. Before Hacha was ushered in, Gerda Daranowski and I had to sit in a small office concealed by a door behind Hitler's desk. We were to hold ourselves in immediate readiness should dictation be necessary during the conversation. We sat and sat, and the hours went by. Shortly after 0430 the door opened at last, and Hitler swept over the step, a happy expression on his face. Standing in the centre of the room he said, exuding a superabundance of endless joy: 'So, children, now there and there,' pointing to his left and right cheeks, 'each of you give me a kiss.' Since he had never made such a request of us before we were rather taken aback, but gathered ourselves and complied warmly with his wish. 'This is the finest day of my life,' he went on, 'I have achieved something which has been striven for in vain for centuries. I have succeeded in unifying Czechoslovakia with the Reich, Hacha has signed the treaty. I shall go down in history as the greatest German.'

Just a couple of hours later we were aboard Hitler's special train and heading for Czechoslovakia. We got out at Leipa in Bohemia where the great convoy of Mercedes from Hitler's vehicle park was

---

4 Emil Hacha (b.12.7.1872 Budweis, Czechoslovakia, d. 26.6.1945 in a Prague prison). 1925 president of administrative court, Vienna; 1939 Czech state president; 15.3.1939 signed the Berlin document making Bohemia and Moravia into a protectorate of the Third Reich; 27 May 1945 as state president of Bohemia and Moravia arrested by the Allies.

already waiting. Then we drove for Prague past endless columns of German soldiers. Snow whirled around us but Hitler ignored it. Most of the time he stood up in the Mercedes saluting. In Prague we went to the Hradschin fortress, like a fairytale castle set deep in snow above the houses of the city. Something was not right. The great wrought-iron gates were shut, and the SS bodyguard had to get out and open them, for me a clear sign that we were not welcome. Inside the Hradschin it was like an army camp. In collaboration with interior minister Frick and Secretary of State Stuckart, Hitler worked until late in the night preparing decrees which he dictated to me at the typewriter. It was so hectic that I failed to notice the photographers there. Many years later I chanced across a photo of myself which appeared at the head of a series of 'Christa Schroeder Exclusive' articles in *Corriere della Sera*.

It was difficult for the Czech officials in the Hradschin to hide their hatred for us. No wonder! They found it impossible even to offer us a snack, and about two in the morning the SS bodyguard went to the *Deutsches Haus* in Prague and rustled up some white bread, ham and Pilsner. We did the food justice and praised the icy cold beer. This made Hitler curious and he asked for a glass. He did not like the beer, however, for he pulled a face and said that it was 'too bitter' for him.

We returned to Berlin on the Führer-train on 19 March, my birthday, and Hitler invited his closest staff to a celebratory coffee afternoon in the saloon coach. He was in the best of spirits and presented me with a bouquet of long-stemmed roses which he had ordered by wire to be sent to a station along the way. He also gave me the present of a gold penholder and pencil engraved with the date and his name. In 1946 this gift gave pleasure to some American souvenir hunter in the Mannheim-Seckenheim internment camp.

From 1939 onwards we did more travelling. In contrast to earlier years when Hitler nearly always went by car, now he began to extol the greater comfort of his pleasant, tastefully furbished special train.

It became his habit on these journeys to invite his intimate staff to the saloon coach in the afternoon and evening, when meals and tea would be taken. His female secretaries were never overlooked. If one or other of us slipped away to avoid one of these sessions, often hours long, he would mount an enquiry into her whereabouts and the manservant distributing the invitations soon learned not to accept No for an answer. Accordingly I spent a great deal of my existence in the saloon coach of the Führer-train.

The coach was mahogany-panelled with a large rectangular table, red leather chairs and indirect lighting. A gramophone and radio were on hand. When stopped at stations the signals crew hooked into the telephone network, or telegraphic messages could be sent. On these train journeys Hitler would insist on having the curtains drawn in the saloon coach even in blinding sunshine. He wanted only electric light because he found bright sunshine unpleasant. Possibly he also liked Dara's make-up better under artificial light. He was for ever paying her compliments which led to the Hitler-impersonators amongst the officers staging their usual impressions once Hitler had retired.

During conversations on the train Hitler liked to talk about car travel. He only used the special train because it was so comfortable. He liked being driven across Germany in the car, not only because it was quicker but also because it gave him a chance to meet the common people close up. Hitler the fanatical car enthusiast had suggested various improvements which found approval with Daimler-Benz. Its director-general, Jakob Werlin,[5] had let him have

5 Jakob Werlin (b. 10.5.1886 Andritz/Graz, d. 23.9.1965 Salzburg). April 1921, head of the Benz & Co branch in Munich at 39 Schelling-Strasse where the *Völkischer Beobachter* was printed; 12.9.1924 visited Hitler at Landsberg; February 1925 sold the penniless Hitler a Mercedes worth 20,000 RM on credit; from the end of the 1920s, Werlin belonged to Hitler's private circle at Haus Wachenfeld; 10.12.1932 joined NSDAP and SS; 24.11.1933 board member of Daimler-Benz AG and later director-general; 16.1.1942 Inspector-General and Plenipotentiary for Automobilism; 30.1.1942 SS-Obergruppenführer; May 1945–9.11.1949 interned.

a car on credit during the period of struggle, which Horch's had declined to do, and so Hitler was especially indebted to him. He once joked to Werlin: 'By the way, do you know that you are the true conqueror of Germany? If you had not given me a car then, it would have been impossible for me to have been it. Therefore you are the true conqueror. You should consider whether you have any demands to make!' Werlin, who came into the sleeper coach where I was smoking a cigarette in the corridor, said to me: 'Fräulein Schroeder, did you hear what the Führer said? I must tell my mother that.'

Chapter 5
Hitler's Birthday

IN THE PREWAR YEARS Hitler's birthdays would begin with a serenade by the band of the *SS-Leibstandarte*. When Hitler then descended the staircase from his first floor apartment in the Radziwill Palace, he would be greeted by a host of ministers' and adjutants' children in their party best holding colourful posies. Hitler evidently enjoyed taking his breakfast with the children, and for the photographers the table scenes were a welcome opportunity. The official chorus of congratulations would follow and then would come the Wehrmacht parade in the Tiergarten-Strasse.

The historical Congress Hall which separated Hitler's apartment on the first floor from the service rooms of the Reich Chancellery would have been cleared a few weeks before 20 April. The presents received would be stacked on the long negotiating table and additional tables brought in for the purpose if necessary. The scent of small almond trees, carnations and roses would perfume the room. There was the widest range of presents imaginable: valuable, useful, beautiful, artistic. Paintings, sculptures, candelabras, carpets, old weapons, rare coins, clocks, accessories for the writing desk, briefcases, books, music scores and much more. Then the handicrafts: pillows and blankets with National Socialist symbols, or legends such as *Heil mein Führer!*. How many thoughts from fanatical, adoring women had been woven into this handiwork! Mountains of baby clothes, bedsheets and blankets finished up later in the archive room of the Private Chancellery to be carefully sorted for distribution to needy families. Cakes with artistic structures and inscriptions, baskets of delicacies and more or less all the edible stuff were sent on Hitler's order to hospitals. Valuable items ended up in the showcases and cabinets of the Führer-flats, handicrafts without National Socialist emblems in visitors' rooms. Later in the war field-grey socks knitted by women of the Nazi Women's organisations were piled into great mountains in the four corners of the Congress Hall.

In the 1950s my friend Johanna Nusser in Berlin returned to me the letters I had written her from the Berghof and Führer-HQs during the war. The following extracts are taken from them.* In a moment of thoughtlessness I made some of them available to David Irving. The opinions they express about the Russian mentality I had assimilated from conversations with Hitler and repeated in chat. Nowadays I am horrified at these opinions of Hitler which I thoughtlessly passed on. How could I pass judgement on people whom I never had the opportunity to know first hand! I am blameworthy, but I let the material stand.

Letter from Berlin, 21 April 1939:

> All my plans to take the cure and convalesce have come to naught again. I wanted to go in March, and when that was not possible in April. That is now out of the question and for the time being I have given up. We have a Reichstag speech on 28th of the month and until then we are on standby for all eventualities.
>
> Dara has been in Munich since last week. I had hoped that Wolfen (Johanna Wolf) would be coming to Berlin, but meanwhile the boss has told her to stay in Munich to catalogue the birthday presents he received and write letters of thanks for them. I have no choice but to wait for the Reichstag speech and see how the general situation looks afterwards.

---

* Extracts from these letters are shown here and in following chapters. (TN)

Meanwhile I have put on a lot of weight, it is really ghastly. If only I had half the willpower of the boss in this respect it would help. As soon as he puts on a few pounds he cuts out this and that at a stroke, goes hungry for three weeks and loses it all.

The birthday was very tiring for him. It lasted for two days, reception after reception. The parade yesterday was fairly large and went on and on. We left at 0930 and got back to the office at 1630, seven hours split by three hours' drive and waiting time, and four hours' march past. I expect you will see it on the cinema newsreels. It is simply amazing to me where he gets the strength from. Hours without a break standing and saluting are damned tiring. Just watching we got dog-tired, or I was at least.

The number and value of the presents this year is staggering. Paintings (Defregger, Waldmüller, Lenbach, even a glorious Titian), then wonderful Meissen sculptures in porcelain, silver table- and centre-pieces, magnificent books, vases, drawings, carpets, handicrafts, globes, radios, watches, etc. Then crates of eggs, huge cakes, boxes of sweets, fruit juice, liquor, a marvellous sailing ship made from fresh blooms, sad that it will soon wither. Then aircraft and ship models and similar military items which give him the greatest pleasure. He is like a kid with them.

The Berliners made a day of it as usual and were on their legs from dawn to dusk. The Charlottenburg Boulevard, which is very wide and has fine, solid lamp standards, was wonderful although like Unter den Linden I found the bunting a bit too theatrical. When these theatre requisites are taken down the street will be back to normal and more imposing than it is now. The Linden has too many of those advertising columns. But perhaps I have no taste and it is actually beautiful. Most people seem to approve of it.

Before we came back to Berlin we were in Austria to review the troops. The boss went off in the car leaving us in the special train for three or four hours just seven kilometres from Vienna. By the way, he calls the train 'The Hotel of the Frenetic Reich Chancellor'.

Recently I have seen some fine theatrical performances and have been mainly in Munich. I never really know where to go in the evenings and so I have made a habit of attending the chamber plays in the Theatre House where almost everything I have seen to date has been wonderfully staged and acted. I have seen for example a glorious *Anthony and Cleopatra* and a short while ago during Festival week *Conspiracy and Love*. I had wanted to see the latter for a long time, but could never get to it in Berlin. It is booked well in advance there and the boss had said one should only see it in Berlin where the setting is fabulous and the casting first class, for example the old city musician Miller with Heinrich George.

The Old Man has been giving very interesting talks recently in the evenings about the Church question. Everything was so clear and straightforward that I regret not having made a note of it. He does not like the Gothic style of architecture because it is strange and unnatural. That is obviously a matter of taste. 'Why suddenly interrupt a naturally fine arch to rise to an unnecessary and senseless point?' he asks. And why the many towers and turrets, only there for the eye, inaccessible and blocked off inside.

Christian mysticism had its origins in the era of the Goths. The dark interior of the buildings favoured it. The period was one of darkness and prudery, the female body, abdomen and everything, hidden. An unmarried painter would never have seen a naked female, hence the false and ugly representations. In that era fables and mysticism would have spread very rapidly. Christianity is based on knowledge 2,000 years old, and this knowledge is confused and layered with mysticism and biblical fable. The question is: Why should it not be possible to base Christianity on our modern knowledge? Luther had attempted to introduce the Reformation but he had been misunderstood, for the Reformation was not a single event but eternally progressive reform, no standing still but advancing together, developing together, etc. The boss knows of course that the Church question is very complicated and should war come could have very unfavourable effects internally. I have the impression he would be happy to see it resolved in a dignified manner.

There is very much more of which I have to unburden my heart to you. For example I have come to realise that there is a big difference in character between my younger colleague and myself. She is too interested in pleasing at all cost and for this purpose anything goes. I have got used to her passing off my opinions on books as her own, and my beliefs about this or that problem, after half an hour, even in my presence, quite openly claiming them to be the product of her own mind.

The balloon went up on our last stay at the Berg when she started to speak for me, i.e. when somebody asked me something directly she got her oar in first and answered on my behalf before I had a chance to open my mouth (if it had been on office matters it would not have bothered me, but these were the most private things), or if I was sitting with somebody in serious conversation she had to come along and butt in with loud comments and so ruin everything. Then in all her glory in the 'I'm convinced of it' type of superior tone she came out with so many well-stretched out 'Isn't its?' and 'Don't you agrees?' that I got furious. Since then I have been very reserved and only speak to her if I have to. The worst thing is that the boss is very taken with her and she naturally used that to her advantage. You know yourself best how unpleasant such things can get. So life is an eternal struggle to get my own point across and that I do not like. It is the case today that men (and particularly those here) like to have around them pretty, nicely made-up, young, totally unproblematical heads. No trouble from a serious face, thank you! On the Berg recently I had enough of it. But then I told myself, I cannot just throw in the towel. I cannot start all over again and in any case you meet struggles and resistance wherever you go. I shall just be glad when it is over at least and I can pack my bags and take the cure . . .

Chapter 6

The Polish Campaign

O N 1 SEPTEMBER 1939 the war with Poland came as a surprise for us all, and at 2100 on the evening of 3 September we left Berlin in Hitler's special train for Poland. As usual we had been given no time to make preparations for the journey. 'In a couple of hours we are leaving Berlin,' I wrote to my friend on the afternoon of 3 September:

> First of all receive a Hallo from me. Now I have to go through thick and thin with the boss. That it could be the thing I do not like to think but if so – then life has nothing more for me. When you write please do so to the address at the head of this letter, I will reply from the same . . .

At the beginning of the Polish campaign Hitler directed operations from his special train in the vicinity of Gogolin. Every morning he was driven to the Front to visit the most forward lines. In the evening he would return covered in muck and dust. Before leaving again he would dictate exhortations and orders of the day to his troops. During the siege of Warsaw he made appeals to the population to abandon the city. Only towards the end of the campaign did he set up his HQ in the Casino Hotel at Zoppot.

Letter from FHQ, Poland, 11 September 1939:

We have been living in the Führer-train for ten days, continually changing sidings, but since we – Dara and I – never leave the train it is very monotonous. The heat is almost insufferable, simply frightful. The sun beats down all day on the roof and one is powerless against the tropical-type heat. I have got really fat, simply ghastly. In addition the worst is that one cannot do anything useful. It is always the same: the boss leaves in the morning with his officers in the car and we are condemned to wait and wait. We have done everything possible to help out somewhere but it is simply impossible because we do not stay long enough in one place.

Recently we spent a night near a transit dressing station. A big transport came along full of wounded. Dr Brandt was operating all night, our people from the SS bodyguard helped out. We, Dara and I, offered to write letters for the wounded to their next of kin and were hoping to be able to help out a little in this way. But once again it was turned down, the senior surgeon was very pleased and thanked us but since it is only a transit unit our offer was inconvenient. How envious I was to hear about your coal-shovelling, I would like to have been there, at least one can see what role one is playing.

Our people who went into Poland with the boss can naturally see what is going on, but it is not safe because they often come under fire from ambushes. They cannot convince the boss not to stand up in the car as he does in Germany, not even in the most exposed areas. I think it is crazy but he will not listen. The first day they drove through a wood infested with partisans. Half an hour before, an unarmed German medical team had been wiped out. The single survivor managed to escape to tell the story.

Polish aircraft were bombing not far away. It is assumed that the Poles saw the Führer-convoy. Visible to all and sundry the boss stood on a hilltop, the soldiers ran towards him from all directions shouting *Heil!* – and the Polish artillery was in the valley. They

74

obviously saw the crowd forming and – since it is no secret that the Führer is spending time at the Front – it was not too difficult for them to guess who was there. Half an hour later their aircraft dropped bombs near him. It is of course a great incentive for the forces and has a colossal effect for morale to see the Führer in the danger zone. All the same, in my opinion the danger is too great.

I am very interested to see how the business with the British and French develops. I hope that the French will soon see that it is not worth the price to sacrifice millions of people for Britain. If the thing with Poland is over with quickly this will take the carpet out from under their feet – or at least that is how I see it.

One of the orderlies[1] died suddenly the day before yesterday of meningitis, the same disease which claimed the Führer's driver, if you remember Schreck. I heard some SS comrades say that he was only twenty-four: 'It would have been better for him to have fallen in the field'. But one cannot pick and choose the way one is to die. There are many we know amongst the dead. The brother of Hans Junge, who was with the *Leibstandarte*, has also fallen . . .

On 26 September 1939 we returned to Berlin.

---

1 This was Ernst Bahls (b. 29.7.1915 Rügen Is., d. 9.9.1939 Poland). 30.7.1934 joined LSSAH; 1.4.1936 SS-Junker; 20.4.1937 SS-Untersturmführer LSSAH; 20.3.1938 detached to Führer's Adjutancy; 11.9.1938 Obersturmführer; died of meningitis aged twenty-four during the Polish campaign.

Chapter 7

The French Campaign

ITLER HAD MANY CONFERENCES with the military in April and May 1940, but none of the content seeped through into the Staircase Room. There was only a suspicion that some thing was in the wind. On the afternoon of 9 May 1940 we, the inner circle, were told to prepare to travel the same evening. The destination was not disclosed, nor could we discover how long we might be away. In response to my enquiry in this respect to Obergruppenführer Schaub, he said in a manner both secretive and showy: 'It could be eight days, it could be fourteen days, it could be a month, but there again it could be years!'

Towards evening we assembled in the Führer-apartment and received the order for the off. Seated in a car with my colleague Daranowski and the representative of the Reich press chief[1] we were driven out of Berlin towards Staaken, leading us to assume that we would be flying from the airport. That was not the case, for the car drove on past Staaken and eventually pulled into the forecourt of a small railway station where the Führer-train stood waiting.

Apart from the military adjutants nobody seemed to know where we were supposed to be going. It was all very mysterious. At dinner in the dining car Schmundt[2] joked: 'Have you all got your sea-sick

---

1 This was Heinz Lorenz.

2 Rudolf Schmundt (b. 13.8.1896 Metz, d. 1.10.1944 Rastenburg). Generalleutnant,

pills?' Was he hinting that we were going to Norway – the train was steaming north? Hitler chipped in: 'If you are good, you might be able to bring home a sealskin as a trophy.' After midnight – past Hannover – the train was suddenly switched to the westbound tracks although this was only noticed by the alert few.[3] Towards dawn we drew into a small station from which the name-shields had been dismounted. We left the train and continued our journey in three-axled open Mercedes cars. In all the villages through which we drove the street signs had been replaced by yellow shields with military designations. Finally we finished up in a hilly, wooded region before a regimental command bunker which the boss had claimed for his HQ. As we stood near this bunker at dawn we could hear artillery fire in the distance. Hitler gestured with his hand towards the West and said: '*Meine Herren*, the offensive against the Western powers has just begun.'

It became clear that we were somewhere near Münstereifel. The FHQ was called Felsennest.* The command post (bunker) was very small with simple wooden walls and chairs of braided fibre. The room accommodated Hitler, Keitel, Jodl, Schmundt, Schaub and one manservant and there was a small dining room for a nucleus of the staff. All other staff members were given quarters in the nearby village. From the point of view of landscape it was the best situated of all FHQs. The wood, fresh with spring, was filled with bird

---

chief Wehrmacht adjutant to the Führer.

3 Reich press chief Dr Otto Dietrich stated at Nuremberg on 9 August 1948: 'An hour before the departure of the Führer-train on the night of 9 May 1940 I was told to pack for a journey with Hitler's staff to inspect a shipyard at Hamburg. At about 0100 just short of Hamburg the train was diverted westwards. I still knew nothing of our destination until we pulled into Euskirchen station in the Eifel at 0600 that morning. It was always done secretly like this.'

* FHQ Felsennest was occupied by Hitler between 10 May and 6 June 1940. The spot height known as Felsennest was a hilltop at 440-metres altitude overlooking the village of Rodert to the northeast, and about thirty kilometres from Bonn and the Belgian border. It had been included prewar in the Westwall air defence zone and from the late 1930s had a bunker and flak installations with barracks. (TN)

song. Hitler called it 'the bird paradise'. He felt very well in this region and since his bunker room was very small he held most of his conferences in the open air. He was never outdoors so often as he was here. He enthused frequently about the glorious scenery and made a plan to bring us all back on a commemorative visit every year once the war was over.

On 5 or 6 June 1940 the FHQ was transferred to Bruly de Pêsche not far from Brussels in order to be closer to the Front. This was a village with an old church and a spacious comfortable schoolhouse set amongst fields in opulent bloom. Never again did I see fields of that kind covered over so great an area with such succulent margaritas and skirted by a wood of wonderful primeval oaks.

Letter, Bruly de Pêsche, 13 June 1940:

We moved forward a week ago and are now in a small village abandoned by its inhabitants. The first few nights I slept with a female colleague in a former pigsty–cowshed of wooden boards and stucco, dreadfully damp. Yesterday thank God they finished the barrack hut and now we are living in the dry. The first few days we had no water, which gave me an insight into how essential this wet element is. We cleaned our teeth with soda water, not totally refreshing.

On the first night we had a fire in our stall. The telephone and lighting wires were close together and the damp started the fire. The hissing and crackling of the flames woke me up, and still half asleep I tried to put it out with my bare hands. When that failed I used a wet handkerchief and got a shock. The same happened with several of the officers. The cabling cooked all night, an uncomfortable feeling lying in bed below it. Anyway, at least the inconveniences are over and we have settled in quite nicely.

As to our successes, our troops have got as far as Fourges (Paris aerodrome) from where I am writing this letter, but I doubt we shall be putting down roots here.

Recently I went through Sedan, Namur, Philippeville, Dinant, etc. There was much devastation. Whole blocks of flats reduced to rubble. Even worse are the highways along the route of the advance, in ditches right and left artillery, tanks, aircraft of all kinds, uniforms, ambulances, ammunition, etc., burnt-out trucks. A sweetish odour of decomposition hangs above these towns, and above the whole thing great hordes of screeching ravens circle. A desolate picture of destruction. Cattle, horses and dogs all ownerless wander between the gutted houses. In the first few days when cows were not milked we could hear them at night bellowing in pain.

The refugees make a sad picture. Large families living in burnt-out cars, old ladies being pushed in children's perambulators; war is the most terrible thing there can be. Our boss does what he can for the poor people. Hilgenfeldt[4] has been detailed to see to it.

Every night we endure the same piece of theatre from 'above'. Punctually at 0200 the enemy aircraft come and circle the village for three hours. A few nights ago they wrecked a house in which some of our RSD policemen were billeted. Thank God nobody was hurt; they took cover in time. We do not know if the aircraft were going for us or the highway. They are apparently invulnerable because they keep so high. If they fail to appear the boss asks: 'Where are our house aircraft tonight?'

Every night we stand in the open with the boss and some staff officers until 0300 or 0330 watching the nightly manoeuvres of the reconnaissance aircraft until they disappear with the dawn. The landscape reminds me of a picture by Caspar David Friedrich.

The food is first class, we have enough butter and milk, we even get tomatoes and fruit now and again. We do not really go short of anything. Yesterday I was invited with Schaub to a slaughter party. About twenty minutes from here by car is our Flight-Squadron where the airmen had slaughtered two pigs. There were about fifty

4 Erich Hilgenfeldt (b. 2.7.1899 Heinitz/Ottweiler, fate after 1945 not known). Head of *Hauptamt für Volkswohlfahrt* (Principal Office for People's Welfare).

people gathered in a former clubhouse (almost certainly YMCA) seated at festively decorated tables illuminated by tall French paraffin lanterns. There was plentiful blood- and liver-sausage and a belly of pork. Later a simply wonderful old French wine was served, not to mention the schnapps. So you see, I am not missing out on anything. For tomorrow evening we are invited for pancakes with the RSD. They are billeted in farmhouses, eat at midday from the field kitchen and in the evening have to forage for themselves. They have picked up a lot of housewifely talent, which they are naturally hoping to show off, hence our invitation tomorrow for pancakes.

There is still so much to tell you but which I cannot for the moment. The time is not so far away however when we can sit together comfortably. Personally I do not believe that the war will last beyond June. Yesterday in Paris General Weygand stated that the Battle for Paris was lost and proposed a special peace in which Pétain supported him. Reynaud and others were violently opposed.

Letter from FHQ Bruly de Pêche (Wolfsschlucht), 20 June 1940:

The Armistice came into force tonight at 0135. How many mothers and wives will thank God that the war with France has ended so quickly. The boss will address the Reichstag briefly. Probably it will contain his final appeal to the British. If they will not quit, he said, he would go ahead ruthlessly! I believe that he is sorry to have to wrestle the British to the ground; he would apparently find it preferable if they would be reasonable about it.

If only they knew that all the boss wants from them is our former colonies back, perhaps they would be more approachable. I am very interested to see how Britain will respond.

By the way, Munich was lovely, great enthusiasm. Dara and I got a lot of surprised looks in our field-grey costumes with the Deutsche Wehrmacht armbands. Meanwhile the boss was in the room where he dictated the appeal for the newspapers. He composed the radio programme himself . . .

Explaining why he had not destroyed the BEF at Dunkirk, Hitler told his intimate circle: 'Their army is the backbone of Britain and the empire. If we had destroyed the BEF, the empire would follow. As we neither wish to be, nor can be, its successor, we had to give it a chance. My generals have not been able to understand that.' Hitler was scuppered, so to speak, by his spurned love for Great Britain. That day in Bruly de Pêsche Hitler was very relaxed and happy. The news of the French offer of peace was given to him while standing with his officers on the road between the church and the schoolhouse. He gave himself a lively slap on the upper thigh and his laugh of relief carried to us two secretaries. A little to one side we watched the scene as Walter Frentz filmed it. Then Keitel gave an address in which he hailed Hitler as the greatest warlord of all times.

Hitler visited the trenches where he had served in the First World War, finding them to be exactly as he remembered them. Later he went to Paris to see the Invalides cathedral, the Opera House and other buildings.[5] After his return he claimed with pride that he knew his way about their corridors better than the guides did: during his youth in Vienna he had made a thorough study of its ground plan and had retained all the architectural details in his head.

A few days later Dara and I were taken by a Wehrmacht driver, whom Oberst Schmundt had placed at our disposal, to Brussels where we were involved in a minor accident. It was nothing serious but Dara was thrown against the car roof and suffered concussion. I found her a hotel to change before our return a couple of hours later. Hitler heard about this accident and banned us from riding

5 Hitler made a lightning visit to Paris first between 0500 and 0600 on 23 June 1940. Architects Speer, Giesler and Breker were with him. Next, on 25 and 26 June 1940, he travelled with First World War comrades Max Amann and Ernst Schmidt to the former German trenches on the Somme.

in Wehrmacht cars. He showed such concern for us. It was a good relationship and one felt protected, even at the beginning of the Russian campaign before much changed.

At the outbreak of war I had a large trunk made with compartments for the office material and stocks of headed stationery. These had the sovereign emblem (eagle with swastika) and the words *Der Führer* below it in gold, while the private notepaper had Adolf Hitler instead of *Der Führer*. There were also cards with the same design.

Since we were now constantly at FHQ, Hitler wanted us to wear uniform. On Hitler's directive the president of the Guild of Stage Designers, Benno von Arent, designed for us a costume in Italian officers' grey cloth with gold buttons and cord trim. In place of the round Party badge Dara and I wore on the left lapel the silver sovereignty emblem designed by Hitler himself and cast by goldsmith Otto Gahr. It consisted of a slim eagle clasping a swastika in its claws. Permission to wear this badge was granted by Hitler only to a chosen few.

Even later Benno von Arent visited Hitler frequently at FHQ and also received invitations to join the evening tea sessions. Hitler would talk with him about the artists they knew. When Arent left, Hitler would always shake his hand warmly and say: 'I am glad to have you visit me from time to time in my loneliness. You are for me a bridge into a better world.'

Letter, Berghof, 22 February 1941:

We have been continually on the move since 21 December 1940. Christmas on the French coast, Calais, Dunkirk, etc. On 23 December at Boulogne, while at dinner in the dining car of our special train, the British bombed us and our flak roared back. Although we were sheltered in a secure tunnel I had 'funny feelings'. I have already told you about Christmas Eve and New Year's Eve, where the mood was less than pleasant.

The six days I spent in Paris with Schaub, Dara and Kempka were free of duty. We had almost too many invitations, from the German embassy and the staff of General Hanesse, and scarcely had time to come up for air. We should have arranged for a rest day afterwards, that would have made it better . . . Probably we will not be staying up here too long. At the moment Daranowski is resting, I am here with (Johanna) Wolf.

Since we shall be spending the whole year sitting in the bunker with nothing to eat day after day but thick pasty stew I would like to take the cure at Niederlindenwiese, even if only for fourteen days. Up here we have an unpleasant thaw with gloomy overcast sky. The boss is in Munich today and so it is really desolate . . .

Letter, Berghof, 7 March 1941:

I am pleased your holiday was so harmonious and that you were able to be with so many nice people. I think it would also be good for me to spend a few weeks with normal people, therefore I really do envy you. One should also definitely maintain contact. By being so cut off from things I feel lonely, dull and ossified. It is time we went back to Berlin, we have been here long enough. We shall be in Berlin probably mid-month.

At the moment it looks as though I shall not be going to Niederlindenwiese. Now we have to be immunised against cholera and typhus (this happened before all our big journeys). Well, if I cannot go, I accept it. War is war. I have just heard today of the heavy work the women have to do in the bomb factories, it makes one feel quite insignificant.

I hope you received my letter from Vienna. We went there on Saturday for the signing of the Bulgarian Pact.[6] On Sunday we were travelling and I could not call you. Meanwhile we had a hefty

6 Signed at Schloss Belvedere, Vienna, on 1 March 1941.

snowfall which spoiled our spring mood. I do not think it will settle long, it is too wet and the sun is trying to break through to melt it.

I am returning Lav's letter to you with this one. He does not seem to be very satisfied but this pessimistic undertone you find in all his letters. Rather skilfully he sent me a few short lines directly through a business friend who visited him there. He seems to be very disappointed not to have heard from me. He ought to be able to understand the problem in itself, but of course he knows nothing about the OKW and Gestapo investigations . . . and if you have not passed on my aquamarine ring I would be glad if I could hold on to a memento of Brückner. Imagine it, Wernicke was also swept out with another colleague in the whirlpool of clearance and reorganisation. I did not hear of it until he had already gone. Nothing surprises me any more. Nobody hears any more said about the 'powder keg'.

Letter, Berlin, 28 April 1941:

I was hoping that the boss would not come back so soon.[7] On this last journey he gave Wolfen a rare outing but now he has arrived and probably we will be off south again in the next few days. The fourteen days when I was alone in Berlin simply sped by . . .

Gretl Slezak[8] secretly married three months ago without her parents' knowledge. He is six years her junior, a conductor who composes heavy and light works, has a terrific temperament and is in the Luftwaffe. She is happy, looks years younger and keeps advising me to do the same. All I am short of is somebody suitable.

A short while ago I got from L(av) a small packet which somebody sent me in Berlin of his behalf. Ahrens at FHQ forwarded it for me to Niederlindenwiese and now I have received it by this roundabout

---

7 Hitler was in Munich 21–24 March 1941, and in Vienna on 25th, when Yugoslavia joined the Axis. He left immediately afterwards for Berlin, where he arrived on 26th.

8 See Chapter 11.

route. It contains twelve socks and a kilo pack of tea with the note: 'On behalf of Herr L.A. with warmest greetings.' No date or other message. Probably he will have handed it over in February. I expect it will be the last sign of life from him, for now he will scarcely dare write.

Owambo[9] has now finally cleared out his room this week. I kept him company and got the last bits of information I was missing. Also the certainty that in our circle there is nobody who will lift a finger to help if one falls into disfavour. I was very sorry for Owambo, apparently nothing military has been arranged for him. He is completely in the dark, nobody amongst his comrades who once sent him photos signed 'in undying friendship' will have anything to do with him, and here I mean those who were once degraded[10] themselves. But that is all forgotten. It is disgusting when people are so selfish and have no sympathy for the sufferings of others, and do not even have the will to imagine what it must be like in the other's shoes. Well, there is still much to be said about it. Damn, now I have to stop, they are laying the table. The boss joins us for coffee every afternoon . . .

Letter, Berghof, 20 May 1941:

The boss left today for Munich, I have stayed behind . . . as my friend now needs money, she decided to sell the handwritten poems by Dietrich Eckart which he had sent to old von Wolzogen. I mentioned this to the boss, who was very close to Eckart, and no sooner said than done, he bought them for 10,000 RM. An amount like that M. would naturally not have got anywhere else . . .

---

9 Nickname of Wilhelm Brückner.

10 In a footnote to her papers Schroeder commented: 'Schaub'. What Schaub had done to merit this note was not recorded.

Chapter 8

The Russian Campaign 1941–1944

THE WAR WITH THE Soviet Union began on 22 June 1941 and next day we left Berlin after making brief preparations. On 28 June I wrote to my friend from the new FHQ Wolfsschanze,[1] eight kilometres in the woods from the miserable little town of Rastenburg in East Prussia:

> After five days here at HQ I can give you a short report on morale . . . the bunkers are dispersed through the woods, divided up into work sections. Every division set aside for itself. Our dormitory bunker is the size of a railway compartment and has light-coloured wood panelling. There is a discreet washbasin, above it a mirror, a small Siemens radio with a wide choice of stations. The bunker even has electric heating, not yet connected up, eye-catching wall lamps and a narrow hard mattress filled with eel-grass. The room is narrow but all in all it will have a nice look once I have hung a few pictures. Common shower rooms are available but until now we have not used them. At first there was no hot water and as usual we slept in until the last possible moment anyway. Because the noise

---

1 FHQ Wolfsschanze in the woods at Görlitz was the largest HQ built by the end of 1944. With various absences elsewhere Hitler inhabited this HQ from 24.6.1941 to 20.11.1944 as military overlord. Originally intended for a four-week Blitzkrieg, it was continually expanded until the installations were destroyed on 24.1.1945.

from the fan in the bunker disturbed us and the draught passed continuously above our heads, which I always hate especially because of the rheumatic pains I have so often, we requested that it be turned off at night with the consequence that we now sleep in a fug and suffer all next day from a leaden heaviness in the limbs.

Despite that it is all fine except for the damned plague of biting midges. I have midge bites all up my legs which are now covered in thick swellings. The anti-midge precautions last us only a short while. The men have better protection than we do (long leather boots and thick uniforms). Their only vulnerable spot is the neck. Some wear a mosquito net all the time. I tried it one afternoon but it becomes a burden after a while. If we spot a midge the hunt for it starts immediately . . .

The awful biting-midge plague did not leave Hitler unaffected. He said that they had searched out for him 'the swampiest, most climatically unfavourable and midge-infested region possible'. Nevertheless he had not yet lost his humour at that time, pointing to 'difficulties in jurisdiction', and concluded, after all hands went for the midges, 'in this work only the Luftwaffe is competent!'

Actually in the initial stages of the Russian campaign I found that Hitler was nearly always good-tempered and ready for a joke. One night after the usual tea hour at Wolfsschanze ended (it always followed the military situation conference and was attended by one personal and one military adjutant, one medical doctor and two secretaries) Hitler accompanied us to outside the bunker doors. There we stood chatting for a while in the darkness (blackout was always strictly observed). Suddenly I realised that I had left my flashlight in Hitler's room, and asked the manservant to fetch it. He returned empty-handed. 'Where could it be then?' I said. Hitler, in jovial frame of mind, defended himself with a smile: 'I have not stolen it. I may be a thief of lands, but not of lamps. And it is better that way, for they hang you for the little item, but for the bigger one they let you go!'

Letter, FHQ Wolfsschanze, 28 June 1941:

Some wire fly-swats have arrived and whoever is free has to join in the great midge hunt. They are saying that this is only a smaller breed and by the end of June an even more unpleasant kind comes and the stings will be even worse. God help us! However, I am pleasantly surprised by the temperature. It is almost too cool in the rooms. One has to dry out the bed first by body heat, it always feels damp. The trees deflect all the heat. Just how much one realises only when in the open on the highway. Then the heat hits you.

Now for my 'busy schedule'. Shortly after 1000 Dara and I go to the officers' mess bunker, dining room 1, an elongated white-painted room set quite deep in the ground so that the small gauze-covered windows are quite high up. The walls are decorated with marquetry: one shows Hutten, the other Heinrich I. A few days after moving in, a captured Soviet flag was fixed to the wall. In this room with seats for twenty at the table, the boss with his generals, general staff officers, adjutants and doctors eat at midday and evenings. At breakfast we two ladies join them. The boss seats himself so that he can gaze at the map of Russia on the opposite wall, which naturally spurs him into new monologues about Soviet Russia and the dangers of Bolshevism. He must have suffered very much in the period after the signing of the so-called Friendship treaty with Russia. Now he speaks of his fears from the heart, always emphasising the great danger which Bolshevism presents to Europe and that, had he waited another year, it would probably have been too late.

Recently he said in Berlin during the usual coffee hour which he takes daily in our room that Russia seemed eerie to him, rather like the ghostly ship in the *Flying Dutchman*. In reply to my question why he always insists that this was his most onerous decision (namely to proceed against Russia), he answered: 'Because one knows next to nothing about Russia, it might be a great soap bubble, or just as well be something else . . .'

The beginning has been so promising. In the first two days at Wolfsschanze Dara and I even attended the military situation conferences when the improvised sessions took place in the mess. So we heard the boss, standing by a large map of Europe and pointing to Moscow, say: 'In four weeks we will be in Moscow. Moscow will be razed to the ground.'

Letter, FHQ Wolfsschanze, 28 June 1941:

Yes, now I have wandered completely off the subject. Therefore in the morning we wait in Dining Room I until the boss, coming from the map room (where he will have received the situation report), arrives for breakfast which, by the way, consists of a cup of milk and a peeled apple. Easily satisfied and modest, isn't he? We girls on the other hand cannot get enough and, after wolfing down our allotted portions (small pat of butter), deftly exchange the cutlery so that we get three portions instead of two. After that we let the boss explain the new situation to us and afterwards attend the general situation conference at 1300, which is held in the map room where reports are made by either Oberst Schmundt or Major Engel (army adjutant).

These reports are extraordinarily interesting. Statistics about the enemy aircraft and tanks destroyed are delivered (the Russians seem to have enormous masses, up to now they have lost over 3,500 aircraft and 1,000 tanks including heavy 40-tonners) and the progress of our troops is demonstrated on the map.

It is made clear how furiously the Russian fights; he could match us man for man if the Soviets had proper military planning which, thank God, is not the case. So, from the experience so far one can say that it is a struggle against wild beasts. If one asks how it is that we have taken so few prisoners, it is important to know that the

Russian soldiers are stirred up by their commissars, who tell them atrocity stories about our 'inhumanity' which they will experience should they be taken prisoner. They are instructed to fight to the last and if overwhelmed to shoot themselves. That is how it plays out and the following happened at Kovno. A Russian prisoner sent by our troops to a bunker in order to ask the Russians there to surrender was probably shot by the commissar himself for having volunteered to carry the message. After that they blew themselves up. Better death than surrender.

Each unit is controlled by a GPU commissar to whom the commander is subordinate. Cut off from the leadership, what remains is a mob, totally primitive but which puts up a dour fight. This is naturally a danger in itself and leads to bitter fighting. The French, Belgians etc. were intelligent and gave up when they saw there was no point in going on, but the Russians keep fighting like madmen, trembling with fear lest something should happen to their families if they surrender – that is in any case what Moscow has threatened.

They cannot take advantage of having so many aircraft because they lack intelligence. In the Russian squadrons, for example, the squadron commander leads the way and the rest follow without knowing the objective, they simply stay on his tail. If he is shot down they cannot find the way back because most of them have not been trained to read a compass. Meanwhile – as I said previously – we have destroyed 3,500 Russian aircraft.

Back to the daily routine: at the end of the situation report the time passes slowly to lunch, which we take in Dining Room II. As the meal is very often stew we give that a miss particularly if peas and beans. If we have nothing important to do we take a nap for a couple of hours after lunch so that we are well rested for the remainder of the day, which usually lasts into the early hours.

Towards 1700 we are ordered to join the boss for coffee, and he treats us to cakes. Whoever eats the most gets a word of praise!

The coffee hour usually lasts until 1900 but often longer. Then we go back to Dining Room II for dinner. After that we have a walk or see a film to kill time until we are invited for 'tea' after the evening situation conference.

In Hitler's study, opposite the main windows, was a large fireplace with a round table before it and rattan chairs. As a rule at teatime the guests of the boss would be a medical doctor, one military and one personal adjutant, Martin Bormann, we two women and Heim,[2] Bormann's adjutant. Heim had been given the task to record 'secretly' the gist of Hitler's talk after the tea session was over. These were first published subsequently under the title *Adolf Hitler: Monologe im Führerhauptquartier 1941–1944* by Werner Jochmann.

Here I have to make some observations about Dr Henry Picker.[3] For a four-month period in 1942 Picker deputised for Heim as temporary adjutant to Martin Bormann at FHQ. On Bormann's instructions but without Hitler's knowledge, he had to make surreptitious notes of Hitler's conversation to keep Bormann abreast of Hitler's thinking. Whatever one may think, the *Monologe*[4]

2 Heinrich Heim (b.156.1900 Munich). 1920 NSDAP Membership No. 1222; from 1927 Munich lawyer; 1928–end 1930 attorney on staff of Hitler's lawyer Hans Frank; 1933 staff of Rudolf Hess; various offices at NSDAP; 1940–end 1942 Martin Bormann's adjutant at FHQ (absent 21.3.1942–31.7.1942); 1943 to end April 1945 head of commission in Munich investigating basic questions of law for the reconstituted Europe; 3.5.1945–mid 1948 interned.

3 Henry Daniel Theodor Picker (b. 6.2.1912 Wilhelmshaven, d. 2.5.1988 Starnberg). NSDAP member from 1.4.1930; Hitler Youth Bannführer and Reichsamtleiter to 1.11.1944 when relieved of his post by Hitler and Bormann; deputised for Heinrich Heim at FHQ 21.3.1942–31.7.1942, secretly noting Hitler's table talks for Bormann. Picker claimed in his book (third edition, 1976) that he was 'Hitler's constant guest' and that Hitler had approved his taking verbatim notes of Hitler's conversations (p.28). Hermann Giesler: *Nachtrag* (Heitz & Höffkes Verlag, Düsseldorf 1988, pp.17–18) states however that 'Picker's place was at the adjutants' table and not with the nightly tea guests.'

4 Werner Jochmann (ed.), *Adolf Hitler: Monologe im Führerhauptquartiere 1941–1944: Aufzeichnungen Heinrich Heims*, Verlag Albrecht Knaus, Hamburg 1980.

(Heim) and the *Tischgespräche*[5] (Picker) are valuable sources for following Hitler's thinking. Many historians have relied on them in the past, and many will in the future. What they may not know, however, is that a red line must be drawn through the Foreword and Commentary of *Tischgespräche*, for it is not true to claim that in 1942 Adolf Hitler gave Henry Picker the exclusive rights to write up the table talks. The facts are that Adolf Hitler had no knowledge of his monologues being secretly noted down. That he did not know, and did not wish a record to be kept, is proved by the following:

(a) a conversation between Heim and Schaub after 1945. 'In the spring of 1951 I met Julius Schaub in the street just after a magazine had published an extract from (Picker's) Bonn book, which was on the point of being released. Schaub assured me that Hitler had had no idea that I was making notes . . .';[6]

(b) a letter from Gerda Christian née Daranowski to Christa Schroeder dated 19 March 1975: '. . . you know how he (Hitler) hated having his thoughts committed to paper, i.e. he strictly forbade it. I remember one night at Wolfsschanze when after some highly interesting talk you said to him something like: "I would like to have got that down in shorthand" and he replied: "No, then I would not be able to speak so freely" etc. etc, do you remember?'

(c) Adolf Hitler often said that after the war he would dictate his memoirs to his two senior female secretaries Wolf and Schroeder. The events, experiences and ideas expressed in his table talks were naturally the major component of his life story. A signed statement in my possession made by stenotyist Gertraud Junge reads: 'The worse the situation got at the fronts, in the small circle at the evening table

5 *Hitlers Tischgespräche*, first published Athenäum Verlag, Bonn 1951, later edition with extensive commentary and notes by Picker, Seewald Verlag, Stuttgart 1976.

6 14.9.1953 for the BBC, London, taped recording, extract from *Klüter-Blättern. Monatshefte für Kultur und Zeitgeschichte*, Jahrgang 32, December 1981, Issue 12, p.29.

talks the happier the Führer would be to talk about his plans for after the war. He talked about the painting gallery and reshaping the city of Linz, to where he was planning his retirement, and mentioned in this context repeatedly that he would then surround himself only with civilians, artists and academics, and never again with 'uniforms', so that he could then finally dictate his memoirs. His two long-serving secretaries Wolf and Schroeder would help him in this, the younger girls would probably marry and leave him. As he would then be older and slower, the women would be able to keep up with his tempo.'

(d) Another myth is that Adolf Hitler allegedly instructed Martin Bormann to give Picker special treatment by ordering that his bags were not to be searched whenever he left FHQ. In fact the bags of FHQ staff were never searched: 'AFFIDAVIT. I hereby swear on oath that during my service as personal adjutant to Adolf Hitler from 1943 to April 1945, my bags and personal effects were never subject to controls on entering or leaving FHQ. This was true for all other personnel at FHQ. There never was an order to search baggage of FHQ personnel upon entering or leaving FHQ or Sperrkreise I and II (Führer-bunker and accommodation of Adolf Hitler's personal staff). Upon entering Sperrkreis I (Führer-bunker) after the assassination attempt of 20 July 1944, visitors from outside were required to surrender their pistols to the RSD, and their hand baggage (file and attaché cases) was examined.' Signed, Otto Günsche, 26.3.1982.

To rebut all of Picker's false assertions would require another volume. I point out here just three glaring examples:

(a) Eva Braun was the lady of the house at the Berghof;
(b) Eva Braun was Hitler's 'great love'; and
(c) Hitler broke off his friendship with Gretl Slezak in 1932 because of her Jewish background.

All three statements lack any basis in fact and are discussed at length later in this book.

It was the custom of Dr Picker to throw a party every year to celebrate his birthday. In the Foreword and Commentary to *Tischgespräche*, Picker includes a tract allegedly signed by the three former military adjutants, von Puttkamer, von Below and Engel, to the effect that all have read the material of the book and vouchsafe its accuracy to the best of their knowledge and belief. In order to lend credit to this authentication, these three former officers were invited to attend the birthday parties. It is unfortunately the fact that hardly any of them had read the Foreword and Commentary. When I asked the wife of one of the former ADCs she replied: 'Ah, you know Christa, we never read stuff like that. We put the book straight on the shelf!'[7] Thus historians may rely on the authentication and in good faith repeat Picker's assertions as historical fact.

Letter, FHQ Wolfsschanze, 28 June 1941:

It is a companionable reunion in the inner circle, coffee and cakes again, etc. You can be sure after reading this that we shall not be returning any slimmer. Occasionally we visit our chef,[8] who came from the Mitropa and who cooks for us on our travels and follows us in all the HQs, in his highly professional, white-tiled kitchen equipped with the most modern electrical equipment, and scrounge whatever catches the eye.

We were very keen to give him a hand the other day, cutting bread, apportioning butter or making the salad garnish, but he simply does not want help. He is a small, slim, agile man whom the boys of the *SS-Begleitkommando* call 'Krümel' – Lump – I do

---

7 Frau von Below, wife of former Luftwaffe adjutant to Hitler Nicolaus von Below (statement by Schroeder to editor).

8 Otto Günther, 1937 employed on the Führer-train, and then at FHQ. He was on Kannenberg's staff and cooked for the 150–200 personnel at FHQ Wolfsschanze.

not know why – and the more work he has to do the happier he is, and the better he feels. He is a cook from passion, so to speak, and it is a joy to see how quickly and skilfully everything flows from his hands. In a trice he arranges something, not tossed together with a prayer, but always into a beautiful garnish. When one sees the happy Lump one realises how important work is for fulfilment and a feeling of contentment. On the other hand I often see myself as useless and unnecessary. When I think how much I do in a day's work I come to the devastating conclusion: nothing. The wife of a plutocrat is active compared to me. I sleep, eat, drink and converse if I can bring myself to it. In a quiet moment – I cannot really change anything since duty condemns me to eternal waiting and readiness, until another blow is to be struck – I set myself a job (I have 1,000 words of French to learn) – but even here it is hard to get involved. I lack verve and motivation. Today I had to really force myself to finally provide you with a long report . . .

Meanwhile you have already heard the batch of Special Announcements for a whole week. The boss said this morning that if the German soldier deserves a laurel wreath it is for this campaign. Everything is going better than anticipated. We have had a lot of luck, e.g. the Russians stood at the frontier and did not allow us to make a deep penetration, which would have caused us problems on all our supply lines, and then by failing to destroy two bridges at Dunaburg.[9] That would have caused a great loss of time if we had had to rebuild the bridges first. I believe that once we have occupied Minsk we will then go forward all out. If there are a few Communists hidden in our soldiers' ranks then they will certainly be converted when they see the 'prosperity' over there. I have talked to several officers who had the chance to look around Moscow.[10] It must be a miserable, harsh life for the Russian people. Their

---

9 On 26.6.1941 the German 8.Panzer Division captured the bridges over the Duna intact.

10 Photographer Heinrich Hoffmann and adjutant Richard Schulze.

insecurity has been used to rob them and lead them astray. It would be interesting to experience something more authentic about it.

Letter, FHQ Wolfsschanze, 13 July 1941:

In our evening discussion with the boss the Church plays a major role. It is a pity that you cannot be there. It is all so enlightening what the boss says when e.g. he explains that Christianity with its lies and hypocrisy has held Western humanity back 2,000 years in its development – from the cultural standpoint. I really must start making notes afterwards about what the boss said, but the sessions last a ridiculously long time and one is by then – if not actually ready to drop – well at least so enervated and bereft of energy as to not feel like writing.

The night before last when we left him it was dawn. Instead of going to bed as normal people do we had a couple of sandwiches in the kitchen and then went for a two-hour run direct into the sunrise. Past horses and cattle in corrals, past hills of red and white clover simply fabulous in the morning sun. I could not get enough of it. Then we went to bed and spent three hours exhausted, unable to bestir ourselves. A mad existence, don't you think? Such a weird occupation as Daranowski and I have would probably never offer itself again. Eat, drink, sleep, now and again write something and be sociable for hours on end. A new idea is to make ourselves useful for the boss picking flowers 'so that his bunker does not look so bare'.

Letter, FHQ Wolfsschanze, 28 July 1941:

The last few days I have been miserable again. It is a thorn in the side of certain people that even in wartime the boss has his personal staff around him which obviously includes two females. An orderly told me about comments made at a late hour after excessive drinking in the officers' mess and which have incensed me. At first I was going

Above: Hitler's secretaries Christa Schroeder and Johanna Wolf at breakfast, Haus Wachenfeld, 1935

Below: Dr Goebbels, Eva Braun, Karl Hanke, Christa Schroeder and Albert Speer waiting for Hitler, Berghof terrace, 1938

Above: At the Hradschin in Prague on 16 March 1939 Hitler signed the edict creating the Protectorate of Bohemia and Moravia. From left, Schaub, Hitler, Dr Frick, Dr Lammers, an adjutant, Dr Stuckart and Christa Schroeder

Below: In the Reich Chancellery, Christa Schroeder and Gerda Daranowski congratulate Hitler on his 50th birthday, 20 April 1939. From left, Heinz Linge, Gerda Daranowski, Christa Schroeder and Hitler

Above: Hitler's personal physician Dr Theo Morell, Wilhelm Brückner, Gerda Daranowski and Christa Schroeder in conversation with Hitler at the Berghof, New Year's Eve, 1940

Right: Christa Schroeder at her typewriter at FHQ Wolfsschanze

Above: Christa Schroeder examining Hitler's world-globe in the Berghof 'Great Hall'

Below: Hitler's guests, Great Hall, Berghof, New Year's Eve 1940. Front row from left: Wilhelm Brückner, Christa Schroeder, Eva Braun, Hitler, Margarete Braun, Adolf Wagner, Dr Dietrich: upper right is Heinrich Heim the stenographer who copied down Hitler's monologues. Contrary to what many assert, as this photo shows, Heim really did belong within Hitler's inner circle

Right: Hitler dictating to Christa Schroeder at FHQ Wolfsschanze, 1941, behind her is Dr Morell

Below: Hitler's intimate staff in the officers' mess at FHQ Wehrwolf near Winniza, 20 September 1942. From left to right: Nicolaus von Below, Christa Schroeder, unknown, Walter Hewel, Albert Bormann, Julius Schaub

Above: Hitler exercises his Alsatian Blondi in the open meadow east of the Wolfsschanze, c. August 1943

Below: The Wolfsschanze's Führerbunker, Rastenburg in East Prussia

The Wolfsschanze was the location of the failed bomb plot of 20 July. This photograph shows Hitler with his would-be assassin Claus von Stauffenberg (far left) at the Wolfsschanze just a few days beforehand on 15 July 1944. During this meeting Stauffenberg had a bomb with him but it did not detonate

Above left: From 1936 Hitler's home in Obersalzberg became known as the Berghof. Along with the Wolfsschanze this was the place where Hitler spent most of his time during the war and was one of the main headquarters

Above right: Hitler with the Berghof in the distance

Below: Hitler walking out of the Berghof with Goebbels to his left

to take it up with the boss, for it is really a mutiny against him, a criticism of his directives and orders. We are not here from choice but only because the boss wants it and maintains that he can only work with us. He has emphasised more than once in the presence of these gentlemen that without us (Dara and me) he would have been in a pickle. Thus I find it arrogant and stupid of these officers to deprecate our presence.

I am exercising an iron reserve towards the parties involved and now they have a bad conscience. Probably it was not a pleasant situation for them when, just a few days after the comment, the boss asked the Wehrmacht adjutant if a tent was available for his ladies at the next HQ. Receiving the answer 'No!', in indignation the Führer ordered that a possibility for our accommodation had to be created immediately – yes, they had been thinking it would be just a short stay for a few days under canvas and we would not be needed. In all these excuses one sees their hope of ditching us by the wayside. But the boss would not let himself be persuaded. A coach will have to be provided for our beds and work, he said.

Earlier when I drank with them I laboured under the delusion that these people were friends, but now I see that the chats we had in those hours were not the outpourings of comradely sentiment but just the effect of the damned alcohol. These social periods changed nothing and created no friendships. The day after, I came across more hostility. Why such deception? It is a bitter fact to realise that one is abandoned and alone and that with the best will in the world and with the purest intentions no friendship is possible.

The men are all obsessed with one thing, to seize the best possible advantage for themselves and appear in the best light. They all want to be more than they are and do not realise how silly they look to those who see through them. The most ridiculous thing is when the boss is standing amongst some of these gentlemen and the photographer picks up his Leica. Then they all come streaming to the boss like moths to the lamp, just to get into the picture. This morbid need to be noticed is simply disgusting. Well, now I have had a good moan. But you can understand how this hollow society revolts me and therefore I had to let off steam again.

Letter, FHQ Wolfsschanze 20 August 1941:

Life has become rather monotonous. We have been here nine weeks already and we gather that we will be staying here until the end of October. That is really a wretchedly long time, little work, often nothing to do all day, always the same faces, the same conversations. I am so sick of this being condemned to inactivity that recently I attempted to convince the boss that he really needs only one secretary, for I kept the shop alone for years. But he stopped me at once, preventing me from making my point that I should spend the war employed usefully somewhere – either in a hospital or an armaments factory. Yes, I have no choice but to soldier on here.

A few days ago we saw a British newsreel which came from the United States. It showed the awful devastation caused to whole sections of streets in London. All the warehouses, the Parliament, etc. have been destroyed. Wandering over whole districts of the city, the camera showed the enormous fires, warehouse after warehouse a sea of flames. The commentary said that the British could take it because they knew that Berlin looked the same. If the poor British only knew that the damage they inflict on Berlin is a mere pinprick compared to London, I am sure they would not want to carry on. Captured British officers say themselves that their own government is acting irresponsibly. If the British – and moreover their officers – admit it, we can hope for the best to happen. I would like nothing better than that the British should sue for peace once we have disposed of Russia. The war with Britain can only lead to each of us reducing the cities of the other to rubble. And Mr Roosevelt laughs and looks forward to his British inheritance. It is really incomprehensible to me that the British do not see sense.

After we have won the war ... we do not need their colonies, I would find it much more practical if we worked together. The Ukraine and Crimea are so fertile, we can grow everything we need there and barter for the rest (coffee, tea, cocoa, etc.) with the South Americans. It is so clear and simple. I pray to God that the British soon see reason.

Letter, FHQ Wolfsschanze, 30 August 1941:

. . . we spent a couple of days in Galicia and I found your letter on my return . . . Our stay here at HQ is dragging on and on. At first we thought we would be back in Berlin at the end of July, then it was mid October and now people are saying we will not be getting away before the end of October or perhaps even later. A perceptible autumn chill is already in the air and if the boss decides to stay for the winter we shall all freeze. This 'living for ever in the bunker' is healthy for none of us. The boss does not look at all well, he gets too little fresh air and is now oversensitive to sun and wind whenever he goes for a few hours' drive.

I would love to have remained in Galicia,* nearly everybody was in favour of it, but it is more difficult to guarantee security there. Incidents occur every day, and as the compound there cannot be fenced off as well as at our present HQ the danger is too great.

The countryside there is so lovely it really surprised me. On one side forests and on the other gently rolling hills. On the hilltops cattle were silhouetted against the blue sky and the farmers followed the plough. The peasants' huts are quite romantic, rounded and protected against the wind by a thatched roof and scarcely a window

---

* During a visit to the Eastern Front, Hitler and Mussolini spent the night of 27 August 1941 on their special trains at FHQ Askania-Süd, a purpose-built surface tunnel to house the train coaches near the village of Frysztak in Galicia (tunnel and other structures remain in existence). Barracks for the security personnel and a tea-house for Hitler were located near Strzyzow, twenty kilometres north of Krosno. Seidler and Zeigert, *Die Führer-Hauptquartiere*, pp.218–21. (TN)

anywhere. In front a well with a rusty chain, a few sunflowers; the womenfolk, suntanned and all barefoot, wear a long dark cloth over the head and down to the hips. They keep close to their cows, a little shady, a little secretive, but totally in keeping with the landscape, which somehow reminded me of home.

That whole region there is freer; here in the woods the atmosphere is depressing after a while. Another thing that struck me there was that I did not have the feeling of being locked in, I could see the farmers working in the fields and this gave me the feeling of being free while here we are always coming across sentries and having to show our identity cards. Even so, of course, we remain perpetually isolated from the world wherever we are: in Berlin, on the Berg or travelling, always the same limited circle, always the same crowd inside the wire. And therein lies the danger of becoming shy of people and losing contact with real life and . . . a great dilemma: one longs to get out, but when one is out one does not know where to begin because one is so utterly and completely set in this fixed existence and no possibility exists for a life beyond this circle. The circle around the boss is held together by the common experience, but woebetide us when he goes away, for then everything comes apart (this is also the opinion of Dr Brandt), and then it is grim for those who have lost contact with the outside world. Excuse me for going on about this, but I see in it a problem for later which will not be easy to resolve.

When the German armies were surprised by the terrible winter of 1941, and stuck fast in the Russian ice, Hitler was frequently depressed, but remained hopeful as before of a quick victory: 'It is no more than a quite thin veil which we have to penetrate', he said, 'we must be patient. The Russian resistance will not endure.' The veil was not torn asunder and our stay at Wolfsschanze grew ever longer.

Letter, FHQ Wolfsschanze, 6 January 1942:

. . . your other observations about morale in the Reich, the Church etc. I found very interesting. I believe that the mood will very soon revive once more great successes begin to be announced, e.g. when Leningrad falls. The harvest will ripen in the next ten days anyhow. The boss has a principle of not making Special Announcements until a battle is definitely won because premature claims can alert the enemy to his danger and imperil lives. He often finds himself in a dilemma over this: he would like to calm the country, but on the other hand deny the enemy any details.

I can well imagine that the churches are full, but I share your opinion (which is also that of the boss) that nothing can be undertaken at the moment. That will have to wait for after the war . . .

Incidentally a gramophone was introduced into the Führerbunker a fortnight ago and now almost every evening we hear the songs of Strauss, Hugo Wolf and primarily Wagner of course. I have a very special liking for the *Heimliche Aufforderung* by Strauss sung by Schlusnus and on another occasion by a tenor from Graz who tends towards being baritone: Peter Anders (you should remember the name when buying records!), he has a very soft, fawning voice, but very clear diction. These songs are wonderful, one is quite lulled into love and warmth which apparently has an effect on the boss too, for yesterday evening he said to us girls: 'Children, you must use every hour!' I should like to have told him: what does he imagine, I should like to know, I can do to enjoy my youth when we crouch down with him day in day out, year in year out and never get away. Yes, yes, theory and practice . . .

Letter, FHQ Wolfsschanze, 15 January 1942:

Scarcely had I posted my letter of moans and groans than your dear letter arrived, which I read voraciously. I wrote to you in reply at once a long, long letter which I held back a few days because my outpourings would surely have been depressing for you. In a way I am sorry but it is better if I save up all these things for my visit in March. I have agreed with my colleague that from now on we will relieve each other regularly so that we have at least some private life. Daranowski has gone on leave now and I shall have the pleasure in March.

I will just tell you today that the holiday here was miserable. In the pre-Christmas period the Führer took over supreme command.[11] His workload has grown immeasurably and scheduled mealtimes have gone by the board. Lunch will now be taken at 1400, but is postponed increasingly to an hour when normal people have their evening meal. The record was set a few days ago when the boss had lunch at 1800. Dinner had to be put back accordingly and our tea session in his bunker, which used to begin at 2200, now usually gets under way after midnight (record to date 0200), which means we turn in between 0400 and 0500.

The natural rhythm of life, which is very important for health, no longer exists, and the mood swings from high to low without a transition period, which I cannot imagine is good for the soul. At New Year for example we were in officers' mess for supper in a contented mood. Then we were ordered to the tea session where the boss was exhausted, and after a while nodded off, which meant we had to keep quiet, and were forced to suppress our merriment. The boss spent three hours in the situation conference and the officers who had arrived to wish him happy New Year waited around with long faces which they dared not crease into a smile. I cannot describe exactly why, but next I had a crying fit in my bunker and went back to the officers' mess where I found a couple of brave

---

11 After dismissing Generalfeldmarschall von Brauchitsch on 19 December 1941, Hitler took over supreme command of the army. He explained: 'Anybody can handle the little bit of operational leadership. The task of the army supreme commander is to educate the Army to be National Socialist. To my way of thinking there is no army general who can fulfil the role.'

lads from the *SS-Begleitkommando*, who naturally also feared that I had been in tears and I promptly started again. They attempted to comfort me with words and alcohol and finally succeeded. Then we sang together that heart-rending sea shanty 'We were lying off Madagascar and had the plague on board.'

One can keep swearing never to touch another drop, but in this miserable life it often seems to me to be the only way to overcome depression. I have not been doing much running. It is too cold, there is too much snow, the roads are so iced over as to make a run a nerve-racking business, and so I prefer to stay in the warm bunker. I have transformed our office, which was formerly a stark, bare room, into a really snug lounge. I needed to exercise my persuasive powers quite often – whenever I saw something I fancied I gave the owner no peace until it was sacrificed to me. Now I have taken to sleeping in the office. I really could not stand the bunker any longer. The fan whirled all night and swept my head constantly until every hair hurt. The so-called couch is not an ideal bed, but at least I have a window in the room . . .

The women who have to work in munitions factories or are recruited for the trams or the subway trains have a damned difficult job but they have a big plus over us in that when their working day is over they can move freely and do what they want. Now I am beginning to pity myself again, so I will stop there . . . a few days ago Sepp Dietrich and General Dietl were here for two days. Two vigorous men who cheered up the monotonous behind-the-front atmosphere wonderfully.

I noted down the following:

A cabin in the bunker with fan. When working, although fresh air came in, it made a terrible din. If it was turned off, we were told we would suffocate. Therefore I slept in the office at the bunker entrance and had a window. No office atmosphere, no fixed work hours. Hitler often maintained that he had been found the swampiest and most climatically unfavourable region rich with biting midges possible, but I found East Prussia very attractive. The giant fields of red clover at sunrise, its expanses, the blue sky and in winter the undisturbed snowy landscape.

Letter, FHQ Wolfsschanze, 27 February 1942:

'. . . and that is essential in this monotony. My colleague, who always used to seem fairly nonchalant about it, is now terribly depressed about the life she is missing. All resolutions to accept with a good demeanour whatever cannot be avoided soon dissolve after a few days. Our mood is eternally Up or Down, which has nothing to do with indiscipline, but with many other things which I hope to be able to discuss with you in March . . .

After two days of warm weather it got cold very suddenly, i.e. the daytime temperature is 17°C, but the keen easterly wind makes you really feel the cold. In itself the cold does not really bother us, so inured have we become to it, it is only the accursed wind. Despite that we now go for at least a one-hour run through the countryside daily, usually to the next village, whose ordinariness was extremely depressing in the summer, but now with its blanket of snow looks rather romantic. The rest of the day one spends more or less idle moping around.

Although the boss is always very tired, he does not spend much time in bed which is often a nuisance. Previously we would often listen to records in the evening and could muse the time away, but since Todt's unfortunate end[12] the music evenings are rare. Since

---

12 Fritz Todt (b. 4.9.1891 Pforzheim, d. 8.2.1942 Görlitz). From 1939 major general of the Luftwaffe; from 17.3.1940 Reich minister for armament and munitions. After visiting Hitler at FHQ Wolfsschanze on 7 February 1942, he took off in his personal He 111 next morning in adverse weather against advice and crashed on the airfield boundary.

the tea circle always consists of the same people and in licoh life come in from outside, and nobody has anything personal to relate, the conversation is often rather indifferent, dragging, tiring and burdensome. The talks go along the same old tracks . . .

I noted later:

Entertainment: every evening cinema, afternoons tea-house. Politics never discussed. Hitler's influence was felt everywhere: either nobody had a private opinion or feared to express it. Whoever dared was cold-shouldered. Hitler was the driving force for everybody in his environment.

Before the disaster at Stalingrad on 2 February 1943 Hitler would organise an evening of record music from time to time. His favourites were Beethoven symphonies, extracts from Wagner operas, and songs by Hugo Wolf. He would then sit, eyes closed, listening to the music. It was always the same records which were played and the tea-hour guests knew the catalogue numbers by heart. If Hitler said: '*Aida*, last act, *Es hat der Stein sich über uns geschlossen*', then one of the guests would call to the waiter: 'Record number 123.'

After Stalingrad, Hitler could no longer relax to music. Then we spent the evenings listening to his monologues. These were invariable: his youth in Vienna, the years of struggle, the history of humanity, macrocosmos–microcosmos and so on. On most topics we knew what was coming next and so the evenings required endurance. World events, the battle front: these were not to be discussed during the tea hour, and in fact anything connected to the war was taboo. It was advisable to broach innocuous themes such as his shepherd dog Blondi's turbulent behaviour and disobedience, or the adventures of the cat which suddenly appeared at FHQ Wolfsschanze one day. He did not actually like cats, apparently because they went for birds, but he gradually accepted 'Peter' to the extent that in the end he would get jealous if the cat selected somebody else's lap to sit on. His jealousy for Blondi was evident from his anger should the dog take an interest in anybody else. He would then tend to suspect that the dog's affections had been undermined by a titbit of meat, an act which was strictly forbidden. According to Hitler, it was useless for anybody else to seek Blondi's affections, for her devotion was limited to him alone.

After breakfast every morning Hitler walked Blondi in the wild area around his bunker. He was very fond of the dog which he entrusted to a keeper (Tarnow). She was a very docile and clever dog, able to do some tricks such as balancing on a pole, jumping a two-metre high wall and climb a ladder. Hitler had no time for smaller dogs. Eva Braun's two Scotch terriers Negus and Stasi he denigrated as 'hand-lickers', to which their owner responded: 'Blondi is a calf'.

How fortunate, [I wrote to my friend,] that we have a cat which often comes to sit and whose funny little games – making us aware of a change in his situation – are something we are grateful for when the conversation palls. I like it especially when he jumps onto my lap, for then I place my aching hands under his soft warm fur: that feels good. We do have a Scotch terrier as well but nobody fawns over him because he is recalcitrant and obstinate (and the boss has sworn never to be photographed with him because the terrier looks like a 'hand-licker'). He is not allowed into the talk circle because of the cat but even when he is absent he enlivens the conversation . . .

Many interesting subjects were addressed which one can read in Heim's *Monologe*. Hitler would often speak about the Japanese. 'I am accused of sympathising with the Japanese', he said, 'but what does sympathising mean? The Japanese are yellow-skinned and slit-eyed, but they are fighting against Britain and the United States and that makes them useful to Germany. In that sense I sympathise with them.' After the fall of Singapore to the Japanese, Ribbentrop appeared before Hitler to deliver a report. Ribbentrop intended to make a big thing of it with the radio and press. In the small bunker office Hitler told him: 'I am not in favour of overdoing this, Ribbentrop. One has to think of the time centuries ahead when we shall have to settle the score with the yellow race.'

Hitler often spoke of people in his wider circle. Of Speer he once remarked:

He is an artist and his soul is linked to mine. I have the closest human relationship towards him because I understand him so well. He is a man of architecture as I am, intelligent, modest and not a dour military head. I did not think he would master his great objective so well, but he has a great talent for organisation and grew to the task. If I show Speer a plan and give him the job, he reflects a while and then says: '*Ja, mein Führer*, I believe it is possible', or he objects: '*Nein*, it cannot be done like that' and then provides the full reason.

Speer was a convinced follower of Hitler and even in internment I could see how deeply Hitler's words 'I take full responsibility for everything!' still had their effect on him. This promise extinguished all feelings of guilt in Hitler's followers, and imbued in them a kind of faith equivalent to belief in God. While Hitler lived, Speer saw in him 'The Extraordinary', but with Hitler's death Speer's fascination for Hitler died too.

Hitler also spoke frequently about photographer Heinrich Hoffmann. 'Hoffmann was once a crazy young man', he told me, 'then he was still slim and agile and went tirelessly about his work with his complicated old apparatus. He had to slip under the black cloth and go through the most neck-breaking operations with the heavy camera to get good photos.' Hoffmann liked his drink. Hitler told him once: 'Hoffmann, your nose looks like a rotten cucumber. I think that if I put a lighted match to your breath it would explode, and soon red wine will replace blood completely in your arteries.' This was said after Hoffmann turned up the worse for drink at the dining table. He had not done so before in Hitler's presence, and it shocked Hitler to see Hoffmann in such a state. Finally he ordered Schaub and Bormann: 'Please ensure that Professor Hoffmann is sober when in my presence. I have invited him so that we can converse, and not so that he can let himself go.' How wounded Hitler must have been only became clear much later.

Professor Hoffmann collected nineteenth-century paintings and bought up all the watercolours Hitler had painted. On visits to his villa on Munich's Ebersberg-Strasse he never neglected to show them. He was extraordinarily proud of the collection. I also remember conversations in which Hitler told Hoffmann not to pay such exorbitant sums for his watercolours since he himself had only received 20 or 30 RM for each. What became of Professor Hoffmann's collection is a mystery, but I think it probably finished up together with all the other paintings and works of art which I saved from destruction at the Berghof after the war. A footnote about a conversation between Hitler and Professor Hoffmann on 12 March 1944 at the Berghof which I noted down indicates Hitler's attitude to his earlier works:

Obersalzberg, 12 March 1944 Rü/Wag
During lunch today Professor Hoffmann showed Hitler a watercolour painted by the Führer in 1910. Professor Hoffmann obtained the picture recently in Vienna.
Der Führer: Hoffmann, I hope you did not buy that picture?
Hoffmann: I received it as a gift, that is to say, the seller told me that for the price it is a gift.
Der Führer: Even today these things should not fetch more than 150 to 200 RM. It is madness if one pays more. It was not my ambition

to be a painter. I only painted these things to support myself in my studies. I would not have received much over 12 RM then. I only ever painted enough to cover my necessities; 80 RM would have kept me for a month; 1 RM would have bought me lunch and supper. I used to study all night. My architectural sketches which I made then, those were my most precious possessions, the fruit of my mental efforts which I would never sell as I did the paintings. One should not forget that all my thinking today, my architectural plans, evolved from the concepts created in night-long work in those years. If I am in a position today to sketch the ground plan of a theatre, it is not done by me while in a trance, it is exclusively the result of my earlier studies. Unfortunately nearly all my sketches of that time are lost to me . . . !

I can confirm that Hitler was very attached to his architectural sketches and would not have disposed of them. When at the end in 1945 Schaub emptied the contents of Hitler's strong box at the Berghof and burned the material on the terrace, many of Hitler's architectural sketches were amongst them, and I saved a bundle from Schaub's bonfire. I did not keep them, however: Albert Zoller failed to return half and the rest I rather stupidly sold to Dr Picker.

In the summer of 1942, Hitler advanced his command post to FHQ Wehrwolf at Vinnitsa in the Ukraine.

Letter. FHQ Wehrwolf, 14 August 1942:

I am only glad that you are sympathetic to my mental inertia. In the four weeks since we have been at the new HQ I have not found the energy for writing private letters, yet I feel really good physically and mentally. I just lack somebody to plug the drain on my spiritual resources and revive me spiritually. Unfortunately so many here have fallen victim to languor that no help can be expected from this quarter. Since the two thick Benrath tomes I have not really read anything. I lack inner calm and the will for it.

The films served up are ancient, stupid, spiritless. The last two evenings Johanna and I have reverted to watching the old silent movies, but only because there is nothing better. The worst is when you get hot under the collar at the stupid films and start to itch everywhere but stay seated because the only alternative is bed. Right, now I shall give you a short report on our new HQ and about the removal to here, etc.

On 17 July, sixteen or seventeen aircraft got ready to fly to the east. It was a very impressive scene on the airfield, all the great machines clustered together, all ready to take off, motors running, the air filled with the deep humming of vibrating wings and wires until one machine after the other rolled down the airstrip and lifted off into the air. The pilot invited me to sit in the cockpit which naturally I accepted gratefully, for from there you get a quite different picture. The fuselage windows give a view to one side only, and a small section at that, but the panorama from the cockpit is greater and freer. And here you really feel that you are flying.

I found it interesting to follow the flight on a map. This is a science I would never be able to master. People who understand it impress me very much, for to say that the landscape below looks like a map is a platitude. Naturally there is a certain similarity, but the reality has a confusing mass of detail which makes it difficult to match the two. Highways coloured red on the map prove to be grey and inconspicuous below (the easiest to spot were railway lines). Here and there the landscape is darkened when clouds hide the sun, or ground mist obscures the ground for a while until a piece of terrain reappears: but where we were on the map I could never determine.

I have wandered completely off the subject. After many hours we reached the destination airfield. Here we had to search for our car, and eventually set off in a heavy Krupp which is not at all suitable for Russian 'highways'. For Johanna Wolf, who had not felt well during the flight, this was the last straw. She was totally exhausted and unable to lend a hand for the first few hours.

Her depression got worse, and mine began, when we saw our office. To the left and right a door opened to reveal a small aperture containing a narrow bed with nightstand and a rack for the cases. This was our world. The office was so narrow and small that we could hardly move in it. Our luggage, giant office cases, crates and five typewriters filled it up completely. Since we have lived long enough in dark, airless bunkers, our hopes were for bright rooms with large windows. Instead, the bedroom had a single square window twenty-five centimetres along each side and covered with a green gauze. This 'window' was our greatest disappointment. Thank God we could have a look round, and after I moved into another room temporarily for eight days finally I ferreted out a decent office with an alcove behind a curtain. By virtue of my organisational skill and experience I have been able to convert it – say it quietly – into the most snug room in the whole HQ.

Only I could have done it: a couch (sofa with coverlet and dark-green/blue padded back rest, above it some wall drapes which would probably be better put to use as bed mats, in front of the couch a little table I made myself from a suitcase rack and a wardrobe shelf, covered with a red-fringed and spotted blanket; two chairs, one upholstered, the other with a rattan seat; a carpet; colourful engravings and prints on the walls; many flowers but mainly zinnias, and then for contrast thistles in a black earthenware jar. We had a housewarming which lasted until 0600 . . . I will tell you orally.

The living accommodation is similar to Wolfsschanze except we have fortified houses instead of concrete bunkers. They look really attractive but are awfully damp inside. It is always the same whenever you start at a new HQ: the beds are always damp, you shiver terribly and it is quite certain that later one will be disabled with rheumatism. Daytime temperatures are really high (it is not unusual to have 45–50°C) but at night it is disproportionately cool, and often the weather changes as quick as a flash.

The mosquito plague is worse here than last year, and here we have the dangerous Anopheles strain whose bites can give you malaria. There is a prophylactic called Atibrin which tastes ghastly and bitter, one revolts against taking it each evening but you have to force yourself; if you get malaria, that counts as a self-inflicted injury, a serious disciplinary offence. On the evening of hot days we have a mad purge on the insects which enter despite the gauzed windows: they get in through every crack and hum around you in bed, and keep on and on until your nerves can stand no more and you get up cursing. Recently at night I have taken to opening the curtain to the living room and lighting all lamps, this attracts the mosquitoes out of the alcove and into the light, and once the whole army of them has gathered I draw the curtain again and creep back to bed leaving the light burning.

The other night scarcely had I laid my head down than I heard a rustling and a nibbling near my bed: I had left some milk to curdle and the mice had found it. With a loud cry I ran out to the couch and lit the lamps in the bedroom to attract the mosquitoes there. That was a damned restless night! Frank Thiess wrote in one of his books that all women are stupid, they shriek equally loudly for an innocent mouse as a tiger. He is probably right.

We have a wonderful innovation – a fifteen by ten metre swimming pool. Unfortunately the water drains away frequently and is in any case barbarously cold. The food has improved enormously. As we live from the local products of the land we have plenty of butter in the morning and often an egg. A large market garden provides us with fresh vegetables.

In the city there is a slaughterhouse on 100,000 hectares, the largest of its kind in Europe. I had a chance to visit and watched the whole process from stunning the animal to the final sausage or meat paste. The factory is designed on American lines, a continuous production line. They skin a cow in the ridiculously short time of thirty seconds, a process that takes two hours in Germany. Some 250–300 cattle are slaughtered there daily and cooked to make 12,000–15,000 tins of meat. A few sample tins are taken from each run for airtightness testing, which is done in a culture cabinet, where they are kept for twenty-four hours in tropical heat. Provided no defective tins are discovered, the batch is then consigned to the Front.

This factory uses every last piece of the animal, which ends up as soap, in buttons, combs and cigarette butts. The skins are salted and stored for four to six weeks, turned every day and freshly salted. It is really an enormous business. Most of the employees are women, chosen because they are more industrious . . .

In the city there is a theatre dating from the Tsarist era, naturally terribly neglected with woodworm in the ceiling, and it is just a question of when it will fall in, tomorrow or in a hundred years. The experts are unable to be precise. As it weighs seventy tonnes, it will be a notable event. The performers make the best of what they have at their disposal. The orchestra plays cleanly, the ballet is grandiose in parts. The ballet master and prima donna could perform in Berlin and receive rapturous applause. They are outstanding in their own field. The pair does a Mongolian dance which brings their racial origins to the fore in the mime, a crass characterisation of the Asiatics. They cannot waltz; it is a ghastly hopping affair which they should drop. It is interesting that every opera house has a large installation for ballet.

I saw *La Traviata* and *Faust*. These were not a success. The actors are like wax figures, the men with fixed expressions and mechanical gestures making them appear wire-operated. Perhaps it is the training. Most of the voices are outstanding. The costumes (e.g. in *La Traviata*) are a cross-section from the twentieth century: short, three-quarter length, fringed (like we had in the 1920–24 period), long and patchwork. The honest presentation allows all these defects to be overlooked, and in a way one finds it enthralling.

I got to know the German city and regional commissars at the beginning of our stay and had the chance to see a few things, e.g.

I took part in a tour of various collective farms. It was a glorious day. We started off at 0800, breakfasted with a district farmers' leader who lives by the inland sea ninety minutes away. There was German rump steak, scrambled egg and cooked cheese, washed down with a glorious egg liqueur. Then we did the tour. The fields needed a lot of initial work because the Bolsheviks never spread manure. It will take much toil until the yield reaches the hoped-for targets. I love the countryside here very much; it makes me feel at home somehow. The fields are so beautiful with black wheat in bloom, sunflowers, the red and pink poppies were wonderful but have now started to seed. Soya bean growing has failed so far, it does not ripen; the Bulgarian variety, which ripens six weeks earlier, has now been introduced.

Our people immigrating here do not have an easy task, but there are many possibilities to achieve great things. The longer one spends in this immense region and recognises the enormous opportunity for development, the more the question presents itself as to who will be carrying through these great projects in the future. One comes to the conclusion that the foreign people* are not suitable for various reasons, and ultimately because in the course of the generations an admixture of blood between the controlling strata, the German element and the foreign people would occur. That would be a cardinal breach of our understanding of the need to preserve our Nordic racial inheritance and our future would then take a similar course to that of, for example, the Roman Empire. Everybody who takes a closer look at things comes to the conclusion that the achievements of our people after the war is won, and their territorial gains, must be at least as large as during the war, and therefore our generation will not be able to sit back and relax.

---

* Foreign people = *Fremdvolk*, i.e. presumably the settled inhabitants of the Ukraine before the Nazis arrived. (TN)

Now I have gone wandering off track again, and so back to the district farmers' leader, an extremely well-fed Schleswig-Holsteiner who has kept the business in wonderful order. After lunch we toured one of the giant sugar factories destroyed by the Bolsheviks, then coffee and doughnuts were followed by a visit to the inland sea. It was a cheery event! I, the only female, and therefore the hen in the basket! It did me really good. In the evening the table almost sagged under the weight of the plates, and we laughed ourselves silly at the stories the regional commissar, a very sharp fellow, told us.

We received invitations to visit the city commissar. He lives in a former convalescent home for children. The house is a ruin, the wild garden romantic (I just loved it, I am not so keen on circular paths and borders), and it is situated on a small mountain (the infantry have named it 'Obersalzberg'). It offers a really entrancing view of the city in the distance and over a fairly broad river which winds through hilly meadows and woods and reminds me of the Weser. In the evening we sat at a long table in the garden by candlelight, which was quite romantic except there were too many people there. I am beginning to favour smaller circles where people can get to know each other.

The district commissar has just rung me with his praises, saying that everybody on the collective farm tour found me inspiring and I should come along next time too!

I think that this letter has gone on too long for you, but now that the mood has caught me I will tell you a little more.

In the evening we often walk to the nearest village where the children always look out for us. They are strikingly beautiful, mostly blond and blue eyed. I have a soldier's dictionary and try to make myself understood. The others laugh at me but I succeed. Anyway, it gives us a lot of fun. Most of the old men from the Tsarist time have fine heads and are very polite. The women and young men have had Bolshevism hammered into them and I should not like to run into them alone on a dark night. The unmade streets are miserable:

after rain, like soap in which one's vehicle bogs down; when dry, like encrusted lava over which the vehicle rocks and shakes. From afar the houses look quite enchanting, white with a thatched roof, the interiors simple. That's enough about the land and people . . .

As already mentioned, in the early phase of the Russian campaign Hitler was nearly always in good humour and not averse to the odd joke. When the bitter winter of 1941 halted the advance, this affected his demeanour. Personally I was suffering very much from the constant inactivity and was glad whenever Dr Brandt, who had a substantial correspondence as president for hospitals and health, gave me a few hours' work. The longer the Russian campaign lasted with its to-ing and fro-ing, the more FHQ Wolfsschanze began to be more permanently equipped. Gradually along came a cinema and tea-house, and gradually life began to be more acceptable for us there.

Unfortunately I had not been able to convince the boss that he only needed one secretary. I was anxious to do useful work elsewhere, but he would not release me. This enforced indolence, this eternal monotony and the repetitive daily tea hours, all made me aggressive. I rebelled inwardly and then something happened one evening at tea which exposed this aggression to everybody.

The day had been as dull as any other. After dinner I saw a film in the hope of relieving my boredom, then I went to the officers' mess from where Hitler's manservant winkled me out just as I was getting comfortable. In the hope that the tea session would perhaps not last too long, I promised to return to the mess afterwards. Torn from a convivial environment, I now came to a Führer who wore a frown. I knew that he would be in a bad mood, for the situation at the Front was not good. Today's theme was that old chestnut, smoking. He would start out with special reference to narrowing of the arteries caused by smoking. How awful a smoker's stomach must look. Smokers lacked consideration for others, forcing them to breathe in polluted air. He had really toyed with the idea of outlawing smoking anywhere in Germany. The campaign would begin by having a death's head printed on every cigarette pack. 'If I should ever discover', he often said, emphasising the depth of his antagonism to smoking, 'that Eva were secretly smoking, then that would be grounds for me to separate from her immediately and for ever.' When her sister Gretl made him the pledge never to smoke again, he made her the present of a valuable sapphire ring with diamonds.

At that time I was a heavy smoker. Hitler said that because tobacco products were distributed to them freely, even young soldiers who had not been smokers previously had now taken up the habit. They should be given chocolate, not cigarettes. Everybody nodded in agreement, but I, already in a rather spirited frame of mind from my visit to the officers' mess, chipped in and declared: 'Ah, *mein Führer*, let the poor boys (I might even have used the word 'swine' here) have this pleasure, they don't get any others!' Ignoring my idiotic outburst, Hitler went on to explain how nicotine and alcohol ruined people's health and addled the mind. Now I brought up the big gun and said, referring to photographer Heinrich Hoffmann: 'One cannot really say that, *mein Führer*. Hoffmann smokes and drinks all day yet is the most agile man in the shop.' At that Hitler understandably clammed up. Without another word he rose quickly and took his leave 'ice-cold' and with an aggrieved expression, from which I finally saw what I had done. Next afternoon when I enquired of the manservant in what mood the boss found himself today, Hans Junge gave Johanna Wolf and myself a long look and said that tea would be taken today without the ladies. Albert Bormann had been told to inform us officially. When I asked him, Bormann admitted in embarrassment that the boss was annoyed with me and would not be requiring the ladies' company at tea.

Later that afternoon when Hitler called me for dictation I attempted to apologise but he cut me short, saying: 'There is no need for you to apologise,' maintaining an attitude of cold reserve. When Johanna Wolf tried to repair the damage, he replied bitterly: 'that he had the feeling that it was a bore for us to be with him and he did not want us to be forced to sacrifice our evenings'. Henceforth I no longer existed for him. Since for example on train journeys he would ignore me even when we were sitting at the same table, I no longer went to the dining car but had the meal served to me in my compartment. This went on for some time until one day Albert Bormann appeared and said: 'Little Miss Schroeder, the boss has asked me why you do not come forward.' I misinterpreted this as a request and a gesture of reconciliation, and went to the dining car thinking that all was forgiven, but there he continued to ignore me. This made me ill, and I was away from FHQ for a few weeks to take the cure.

During my absence, Dara, who had meanwhile married, resumed her duties. A dietician-cook skilled in specialised diets, Frau von Exner had been given employment and the convivial tea sessions had been resumed. On the evening of my return I sat at Hitler's right and left of Frau von Exner. After the usual kiss of the hand in greeting and an enquiry after my health he did not speak to me again. It was to be many months before Hitler forgave me for my *faux pas*.

In September 1943, as the Front began to pull back, he decided to fly to the most advanced line near Zaporozhye-Dnepropetrovsk and requested me to accompany him. During the night flight he dictated his orders to the troops to stand firm and spoke to me for the first time again on a personal note although the actual reconciliation did not follow until March 1944. I had severe sciatica and had gone to Bad Gastein to take the cure. On my birthday he sent me a bouquet of long-stemmed roses and a handwritten message of good wishes. This white card bearing his name and the sovereignty symbol engraved in gold was a very special honour which he used only for messages to ladies he held in high esteem such as Frau Goebbels, Frau Göring, Frau Troost, Winfred Wagner etc. I was very moved and mentioned in my letter of thanks that I had now made a vow never to smoke again. This letter apparently impressed him, for it became a conversation piece on several evenings around the fireplace at the Berghof where he was then staying temporarily. After the cure at Bad Gastein I was told to take a slimming course with Professor Zabel at Bischofswiesen near Berchtesgaden, which terminated with a special diet course at Bircher-Benner.

Here I would like to add something about Hitler's two dietician-cooks, Frau Marlene von Exner and later Constanze Manziarly. During the Russian campaign Hitler's stomach troubles had begun to cause him concern, and he had discussed the matter with the Romanian head of state Antonescu who had suffered for years from the same thing. Antonescu recalled an assistant in special diets at the University Clinic of Vienna, Frau Marlene von Exner, who had cured him by means of a strict but tasty regimen. On Hitler's instructions Dr Morell sought a good dietician-cook at the Vienna Clinic and succeeded in hiring Frau von Exner. A small diet-kitchen was set up at FHQ and Frau von Exner set to work with a will. Hitler enthused over the varied menu, especially the Viennese desserts and the wonderful apple pies, which everybody agreed tasted wonderful (very thin pastry with thick layers of apple slices and if possible a small topping of whipped cream). The nightly tea session had been abandoned some time previously after an altercation when Hitler had gone into reclusion, but when I returned I found that it had been resumed, with Frau von Exner as an extra guest. She enlivened the conversation especially when she spoke about her home town of Vienna, this being very acceptable to Hitler.

On a visit to FHQ, Marshall Antonescu met Frau von Exner again. This delighted him and he made her the present of a tiny dog similar to a Yorkshire terrier, very temperamental and intelligent. Hitler considered this dog to be unworthy of a statesman because it was below Hitler's approved size for dogs, and Reichsleiter Martin Bormann was given the job of finding a prize-winning fox terrier for

Frau von Exner. Unfortunately the luck of the charming Viennese cook took a tragic turn when she fell in love with one of Martin Bormann's adjutants.[13] Her racial origins were examined, and it was discovered that a grandmother of hers had been a foundling, which called into question her pure descent under the Aryan Law. Hitler would no longer touch the food she prepared, and his stomach symptoms reappeared. This all happened at a time when consideration was being given to reinforcing the bunker at Wolfsschanze against air attack and therefore FHQ was transferred temporarily to Obersalzberg.[14] Frau von Exner was sent on leave using this as an excuse, and she was dismissed from service shortly afterwards. Reichsleiter Bormann was ordered to 'arianise'[15] the von Exner family.

During Hitler's stay on the Berg his food was prepared by the young Tyolean Constanze Manziarly (not Manzialy as often misspelled) who was employed at Professor Zabel's sanatorium in Bischofswiesen, to the Swiss Bircher-Benner recipe and then brought up to the Berg by car. Shortly before returning to the Rastenburg HQ at the beginning of July 1944, Fräulein Manziarly was invited to join the staff. I was taking the cure at the Zabel sanatorium at the time and she asked my advice. Unfortunately I recommended that she should accept and so this beautiful, tall, young brunette,

---

13 This was SS-Obersturmbannführer Friedrich Darges (b. 8.2.1913 Dülseberg/ Altmark). Hitler wanted Darges to marry Eva Braun's sister Margarete, but Darges preferred Frau von Exner. It is assumed that Hitler was not happy with this arrangement and on 28 July 1944 Darges found himself on the Eastern Front with 5.SS-Panzer Division Wiking; 8.5.1945 interned by US Army; 30.4.1948 released.

14 Hitler left FHQ Wolfsschanze on 23 February 1944 and remained at the Berghof with short breaks until 14 July 1944, his last day there.

15 Helene Maria 'Marlene' von Exner (b. 16.4.1917 Vienna). 15.7.1943 employed by Hitler; end 1943 Aryan genealogy examined and found defective (Jewish grandmother); 8.5.1944 dismissed from service; Bormann was ordered to 'arianize' the family. This was easier done in Austria than Germany and involved juggling old birth certificates to change the line of descent. Frau von Exner survived the war and was living in Austria when this book first appeared in Germany.

a gifted pianist, served Hitler as his dietician-cook. He was quite taken with her, saying: 'I have a cook with a Mozart name.' At the end in 1945 Fräulein Manziarly had her diet-kitchen in the Führerbunker in Berlin and often dined with Hitler. After leaving the Reich Chancellery at the beginning of May 1945 she disappeared mysteriously. Nothing more was ever heard of her, although it is said that she took her own life using a cyanide capsule provided by Hitler.[16]

After completing the supplementary cure with Professor Zabel in July 1944 I resumed my duties at FHQ Wolfsschanze where the bunkers had been reinforced against air attack. The flat roofs had been camouflaged with grass and trees to prevent their being spotted by air reconnaissance. Upon my return Hitler was as warm to me as he had been in earlier times. Knowing that I was also persevering with the Bircher-Benner diet he asked me if I would be eating in the officers' mess or alone. When I said 'alone' he invited me to dine with him in his bunker. On 19 July 1944, the day before the assassination attempt, he was not feeling quite well. He always had premonitions. He felt that an attempt on his life was being planned. He told me this and even said: 'I note that there is something afoot', and again: 'Nothing must happen to me, there is nobody who can carry on the business.'

The situation conferences at that time were being held in the social room in the guests' barrack hut. It was a very hot summer with swarms of mosquitoes and biting midges in the swampy meadows. The sentries wore mosquito nets over their heads. Around midday on 20 July I heard an explosion. This often happened because landmines were laid off the paths and wild animals frequently set them off. This time it was different. People were shouting excitedly for doctors: 'A bomb has gone off, probably in the guest hut!' Suddenly the barriers

---

16 Constanze Manziarly (b. 14.4.1920 Innsbruck). Greek father, Austrian mother; September 1944 employed by Hitler as dietician-cook; after April 1945 fate unknown.

were up everywhere. I was just thinking that today I would definitely not be dining with the boss when I heard: 'Nothing has happened to the chief, but the hut has been blown up!'

Contrary to my expectations, towards 1500 that afternoon he summoned me. As I entered his bunker he rose with some effort and gave me his hand. He looked surprisingly fresh and spoke about the assassination attempt: 'The heavy table leg diverted the explosion. The stenotyist sitting near me had both legs blown off. I had extraordinary luck! If the explosion had happened in the bunker and not in the wooden hut, nobody would have survived it. But haven't I always anticipated that happening? I told you yesterday, don't you remember?'

Hitler then asked if I had seen the conference room, it was wrecked beyond imagining. When I said I had not, since the area was cordoned off, he said I should at least see his tattered uniform. He had his manservant bring it to him and showed me the trousers, in strips and ribbons from top to bottom and only held together by the waistband. A square piece of cloth had been torn from the tunic. He was proud of these trophies and asked me to send them to Eva Braun at the Berghof with the instruction that they should be carefully preserved. Hitler then described how the attempt had affected his valets: 'Linge was absolutely furious and Arndt stood there with tears in his eyes.[17]

Dr Morell was terribly shaken and emotional after the incident and Hitler had to calm him before the doctor could tend to Hitler's injuries. Although Hitler suffered concussion, a ruptured eardrum and flaking of the skin, he refused to lay up in bed as the other officers had done and was kept going by Dr Morell's injections, as I confirmed from him at lunch. A visit by the former Duce was

---

17 Wilhelm Arndt (b. 6.7.1913, d. 22.4.1945). 1944 appointed manservant in rank of SS-Hauptscharführer. He was tall and blue eyed, and Schroeder stated of him that he was Hitler's favourite valet. Killed when a Ju 352 of the *Führer-Staffel* from Berlin-Staaken in which he was a passenger crashed at Börnersdorf.

listed for the afternoon, and I expected Hitler to postpone it, but in response to my enquiry he assured me: 'Certainly I shall receive him, I have no choice, for imagine what lies they would tell the world about me if I did not!'

When we assembled with Hitler for afternoon tea we had already received news of Stauffenberg's arrest. At first Hitler was infuriated that Stauffenberg had managed to make it as far as Berlin, but when he found out that this had led to the arrest of all the close conspirators he stated in satisfaction: 'Now I am calm. It is the salvation of Germany. Now I finally have the swine who have been sabotaging my work over the years. I always told Schmundt but he is a Parsival and would not believe it. Now I have the proof: the whole general staff is infected.'

Hitler continued:

> These criminals who wanted to rid themselves of me have no idea of what would happen to the German people. They do not know the plans of our enemies who intend to destroy Germany so that it can never rise again. And if they think that the Western Powers without Germany are strong enough to resist Bolshevism, then they are deceiving themselves. I will ensure that nobody will ever again be able to displace me. I am the only person who knows the danger, and the only person who can avert it.

A radio van was ordered from Königsberg and a transmitter unit installed in the FHQ tea-house. Shortly before midnight we went there with Hitler. The lightly wounded officers who had survived the attempt were also there: Jodl with bandaged head, Keitel with bandaged hands. Just after midnight on 21 July 1944 Hitler made a short speech to convince the German people that he had survived unscathed. It was thanks to Providence that the German people had been spared great misfortune.

In early September 1944 Hitler suffered severe stomach and intestinal problems. He put himself to bed but did not improve. Dr Morell diagnosed retention of bile caused by gall bladder spasms. Hitler lay apathetic for several days but then made a gradual return to work at the beginning of October 1944. The death of Wehrmacht chief adjutant Generalleutnant Schmundt made a deep impression on Hitler, for he had held weighty and portentous conversations with him. 'We liquidated the class enemy on the Left', Hitler said, 'but unfortunately we forgot to do the same with the Right. That has been our great sin of omission.' He went on: 'One cannot fight a war with incapable generals, one should take a leaf out of Stalin's book, he purged his army ruthlessly.' Here he was talking more to himself and suddenly changed the subject as if he had said too much.

In September 1944 Himmler provided him with a report on the Resistance involving the military in 1939. Hitler did not like the officer caste. At the Berghof he once said:

After the war I shall hang my uniform on a peg, withdraw, and let somebody else take over the affairs of government. Then I will write my memoirs, surround myself with intelligent, clever people and refuse to receive another officer. They are all strawheads and simple-minded. My two senior-serving secretaries will stay with me and write for me. The younger ones will get married and leave, and when I am old the elder ones can fall in with my tempo.

Towards the end of 1944 the stay at FHQ Wolfsschanze became increasingly anxious. Every day enemy aircraft overflew the HQ. Hitler expected a surprise air raid at any moment and warned people to use the air raid bunkers. He did not want to hear talk of transferring the FHQ to Berlin although he was being urged to do so from all sides. He explained: 'It is my duty to remain here. It keeps the people calm. My soldiers will also never permit the frontline to be pulled back to the Führer's HQ. And so long as they know that

I am holding out here, they will be all the more determined in their struggle to stabilise the Front.' All the same the HQ was removed to Berlin at the end of November 1944 as the Front edged back ever closer.[18]

The preparations for the Ardennes offensive, which Hitler promised would bring the turn in our fortunes in the West, were begun at FHQ Wolfsschanze. Towards the end of 1944 he waited impatiently for the right moment to give the order to strike. His intuition played no decisive role in setting X-Day, however: this was left to the meteorologists. He consulted them daily. The expert who predicted a period of fog during December 1944, which favoured the concentration of troops before the Offensive began, received a gold watch in gratitude for his correct forecast.

From mid December 1944 to mid January 1945 we inhabited FHQ Adlerhorst[19] and spent Christmas there. It was near Bad Nauheim, the nearest railway station was called Hunger. The FHQ consisted of small fortified huts in wooded terrain and also had subterranean bunkers. Hitler, Dara and I once stood under the trees in the open watching the great formations of Allied bombers heading into the Reich in bright sunshine. I asked the Führer: 'Do you believe, *mein Führer*, that we can still win the war?' He replied: 'We have to.' Dara reminded me of this conversation later and said she had wanted the ground to open up beneath her when she heard my question.

After the failure of the Ardennes offensive we returned to Berlin. At first Hitler held situation conferences in his study in the new Reich Chancellery and his meals in our Staircase Room. Since both events were later interrupted frequently by sudden air raid alarms, he then tended to remain in his bunker.

---

18 Hitler left FHQ Wolfsschanze on his special train on 20 November 1944. The enemy remained unaware of the location of FHQ Wolfsschanze throughout its period of occupation.

19 Hitler left Berlin on his special train on 10 December 1944 and returned to Berlin aboard it on 16 January 1945.

Chapter 9

The Women Around Hitler

ANY LIES HAVE BEEN presented to the world respecting Hitler's relationships with women under this alluring heading. It may be that before and during the First World War he had sexual experiences with women. In December 1933 he contradicted my assertion, as already described, that Emilie was an ugly name by observing: 'Don't say that, Emilie is a lovely name, it was the name of my first sweetheart!'

In 1917 during the First World War Hitler is alleged to have deserted an eighteen-year old French girl whom he had made pregnant in France, and an illegitimate son, Jean-Marie Loret, is supposed to have been the result. The boy discovered from his mother shortly before her death the identity of his father – allegedly Adolf Hitler. Subsequently he attempted to establish Hitler's paternity by genetic research at a Heidelberg institute and elsewhere.

As I have said, these two cases may be true, but it seems likely from the moment when he decided to become a politician that Hitler renounced such pleasures. For Hitler, gratification came from the ecstasy of the masses. He was erotic with the women by whom he surrounded himself, but never sexual. 'My lover is Germany', he emphasised repeatedly.[1] Perhaps the frequently rumoured missing

---

1 Walter Buch mentioned after the war in 1945 that Hitler had told him: 'The lady I love is called Germania.'

testicle is also true.[2] When Professor Kielleutner the Munich urologist returned to Henriette von Schirach a book he had borrowed from her about the residences of well-known Munich townspeople, he told her that he had underlined in pencil the names of all the prominent people he had treated. When she read through and saw Hitler's name underlined, she asked him: 'What did you treat Hitler for?' Kielleutner replied: 'Hitler had only one testicle but I was not able to help him because he was too old.' This happened allegedly in the 1920s. It is possible that Hitler might have been mocked by a woman, which led to his abandoning all further sexual activities.

Maser quotes Linge as saying that Hitler had perfectly normal genitalia, which Linge had seen on a picnic when both urinated against a tree.[3] In my opinion Maser puts these words in Linge's mouth in order to prove the possibility of the Hitler-son. Undoubtedly Hitler enjoyed the company of beautiful women and was inspired by them. He used eroticism, but not sex. Because of the great objective he had set himself and to which he was totally committed, sexual gratification occurred mentally. Emil Maurice,[4] Hitler's chauffeur, told me that whenever he drove Hitler to this or that town, he – Maurice – had to search for girls for Hitler while he was engaged in

---

2 Dr von Hasselbach, one of Hitler's official surgeons, stated after the war that Hitler had a definite aversion to showing his body, and the doctor had never seen or examined his lower regions.

3 Heinz Linge, *Bis zum Untergang*, Werner Maser (ed.), Herbig, Munich-Berlin 1980. Schroeder wrote that she considered Linge's 'looking at Hitler's genitals while he was urinating' to be a fabrication. 'What type of wood was it that everybody used the same tree for peeing?' she asked. 'Who would have dared to make a point of looking at Hitler's genitals while he was urinating?' And in any case: 'Every man I asked assured me that it would not be possible to catch sight of a man's testicles in the manner stated.'

4 Emil Maurice (b. 19.1.1897 Westermoor/Schleswig-Holstein, d. 6.2.1972 Starnberg). 1919 Nazi Party member No. 594 (Hitler was No. 555); from 1921 Hitler's chauffeur; imprisoned at Lansberg with Hitler for his part in the 1923 putsch: 1925 entered SS; in December 1927 terminated friendship with Hitler following an argument over Maurice's engagement to Geli Raubal.

conferences. Afterwards he would sit down with them and converse. He paid them, but never requested services.

The exception was Angelika 'Geli' Raubal, the daughter of Hitler's half-sister Angela Raubal. He loved this girl very much but apparently did not have sex with her. Here I must correct an error in the book by Dr Wagener, *Hitler aus nächster Nähe*, p.98: in the apartment at Prinzregenten-Platz 16 (actually two apartments, left and right), the household was run from the outset by Frau Winter and not Frau Raubal. After moving from Thierschstrasse,[5] Hitler brought along his old landladies Frau Reichel and her mother Frau Dachs. Later Geli Raubal occupied one of these rooms. According to Ada Klein it is also incorrect for Dr Wagener to have said that Hitler would not allow Geli to perform on stage. Geli did not want to take singing lessons! Finally she allowed herself to be convinced by her uncle, who would have liked her to have become a Wagner opera singer. From 1929 this attractive lusty girl was installed in Hitler's flat at Prinzregenten-Platz 16. He pampered her and did everything he could for her out of fondness. Geli was flattered that her famous uncle should be so devoted, but he controlled her every move and jealously fended off all her admirers. When she announced her intention to marry a painter from Linz,[6] Hitler convinced Geli's mother to impose a one-year separation so that the couple should prove their love for each other.[7] A letter from the painter which I

---

5 Hitler rented a room at Thierschstrasse 41/I from 1 May 1920 to 10 September 1929.

6 Geli Raubal had several relationships with men whom she hoped to marry (e.g. Hitler's chauffeur Emil Maurice in 1927). According to a statement by Geli's mother to American CIC interrogators in 1945, the man who wrote this letter was a violinist from Linz sixteen years Geli's senior.

7 Schroeder had this letter with her in internment at Augsburg and lent it to Albert Zoller who failed to return it. These passages appear in Zoller's book and are therefore authentic.

salvaged from Schaub's bonfire at the Berghof in 1945 contained
the following extract: *

> Now your uncle, whose influence on your mother is well-known,
> is attempting to manipulate her weakness with unlimited cynicism.
> Unfortunately we are not able to respond to this repression *until you
> reach your majority*. He always puts obstructions in our path to block
> our mutual happiness although he knows that we are made for each
> other. The year of separation that your mother has imposed on us will
> only bind us closer to each other inwardly. As I always make the effort
> to think and act honestly, I find it difficult to accept the existence of
> these faults in others. However I can only explain your uncle's actions
> as being grounded in selfish motives towards yourself. He simply
> intends that one day you will belong to nobody but him . . .

And at another place:

> Your uncle continues to see you as the 'inexperienced child' and
> cannot understand that you have matured meanwhile and want to
> shape your own future. Your uncle has an overbearing personality.
> In his Party they all cower before him like slaves. I do not understand

---

* In fact, this extract from the letter of her unnamed fiancé must have been written
long before the suicide, for Geli Raubal reached her majority at age twenty-one on
4 January 1929. Since the period of one year's separation would fall entirely within
the period when the girl was not of legal maturity, the date of the letter must have
been before 4 January 1928. Whether Schroeder knew the actual date when the
letter was written, and the identity of the writer, we shall never know, but if she did
one must question her motives in including it at the place in the narrative where it
appears. Another mystery about the letter writer is the fact that whereas Schroeder
confirmed in her shorthand notes that the suitor had previously obtained the consent
of Frau Raubal to her daughter's marriage, by 1945 Frau Raubal remembered
nothing of the man except that he was a 'violinist from Linz' sixteen years older
than her daughter. The mystery of the fiancé's identity, the miraculous saving of
the letter from Schaub's bonfire (see Chapter 15 for the full story) and its use in
Schroeder's narrative, pose some intriguing questions about Geli Raubal´s death,
and the extent to which Schroeder knew the circumstances. (TN)

how, with his keen intelligence, he can deceive himself into believing that his obstinacy and theories about marriage can break our love and determination. He hopes that during this year (of separation) he will change your mind, but how little he knows your soul.

And in that he was surely right, for one day Geli could stand the pressure no longer and shot herself on the day of a quarrel with her uncle.

During internment postwar I got to know Frau Winter.[8] She was discreet and tight-lipped and thus enjoyed Hitler's confidence during the period between 1929 and 1945 when she was his housekeeper-cook at Prinzregenten-Platz 16/II. What she told me about Geli Raubal, the daughter of Hitler's half-sister Angela Raubal, I found very interesting. This had nothing to do with any immorality between Hitler and Geli, but of a platonic love saturated with jealousy. According to Frau Winter, Geli, who wanted to study singing, was installed by Hitler in his apartment. He had a room converted for her there. Geli accompanied him everywhere and was the only woman at his side on his visits to the theatre. During the Prinzregenten Theatre festival in early 1930 a beautiful silver-fox fur she was wearing caught my eye.

During the tea hour in the Staircase Room at the Radziwill Palace, Hitler's thoughts very often turned to Geli, and he needed to speak about her. One inferred distinctly that he was grooming her to be his wife. When concluding some anecdotes about Geli he said once: 'There was only one woman I would have married!' and for me the sense of this declaration was unmistakeable. I also understood now why he had watched over the activities of the beloved like a hawk. Frau Winter was firmly convinced that Geli

---

8 Anni Winter née Schuler (b. 29.2.1905 Pfakofen/Regensburg, d. 17.10.1970 Munich). 1.5.1929 married Georg Winter, a former NCO and manservant to General Epp the *Freikorps* leader; 1.10.1929–May 1945 Hitler's housekeeper at Prinzregenten-Platz 16/II; 8.6.1945 interned by US Army.

dreamed of marrying her uncle, for no other man was in a position to pamper her permanently in the manner to which she had become accustomed.

After the war the US archives declassified invoices for extravagant purchases of clothing made for Geli, a sure reason why she was prepared to be submissive and allow Hitler to drive off all her other suitors. Frau Winter stated that the circumstances surrounding Geli's suicide were as follows. Hitler asked Geli, who was visiting her mother at Berchtesgaden, to come to Munich. After her arrival on the morning of 18 September 1931, he had to go into town, but promised to return for lunch. He did not return until four that afternoon, when he informed her that he had to travel immediately to Nuremberg. Geli was upset because she could have stayed with her mother at Berchtesgaden. She asked Hitler for permission to go to Vienna for a vocal test which she had had planned for some time but he refused outright. Thus they parted under a cloud. Geli now went through Hitler's possessions and found items of correspondence. She told Frau Winter that she was intending to go to the cinema, but instead stayed in her room. When Frau Winter brought her breakfast next morning, there was no answer to her knock. Seeing the key in the lock on the other side of the door she feared the worst and asked her husband to break in. There they found Geli shot dead, lying on a *chaise-longue*.

After Geli's death, Hitler was a completely changed man and his supporters feared that he might also take his own life. Heinrich Hoffmann took a close interest in Hitler's well-being and succeeded in the next few months in bringing Hitler out of his self-imposed isolation. Geli's suicide hit Hitler hard, and at this point he converted to vegetarianism.[9] His memory of Geli became a cult for Hitler. Her room at his Munich flat had to remain precisely in the condition it was at the moment of her death. Until the outbreak of war he carried

---

9 According to Schaub's statement in 1945.

the key to the room on his person, and the room which Geli used to occupy at Haus Wachenfeld remained permanently locked. When the structure was enlarged later into the Berghof, the part where Geli's room was located was left untouched. All her clothes, toilet items and whatever else had belonged to her remained in their place. He even refused Geli's mother the return of mementoes or letters.

Towards the end of the war Hitler gave Schaub the job of destroying Geli's personal effects. Beside the photos there was a bust of her. When I knew all this and that Hitler came between the couple whenever a love relationship threatened to take solid form, and when I heard him say in the Staircase Room: 'There was only one women I would have married . . .' there was no doubt for me but that Geli had been this woman. In the Staircase Room we asked Hitler once: 'Why have you never married?' He replied:

> I would not have made a good father and I would consider it irresponsible to have founded a family if I had not been able to devote myself sufficiently to the wife. Moreover I do not want children of my own. I find that the descendants of a genius mostly have it very difficult in the world. One expects them to have the same ability as their famous forebear and do not forgive them for being average. Apart from that they mostly turn out cretins.

Hitler appears to have kept his love life platonic throughout, beginning with the blonde Stefanie in Linz, whom he worshipped from afar, then Maria Reiter, Ada Klein, Sigrid von Laffert to the various female theatrical performers and artistes who were invited to be entertained in the Führer-apartment at the Reich Chancellery in the first years after 1933. His admiration for famous actresses and dancers was sincere. At a premiere and on their birthdays he would send valuable presents, and in wartime took great pleasure in having parcels of coffee and food delivered to them, relishing the letters of gratitude they sent him for the gifts. His custom of throwing a brilliant reception for the German art world every year had to be abandoned once war came.

I remember for example the dancers the Höpfner sisters, the film actress Jenny Jugo, Magda Goebbels, her sister-in-law Ello Quandt, Gretl Slezak, Leni Riefenstahl, Unity Mitford and Eva Braun – yes, even his relationshiop with Eva Braun was a façade. Hitler's personal photographer Heinrich Hoffmann was convinced that Hitler had nothing with Eva Braun.[10] He went out with her, but when he began to find less time for her while electioneering she made some sly suicide attempts. These were successful, for Hitler as a politician could not afford a second suicide of a young woman in his close circle. I repeat, the only woman he loved and would later have married was his niece Geli Raubal.

Eva Braun's calculations worked out: Hitler drew her increasingly into his life. This protected him against future suicide attempts and was also a shield against all his other ardent female admirers. Eva Braun confided to her hairdresser (statement by Klaus von Schirach) that Hitler never had sexual intercourse with her. Ada Klein said the same to Nelly Scholter, wife of Bormann's gynaecologist Dr Scholter, who was friendly with Hitler in the 1920s. There were never sexual intimacies between them, and Hitler exercised the same abstinence towards Gretl Slezak.[11]

---

10 Two statements made after the war show unequivocally that Hitler was not the lover of Eva Braun, contrary to assertions in the literature and periodicals. In 1945 Julius Schaub was asked: 'Did Hitler love Eva Braun?'
Schaub: 'He liked her.'
Q: 'What is that supposed to mean? What did you mean when you said in Munich "He liked her." Did he love her?'
Schaub: 'He was fond of her.'
In 1945 Heinrich Hoffmann said: 'From 1930 onwards Hitler often came to my studios and on such occasions took the opportunity to get to know Eva Braun and saw her often. In my opinion Hitler's relationship with Eva Braun was always platonic.'
11 See Chapter 11.

Chapter 10

Ada Klein

ITLER SAW ADA KLEIN[1] for the first time at the refounding ceremony for the NSDAP at the Bürgerbräukeller on 27 February 1925. She was a very beautiful Geli-type girl, and stood in a visible position on a stool listening to him speak, as did many others. Hitler noticed her and asked Emil Maurice his chauffeur to find out about her, but in this he was unsuccessful. Ada Klein worked for a small ethnic-racist newspaper, *Völkischer Kurier*, from where Max Amann recruited her to the *Völkischer Beobachter*. As she was leaving the Schelling-Strasse offices one day she bumped into Hitler. He exclaimed: 'Ah, here you are!' Subsequently they met frequently at Party occasions. Once she was alone with him in the old Haus Wachenfeld on the Obersalzberg where he prepared the coffee himself and discovered that Schaub had left the biscuit tin empty. On another occasion he invited her to Emil Maurice's two rooms. Shortly after their arrival Emil Maurice took his leave. The door to the second room was open, and Ada saw a bed in it. As she told me, there were never any intimacies. He told her: 'that he could not marry', but also: 'You make me more light-headed than when

---

1 Adelheid Klein (b. 12.8.1902 Weingarten). Educated in Switzerland; from August 1927 worked as a secretary for Max Amann at Fritz Eher Verlag, Munich; 1936 married Dr Walter Schultze.

I add the strongest rum to my tea!' and: 'It was you who taught me how to kiss!'

Ada Klein's friendship with Hitler lasted two years (1925–6). He called her 'Deli' and wrote her a few short letters which she kept. When one of her nieces (the two pretty Epps girls were revue dancers occasionally invited by Hitler to his flat on the Prinzregenten-Platz) told him in 1936 that Ada was going to marry Dr Walter Schultze, Hitler said: 'Then Dr Schultze has found himself a good comrade!' Dr Schultze was later head of the Department of Health at the Bavarian Interior Ministry.[2]

I met Ada Klein in 1930 on a gymnastics course on Munich's Carolinen-Platz which was frequented by many employees of the Braunes Haus and the Eher Verlag. After that we lost contact and it was not until the late 1970s that we met again. One day when she visited me in my apartment I told her of my meeting at Easter 1979 with Jean-Marie Loret who was hoping that I might recognise him as the illegitimate son of Hitler, sired during a sexual relationship during the First World War with French girl Charlotte Lobjoies. As neither he nor I spoke the other's language I was unable to make the identification for this and other reasons. While out walking with him in the Blumenau, when he went ahead of me I think I saw a similarity to Hitler in the gait and posture, but it is easy to deceive oneself in such things.

---

2 Walter Schultze, (b.1.1.1894 Hersbruck, d.27.11.1979 Krailing). SS-Gruppen-führer; in May 1945 as head of the Department of Health at the Bavarian Interior Ministry he was interned, and subsequently tried and convicted as a war criminal on two charges of collaborating in the euthanasia programme.

Chapter 11

Gretl Slezak

GRETL SLEZAK[1] WAS THE daughter of the renowned heroic tenor Leo Slezak who even when old remained an inspiration. Hitler got to know his daughter at the Munich Gärtner-Platz theatre where she played the leading role of the sweet Viennese maiden in *Goldene Meisterin*. She exuded a magic so captivating that Hitler was blind to her having a Jewish grandparent. Here I must contradict Dr Picker's assertion on p.288 of *Hitlers Tischgespräche*[2] where he says that: 'Hitler's convictions forced him at Christmas 1932 to break off his especially warm friendship with the much-loved Berlin singer Gretl Slezak.' The contrary was the case! Hitler maintained his friendship with the charming singer, who had inherited the devastating humour of her father, even after he took power, and he looked forward to every meeting with her. Without his agreement, as a person of some Jewish racial heritage she would never have obtained years of successive contracts at the Deutsche Oper in Berlin in the 1930s.

---

1 Gretl Slezak (b. 9.1.1901 Breslau, d. 30.8.1953 Rottach-Egern). Was trained by her father as a soprano; in 1930 came to the Deutsche Staatsoper in Berlin; 1933–1943 appeared at the Städtisches Opernhaus in Berlin Charlottenburg. Although a quarter-Jewish, Hitler continued to receive her until the war's end and often invited her to the Reich Chancellery.

2 Seewald Verlag, third expanded and fully revised edition.

136

In March 1938, on the Sunday before the annexation of Austria to the Reich, Hitler invited Gretl Slezak and myself to tea at his flat in the Radziwill Palace. In the so-called Music Room, used for film shows in the evenings at which, apart from the close staff, the *SS-Begleitkommando* and the house personnel were also present, the tea table before the fireplace was crowded. Hitler enjoyed hearing about the interminable scandals from the performers' circles and delighted in the stories which Gretl Slezak knew how to deliver with just the right amount of charming malice.

That Sunday nobody knew what Hitler had afoot for the coming week. I had no suspicion that he was on the edge of his seat waiting for the off with Austria and as I see now he was doing what he could to bridge the time gap, i.e. suppress his impatience. The tea hour had already gone on far longer than scheduled, and since we could not remain forever at the fireplace I asked Hitler if he would like to see my apartment, which I had been promising to show him for some time. He agreed immediately and arrived during the evening with a manservant who withdrew after handing me a bottle of Fachinger.

My apartment was located in the Reich Chancellery park. In 1936 Hitler had commissioned Speer to build two houses in the English country-house style on the park side of Hermann-Göring-Strasse. These were originally to have been occupied solely by members of the *SS-Begleitkommando* and their families. Shortly before they were completed it occurred to me how practical it would be if we secretaries could also live there. In accordance with Hitler's ruling 'Nobody should know anything he does not need to know, and if he does need to know then at the last possible moment', trips out were always advised at very short notice. It always enraged me when I had to drive to my flat on the Savigny Platz not only to fetch my trunk but to pack it first, and so one day after dictation I asked Hitler if it would not be possible for his three female secretaries also to have a flat each on the Hermann-Göring-Strasse. He thought about this and said: 'Yes, child, that would be good, I would always have you people with me!' Speer was asked to call by with the architectural plans and Hitler told him to include three apartments for his secretaries. When these were ready for occupation, Hitler instructed Schaub to make me an allowance of 3,000 RM to furnish them and promised to pay a brief visit to see the final result.

To return to that tea night. After leaving the Reich Chancellery, Gretl Slezak had driven quickly to her apartment on the Kurfürstendamm in order to dress for the evening. She arrived with two large five-armed candelabras which she placed strategically in the hope that the candlelight would have a magical effect on Hitler when he arrived. No effort was to be spared! Sitting next to him on the English sofa she tried to stroke his hand but he fended her off gently saying: 'Gretl, you know that I cannot allow that!' Although I had discreetly left the room a few times Hitler maintained his reserve and a few hours later his manservant retrieved him intact.

Gretl would not give up hope and thought she might at least have a closer relationship with Hitler. She was playing the lead role of Catherine the Great at the Deutsche Oper in Berlin and before her next performance, convinced of her ultimate victory over him, gave me a photograph of herself in costume with a message in a large, triumphant hand: 'Tinchen (her nickname for me), to my first Lady at Court, from her Gretl.' Just before New Year 1939 she gave me a letter to forward to Hitler at the Berghof. What it said I have no idea but it would have done her courtship no good whatever. After taking power Hitler would never have committed himself to anybody in the theatre because the risk would have been too great, all of them would have used it to advance their careers. He was always careful to maintain discretion with regard to his position.

Now I would like to address the assertion that Hitler painted Gretl Slezak. In the 1920s he produced no more watercolours, only architectural sketches. In 1932 when he is supposed to have painted Gretl Slezak he was on the hunt for electoral support and in a single day might have spoken at three different locations. He had neither the time for, nor interest in, painting, and in any case in the past had only turned out watercolours to survive. He had not found that necessary from 1919 onwards when he was active in the *Reichswehr*, and was sent to report on the newly formed *Deutsche Arbeiter Partei* of Anton Drexler. From then on his life was devoted to that Party and politics.

From 1935 Margarete Slezak was my close friend. If Hitler had ever painted her I would certainly have found out about it. Hitler's alleged letters to her are crude forgeries. Margarete Slezak was a divorcée with a daughter. Hitler knew all about it. He was not so ignorant that he would have written to a divorced woman as 'Fräulein Slezak'. In any case he always called her 'Gretl' and used the formal pronoun 'Sie' and not the familiar 'Du' when speaking to her. He never called her 'Tschapperl' – 'little idiot' – an obvious fabrication.

I knew Hitler's erstwhile lady friend Ada Klein. In the 1920s she was a regular visitor to his flat in the Thierschstrasse and knew from these visits that Hitler had given up painting. She shared my opinion that he had never painted flowers, only buildings and landscapes. To suggest otherwise is an unprincipled deception.

Chapter 12

Eva Braun

F EW PEOPLE KNEW ANYTHING about Eva Braun before the end of the Second World War. I first knew her in the summer of 1933 on the Obersalzberg. The daughter of a Munich teacher of commerce, she was employed upon completing her education as a salesgirl in Heinrich Hoffmann's photography business. Although outwardly soft, blonde and womanly, she had great energy and will and to get her own way she could be very persuasive if necessary. Eva Braun enjoyed sport, was a competent skier, outstanding swimmer and a passionate dancer. Hitler never danced. Hitler met Eva Braun at Hoffmann's business establishment in 1929. She found him to be a very interesting man. His name was always in the newspapers, he had men to protect him and he was driven about in a large Mercedes by a chauffeur. Her boss Heinrich Hoffmann forecast a great future for Hitler.

Six months after Geli Raubal's death in September 1931, Hitler's friends finally succeeded in rousing him from his lethargy. Heinrich Hoffmann took him to a cinema one day and 'purely by chance' sat Hitler next to Eva Braun, whom Hitler had often invited to the ice rink when Geli was alive. He had met her afterwards now and again without having any serious interest in her.[1] Eva Braun told her

---

1 See Dr Otto Wagener, *Hitler aus Nächster Nähe*. 'On Hitler's election tours in 1932, photographer Heinrich Hoffmann often took along his petite laboratory

friends however that Hitler was enamoured of her, and she now spun her web. Hitler had no hint of her intentions and was therefore more than surprised when Heinrich Hoffmann informed him one day in November 1932 that Eva Braun had attempted suicide because of him. Hoffmann was naturally very anxious to protect his commercial relationship with Hitler, and the first meeting between Hitler and Eva Braun after her suicide attempt was held at Hoffmann's house in the Wasserburger-Strasse.

Marion Schönmann[2] who was there told me in the 1960s of the manoeuvre: Heinrich Hoffmann's wife Erna had used make-up on Eva Braun upstairs so that she appeared to be 'in distress' for Hitler's arrival. Success was guaranteed when Hitler saw Eva Braun 'still pallid' coming slowly downstairs. Hitler was of the opinion that he had given her no cause for her action, but the fear that a second suicide by a young woman of his close acquaintance must cast its shadow across his political career disturbed him. With female cunning Eva had realised that fact after Geli's suicide. Hitler was left with no choice but to concern himself more for Eva Braun,[3] and henceforth he included her in his life and cared for her. She was subsequently an occasional guest at Obersalzberg, but never stayed at Haus Wachenfeld because of Frau Raubal's antagonism towards her. Initially Hitler rented her an apartment on the Widemayer-Strasse, and some years later made her a gift of a small house and garden at Wasserburger-Strasse 12. Frau Raubal, Hitler's half-sister

assistant Eva Braun, whom Hitler liked to have at table in the evening for diversion', but in his opinion she 'played no role'.

2 Marianne Schönmann née Petzl (b. 19.12.1899 Vienna, d.17.3.1981 Munich). Daughter of opera singer Maria Petzl, whom Hitler knew and admired from his youth in Vienna; 1935–44 often invited to the Obersalzberg where Marianne befriended Eva Braun; August 1937 married architect Fritz Schönmann, Hitler was present at the ceremony.

3 Frau Winter, Hitler's housekeeper in Munich, said after the war that 'despite her submissiveness, Hitler would have found some way to have rid himself of her had the war not intervened' (Musmanno Papers, Univ. Library, Duquesne Univ., Pittsburgh).

and his housekeeper on the Berg, made no secret of her dislike for Eva Braun and would deliberately ignore her. If obliged to speak to her she would address her only as 'Fräulein' without using her name. She was quite open about her feelings and once told Göring: 'I envy you two things for my brother: the first is Frau Sonnemann[4] and the other Robert.'[5] I heard Göring reply: 'If necessary I would give up Robert, but never Frau Sonnemann.'

From the beginning Eva Braun had an aversion to Göring and particularly his wife Emmy. In the second year of the war, Emmy Göring invited all the Berghof ladies to tea at her country house. The real reason was to subject Eva Braun to close scrutiny. Hitler intervened and when all the women, Frau Brandt, Frau Morell, Frau Göring and we secretaries assembled, we found that Eva Braun and her sister had stayed away. At the 1935 Nuremberg Rally,[6] the wives of ministers and Gauleiters, Hitler's sister and Eva Braun and their friends sat on the tribune for guests of honour. Frau Raubal was of the opinion that Eva Braun had drawn attention to herself, and said so to Hitler in the hope that he would rid himself of her afterwards.[7] This backfired, and Frau Raubal was ordered to leave the Berg together with all the other women who had made adverse comments about Eva Braun in the affair, and they were not invited to enjoy the hospitality at Haus Wachenfeld again for a considerable time.

As previously mentioned, the first 'suicide attempt' by Eva Braun had had the desired effect, and she was now integrated into Hitler's circle. Perhaps by now he had had enough of Geli's mother and so

---

4 Emmy Göring née Sonnemann.

5 Robert was Göring's capable manservant.

6 The Seventh NSDAP *Reichsparteitag* covered the period 10–17 September 1935 at Nuremberg.

7 In her notes, Schroeder recounted a conversation with Eva Braun subsequently in which Eva had become aware of the campaign to uproot her. For this reason she had been making the fuss on the guests' platform, and this was the gist of Frau Raubal's complaint. Afterwards Eva Braun took Veronal in anticipation of the possible reaction but 'was found in time'.

used the campaign against Eva Braun instigated by his half-sister as an excuse to remove Frau Raubal from the Berg. It is suggested elsewhere[8] that: 'his half-sister Angela Raubal kept house for him for years in Munich and on the Obersalzberg. She was forced out when Bormann converted the Berghof. For a large house appropriate to a head of state, she was no longer adequate.' No further commentary is necessary.

In 1936 Frau Raubal left Obersalzberg and, her heart weakened by all the excitement, she took the cure at Bad Nauheim, where she met and married Professor Hammitzsch of Dresden University. She rarely saw her half-brother again, and only officially on his birthdays, when she was forced to wait at the Hotel Kaiserhof like an outsider for one of the adjutants to convey her to the Reich Chancellery.

From now on Eva Braun's position was apparently assured. This was noticeable at Haus Wachenfeld even if she did not appear at official functions. When Haus Wachenfeld was revamped into the Berghof in the summer of 1936, she moved into a room on the first floor of the annexe adjoining Hitler's bedroom, while her sisters and friends who were always around her even had guest rooms at their disposal. She looked after their needs herself but her gratitude was tangible if one accepted them wholeheartedly. Her friendships with women were very variable and generally short-lived. Like all other females in Hitler's circle she was ignorant of politics. In the presence of women Hitler avoided all political talk regarding ongoing or planned operations. Often one would hear Eva Braun complain: 'I never know anything, everything is kept secret from me.'

In her appraisals, particularly of artistes, she lacked objectivity: if a face did not fit well with her that person's good qualities were irrelevant, he or she had to go. Eva changed her clothing a couple of times daily, employed a hairdresser and always gave the impression of being well-groomed. Her wardrobe was always well-stocked with

---

8 Jochen von Lang, *Der Sekretär*, Deutsche Verlags-Anstalt, 1977, p.122.

clothing 'for materials testing'. She had two Scotch terriers, Stasi and Negus, which she often walked. She was keen on sport, practising frequently. She also had a bullfinch which she taught a popular song by whistling to the bird through pursed lips. She liked listening to gramophone records, particularly the tragic songs of Mimi Thoma, reading periodicals and crime novels, and kept up to date about the latest film releases, and so filled her time well.

All accounts which allege that Eva Braun was employed as a housekeeper and ran the Berghof outstandingly well have no foundation in fact.[9] After Frau Raubal's departure, Frau Endres, Herr and Frau Döhring and later the Mittelstrassers were the competent housekeepers. For special receptions, at which Eva Braun never appeared, house manager Kannenberg and his wife Freda would travel down from the Führer-apartment in Berlin to do the necessary in their expert, routine manner.

When Hermann Fegelein,[10] Waffen-SS liaison officer to Hitler at FHQ, was on duty for the first time at the Berghof, he asked Marion Schönmann how he could arrange to be invited for lunch. That was at the beginning of 1944, when he arrived in Obersalzberg with Himmler. Marion introduced Fegelein to Eva Braun and he obtained his lunch invitation through her. After Fegelein had left the Berghof she confided to Marion Schönmann that Fegelein had made a big impression on her and added: 'A few years ago the boss said that if I fell in love one day with another man, then I should let

9 See Picker, *Hitlers Tischgespräche*, third edition, p.228.

10 Herrmann Fegelein (b. 30.10.1906 Ansbach, d. 28.4.1945 Berlin). 10.4.1933 joined SS; 1935 founded SS Cavalry School at Munich; 1937 commander, SS Cavalry School; 30.1.1936 SS-Sturmbannführer; 1.3.1940 SS-Obersturmbannführer and commander, SS-Totenkopf-Reiterstandarte; 5.8.1941–end 1943 leader, SS-Cavalry-Brigade and commander, Kampfbrigade *Fegelein*; 1.1.1944 Waffen-SS liaison officer to Hitler at FHQ; 3.6.1944 married Eva Braun's sister Margarete at Salzburg; 21.6.1944 Generalleutnant der Waffen-SS; 25.4.1945 absented himself without leave from Reich Chancellery bunker; 27.4.1945 arrested by RSD at his flat in Berlin, executed by firing squad in Reich Chancellery gardens for desertion.

him know and he would release me.' Now she said to Marion: 'If I had known Fegelein ten years ago I would have asked the boss to let me go!' But the problem was to be resolved in another way.

After the failure of various efforts to marry off her younger sister Greta to men in Hitler's wider circle (e.g. to diplomat Hewel, adjutant Darges, minister Wagner), Eva Braun now matched her sister with Fegelein. He was a recognised heroic figure for women. Greta Braun was, as one would say today, sexy, and Fegelein might have been thinking of the advantages of one day being Hitler's brother-in-law. Thus the marriage took place and was celebrated as a great occasion on the Obersalzberg and in the tea-house on the Kehlstein. Eva said: 'I would like this marriage to be as wonderful as if it were my own!' And so it was.

Eva expressed her gratitude thus: 'I am so grateful to Fegelein for marrying my sister. Now I am somebody, I am the sister-in-law of Fegelein!' Clearly she suffered from the anonymity to which she was condemned. She was never permitted to appear in public, but as Fegelein's sister-in-law there was a basis for her presence in Hitler's circle, and she could now be close to the man who had won her heart.

Against Hitler's wishes Eva came to the Reich Chancellery in February 1945 and moved into her apartment next to Hitler's private rooms. She expressed the wish for music but had no gramophone. I lent her mine which had been in the Voss-Strasse bunker. While Hitler was attending his military conferences we used to play records, drink champagne and quite often dance with off-duty officers. Hermann Fegelein was frequently amongst those who danced with Eva Braun. Today I can recall clearly the unforgettable scene. After a dance Fegelein would lift Eva chest high. At eye level they would gaze at each other full of tenderness and loving: Eva was obviously strongly attracted to Fegelein. I am convinced that her feelings for him went well beyond those feelings for a brother-in-law, but I do not believe anything went on between them. Upon her arrival in

Berlin in February 1945 she said to me: 'I have come because I owe the boss for everything wonderful in my life.' In my opinion she remained faithful to him although undoubtedly she and Fegelein had to struggle against the overwhelming feelings that attracted them mutually. A tragedy, for at this time and place they were made for each other. The fact that Fegelein, after deserting his post at the Reich Chancellery in April 1945, rang Eva Braun there and urged her 'to leave the Reich Chancellery and come to him' supports my presumption and observations.

What thoughts must have assailed her when it became known that Fegelein had been found with another woman at his flat![11] Her decision to die alongside Hitler was that much easier to take knowing that Fegelein was dead, shot by firing squad on Hitler's order. The most amazing thing of all at this time was how normally things proceeded as the end of the Third Reich approached.

---

11 Upon his arrest on 27 April 1945 at his flat at Bleibtreu-Strasse 10–11 by RSD officer Peter Högl, a red-haired woman was found with Fegelein. She was allowed to escape on a pretext and her identity remains unknown.

Chapter 13

Obersalzberg

I N 1877 MAURITIA 'MORITZ' Mayer bought the equestrian establishment and Steinhaus estate together with all the summer pasture around the Kehlstein mountain. She turned the Steinhaus into the first hotel on the Obersalzberg. Under her proprietorship 'Pension Moritz' became a much-visited resort for guests and convalescents. Rich people from the city arrived as a result, buying up old farms or building their own mountain retreats. Professor Karl von Linde for example purchased the so-called Baumgarten estate and laid a road, later called the Professor von Linde Weg, to the Hochlenzer.* The Berlin piano manufacturer Bechstein built a house there, and Dr Seitz, a paediatrician, set up a sanatorium for children. A Buxtehude businessman, Herr Winter, had an all-weather alpine chalet built there.

In the 1920s Adolf Hitler and senior NSDAP men Hermann Esser and Christian Weber came often to the Obersalzberg because the hunted NSDAP fugitive Dietrich Eckart, Hitler's mentor, had found shelter there. It was through Christian Weber, who found lodgings for Eckart at the Brückner house, that Hitler came to the Obersalzberg for the first time. He was fascinated by the scenery. Hitler told us the story at tea one day. One can read all about it

---

* The Hochlenzer, built in 1672, was an old settlement on the salt road from Hallein to Augsburg which crossed the Obersalzberg. (TN)

in Heim's *Monologe im Führerhauptquartier*,* since a stenographic note was kept. Dietrich Eckart introduced Hitler to many of the local inhabitants including Frau Bechstein, with whose help he rented Haus Wachenfeld from Frau Winter of Buxtehude for 100 RM. The tenancy was put into the name of his half-sister Angela Raubal at first, and in 1927 he transferred it to his own name before eventually purchasing the house outright from the executors of Frau Winter's estate in 1934.

In August 1933 I was summoned by telephone to Obersalzberg** unexpectedly. At the time I was working with the Liaison Staff. I arrived at Haus Wachenfeld in the afternoon to be welcomed by Frau Raubal. She was a widow six years older than her half-brother. She had had three children by her marriage to a taxation official: Friedl and Geli, and a son, Leo, who taught in Linz. Frau Raubal ran the household for Hitler. She was capable, active and a person who maintained discipline, often hitting the table with her fist impulsively at mealtimes to make a point. She was a figure who inspired respect. She controlled her staff with a rod of iron and also felt responsible for ensuring the well-being of her half-brother, although he did not seem to want this particularly.

In an obviously distressed state she told me that Hitler had gone off on a car trip with the gentlemen of his staff and some ladies, and were overdue. Greatly worried that some accident had befallen them, she was apparently glad to see me as it would help to take her mind off the matter. She volunteered to show me the ground-floor rooms of the Bavarian shingle-roofed house. A wooden balcony decorated with bright geraniums encircled the structure. The living room was typically Bavarian. A green dresser with farming scenes,

* Table-talk of 16 January 1942, Orbis edition 2000, pp.202–5. (TN)

** Obersalzberg overlooks Berchtesgaden from the northern foot of the Hoher Göll. The mountain was owned by the NSDAP and was never the seat of government. The terrain of about 1,000 hectares was 278 hectares farmland and 716 hectares woods and mountainside. Seider and Zeigert, *Die Führerhauptquartiere*, Herbig, pp.259, 265. (TN)

a commode and rustic chairs, a grandfather clock and, on a corner table, statuettes of a farmer with canary and a Moorish dancer. Not very Bavarian on the other hand were the many cushions and rugs embroidered with the swastika and mountain blooms in all colours which lay everywhere in abundance, all presents from Hitler's female admirers. Frau Raubal had apparently not had the heart to throw out all this evidence of the love and affection which these handicrafts manifested, and only after the conversion work to the house and the departure of Frau Raubal in 1936 did they disappear.

She took me to the glass veranda annexed to the employee's rooms. It was built by Munich architect Neumayer together with the garage and terrace in April 1933. Meals were taken in the glass veranda, she told me. During my stay I was able to confirm what a careful housekeeper and outstanding cook Frau Raubal was. A real delicacy were the little apple pies she made, which were something new for me. Then she led me to the terrace and showed me the view over Berchtesgaden which stretched out below in the valley to the north. To the right of it was the Salzburg region. Opposite the house was the very impressive sight of the Watzmann (2,715 metres) and Untersberg (today Ettenberg, this latter mountain being the seat of legend, the place where Barbarossa is said to be entombed awaiting the day of his return, rather like King Arthur), the Hohe Göll and the Steinernes Meer. Well-maintained paths led from the terrace to the lawn at the side of the house: there used to be a rock garden on the southern slope with a number of paths crisscrossing it.

At the foot of the northern rock wall was a weathered, elongated, low, wooden annexe fronted by a wooden gallery decorated with a mass of red geraniums. The balustrade had supporting columns to the roof. It formed an enchanting, living contrast to the brooding, gloomy mountains to the south of the house. This single-storey structure adjoining Haus Wachenfeld had five rooms: a simple office, three guest rooms and a large dormitory for the *SS-Begleitkommando*. Later two of the guest rooms were converted into a medical surgery and the surgery of Dr Blaschke, Hitler's dentist. In the summer of 1933 all guests booked into the nearby pensions on the Obersalzberg. At the end of the elongated annexe was the so-called 'adjutants' shack'. A narrow wooden stairway on the outside at the front led up to two small rooms: a bedroom with bath and an office for the duty adjutant. A telephone switchboard was located on the ground floor.

At sunset that day Frau Raubal and I stood on the terrace overlooking the road leading upwards, awaiting the return of the overdue excursionists. I could hear one of the maids, dressed in Tyrolean costume, setting the table for dinner in the glass veranda. Finally some cars came up the mountain, the small house filled with the voices of the arrivals and a short time later Hitler's guests assembled in the veranda. Hitler and Frau Raubal occupied the table ends while the guests sat where they fancied. On that occasion I remember Hitler's photographer Heinrich Hoffmann with his wife Erna, Hitler's long term chauffeur SS-Staffelführer Julius Schreck and female friend, Reich press chief Dr Otto Dietrich with his wife, Julius Schaub, Eva Braun and Anni Rehborn.

Of the last, 'Rehlein', I would like to say something. In 1923 and 1924 she won the German swimming championships in the hundred-metres crawl and backstroke. When the *Berliner Illustrierte* published her photograph on the title page – it was seen by Hitler's followers sharing his imprisonment at Landsberg – Hitler's chauffeur Emil Maurice was inspired to send Anni Rehborn his congratulations. After their release a meeting took place at which Hitler was present, and at Christmas 1925 he sent her a copy of *Mein Kampf* bound in red leather with the inscription 'To Fräulein Anni Rehborn in sincere admiration', and encouraged her to visit whenever she was in Bavaria. She took him up on this offer frequently. In July 1933 while touring Germany in her small red DIXI car with her fiancé Dr Karl Brandt, Hitler invited them both to stay for a few days on the

Berg, where they were booked into one of the pensions as his guests, and came up to Haus Wachenfeld for lunch and dinner.

One afternoon a telephone message brought the news that chief adjutant Wilhelm Brückner and his friend Sophie Stork had been badly injured in a road accident at Reit im Winkel and had been taken to the hospital at Traunstein. Brückner had fallen asleep at the wheel and collided with a telegraph pole. How lucky he was to have had Dr Brandt along as a passenger. Calmly and carefully he took the initiative, did everything necessary to make the casualties comfortable and carried out the operation himself at Traunstein hospital. While Sophie Stork escaped with a broken arm, Brückner was seriously hurt, sustaining a skull fracture and losing an eye. Göring, who was also a passenger, was so impressed by the skill of the young doctor that he exclaimed: 'If ever I have to be operated on, then only by Dr Brandt!' Until then Hitler had never had a medical aide on his various trips, but now he saw the necessity. It was therefore not surprising that he should ask the pleasant young Brandt if he would like to join his staff as doctor (*Begleitarzt*) and he agreed. A short while later Brandt married Anni Rehborn. Both Hitler and Göring were guests at the wedding.

The ability of Dr Brandt was proverbial, as was his joviality: a doctor with the soul of a Paracelsus: to the last his life was devoted to his calling. In the true sense of the term he embraced the higher life and let it embrace him too. He matured to a greatness in which he overshadowed the death sentence which awaited him at the end of the road. Brandt was the Führer's 'emergencies-only doctor' but his role was actually only as a surgeon while Hitler was travelling: otherwise he worked at the Surgical University Clinic in Berlin's Ziegel-Strasse where Dr Werner Haase and Dr von Hasselbach also worked as surgeons and occasionally deputised for Brandt on journeys and when Hitler was at the Berg.

At this time Hitler and his guests used to go on short rambles. A favourite destination was the Hochlenzer, where they would sit in front of the small house on wooden benches in the sun and enjoy the glorious view to Königssee, which glittered in the distance. At Hochlenzer a very refreshing curds and whey was scooped up and served in brown earthenware bowls. It was a rare delicacy. The milk was never moved until it curdled to prevent bubbles forming in the curd. Other walks went to Scharitzkehl and the Vorderbrand. They were glorious little treks. Hitler would wear a bright blue corduroy jacket. In later years the walks were dropped, and after lunch he would venture no further than the small tea-house on the Mooslahner Kopf.

In the 1930s Hitler would always spend Christmas on the Berg although after Geli's suicide in 1931 Christmas was a difficult period for him and awkward for his guests. He would allow a tree to be erected in a corner of the Great Hall but no carols were sung. New Year on the other hand was celebrated in the traditional manner. The meals were festive, and everybody was served sparkling wine. At the stroke of midnight Hitler would touch glasses with his guest and sip, though he always pulled a face as he did so for he 'could not understand how a person could take pleasure in drinking vinegar water'. He would then lead his guests to the terrace to watch the fireworks display at Berchtesgaden. Afterwards he would autograph the table-cards of all his guests and a group photo would be taken before the fireplace.

Chapter 14

The Berghof

BEFORE HITLER BEGAN WITH the conversion, or rather the extension, of Haus Wachenfeld,* the steep road from Berchtesgaden to the Obersalzberg, which was very dangerous in winter due to ice, was widened. Amongst other things it was Hitler's idea to install heating below the road. At his wish the small old house was left untouched by the extension work creating the Berghof which began in March 1936 after Hitler conferred with architect Degano from Gmund am Tegernsee on the plans. A breach was made in the wall of the former staff room on the first floor allowing a Roman arch and corridor to be built for access to the Great Hall of the new structure. On this new floor were also located the private rooms of Hitler and Eva Braun, the apartment of the house manager and the staff rooms. We had two secretaries' rooms in the old house, the smaller being kept bright blue and white; mine, rather larger, was painted red and had a balcony.

Beyond the Roman arch, hung with heavy bordeaux-red velvet curtains, were broad wooden steps leading into the Great Hall. Its interior furnishings carried the hallmark of Professor Gerhardine ('Gerdy') Troost, widow of Professor Paul Ludwig Troost, whom Hitler valued highly. When Hitler equipped his Munich apartment

---

* According to Hitler in Heim, *Monologe*, the house was built in 1917. (TN)

he had been referred by Frau Bruckmann to the *Vereinigte Werkstätten* where he saw furniture which Professor Troost had designed, and which impressed him by its simplicity of style. Troost showed him his plans for the reconstruction of the burned-down Munich Glass Palace which the City Jury had rejected. Hitler was enthusiastic about the design and included it later in the construction of the *Haus der Deutschen Kunst*. Troost also built the NSDAP Braunes Haus and the Führer-building in Munich. Hitler awarded him the honorary title of 'Professor' which passed to his wife after Troost's death in April 1934. Frau Troost was an interior designer and for a while continued her husband's work. She designed tapestries and interior furnishings on commission for Hitler, as well as the document appointing Göring as Reichsmarschall, and his marshal's baton. Frau Troost and Heinrich Hoffmann exhibited a display of sculpture and photographs in the *Haus der Deutschen Kunst*. She was a very intelligent, temperamental woman.

The former staff room at Haus Wachenfeld became the living room. The green stove with its much-admired tiles made it the most comfortable room at the Berghof. Once the ban on smoking was lifted for the early and late hours it became a great favourite. Sophie Stork, Brückner's friend, was a very gifted artist and had painted various scenes on the stove tiles. In the interior of the house, particularly the Great Hall, it was always cool especially when the house was fog-bound or when it rained, and so the female guests particularly would settle on the sofa near the warm stove. Another well-loved spot was the bookcase to the right of the window which contained Meyer's *Lexikon*, often used to resolve arguments. Should the guests have a difference of opinion on details such as the length of a river or the population of a town, the *Lexikon* would always be called upon. Hitler, painfully exact on all matters, would then consult the two different editions of the *Lexikon* just to be on the safe side.

Although the seating below the underpart of the bookcase did not project much and was very uncomfortable, most people were keen to secure a place there because it adjoined the sofa under the window favoured by Hitler. After Hitler and Eva Braun retired upstairs the guests would gather for a glass of sparkling wine before going to bed. This was a chance to relax after the 'official fireplace session' in which not everybody felt free and unrestricted. Here on the wooden sofa covered with cushions one could sit comfortably and rest one's arms on the table. The volume of conversation would often build up, particularly when Schaub and Hoffmann went for each other.

After the conversion, the door next to the bookcase led to the terrace, passing through the former veranda now renamed the 'Winter Garden'. This was an assembly point for guests waiting for the appearance of Hitler before mealtimes in fine weather (in inclement weather the living room was used instead). Eva Braun would usually come down last. Hitler would always greet the women by kissing the hand of each, including the secretaries. Once all were present the manservant, dressed in white dinner jacket and black trousers, would announce: '*Mein Führer*, it is arranged for you to escort Frau X . . .' Hitler would then offer this lady his arm and lead her forward. The second pair was always Martin Bormann and Eva Braun. The other guests chose a partner freely. The train of guests then moved through the sizeable vestibule, its beautifully curved ceiling supported by imposing columns, past the broad stairway leading to the upper rooms and into the dining room finished in finely grained pine, its two wing doors flanked by two servants. The long dining table had twenty-four red leather armchairs. The window front of the elongated dining room ended in a semi-circular balcony where the early risers breakfasted in inclement weather at a round table, although most took breakfast in their rooms. In fine weather breakfast was taken on the terrace. Crockery was white, thin-shell porcelain with hand-painted alpine flowers, e.g. gentian, alpine roses and lady's slipper.

If the big table in the dining room lacked places for all lunch or dinner guests, the round table in the ante-room would be used additionally, primarily to seat the adjutants. Nearby was a sideboard with hand-painted tiles depicting scenes from Berghof life, e.g. some showing Frau Endres, who ran the household for a short while after the departure of Frau Raubal, carrying a bowl of heaped meatballs. There was also a built-in glass showcase in which very beautiful porcelain, a present from Winifred Wagner to Hitler, was displayed, together with hand-painted crockery.

At the Berghof Hitler always sat at the centre of the table opposite the window overlooking the Untersberg mountain. He would have a different female partner at his right hand for each mealtime, the secretaries also had their turn, while at his left Eva Braun and Martin Bormann had a permanent place together. The special invitees were placed directly opposite Hitler. He laid stress on having a beautiful floral decoration at table. It was essential that the best blooms should be supplied from the most exclusive florists in Berlin and Munich. Excellent floral decorations were set for state dinners. When I think of the almond bushes, the long-stemmed roses, rare orchids and gerbera amongst other expensive blooms which transformed the rooms into a literal paradise of flowers then I definitely believe that these decorations far exceeded the costs of the menu on such occasions. That at least was what was whispered.

The porcelain and silver cutlery were made to Hitler's design. They bore the sovereignty symbol, the eagle with spread wings with right and left the initials 'A' and 'H' in the old script, the design on the porcelain being in gold. The fare was simple and traditional: as a rule soup, meat, vegetables, salad and dessert. Hitler's household functioned like a well-run hotel. From Martin Bormann's market garden on the Berg fresh vegetables and salads were delivered daily. The farm provided milk, eggs, red- and blackcurrant juice, grape and apple juice, honey from hives in the wooded regions of Obersalzberg and the Kehlstein. When Hitler recognised the medicinal qualities of hops he would indulge himself later in a beer brewed for him specially. His favourite meals at the beginning of the 1930s were white beans, peas and lentils, vegetable dishes and salads. During the war when a dietician-cook was employed he followed the Bircher-Benner diet. He was sincerely opposed to meat eating, and according to Julius Schaub became vegetarian after the death of Geli Raubal. He was absolutely convinced that meat eating was harmful. As an example he cited horses, bulls and elephants, all plant-eaters, which had great strength and endurance. 'Contrast them with dogs,' he would say, 'which are confirmed meat eaters and, after a bit of effort, finish up panting with their tongues hanging out.' In his opinion meat was dead, putrefied matter, and in addition he disapproved of the cruel manner in which animals were slaughtered in the abattoirs.

Once I discussed this with Ada Klein. When I mentioned Hitler's remarks about meat eaters she recalled an incident at Easter 1926 when she visited a matinée of the *Zigeunerbaron* in the Gärtner-Platz theatre. Afterwards they ate at the Café Viktoria in the Maximilian-Strasse opposite the Thierschstrasse (now the Restaurant Roma). Hitler ordered kid liver. The waiter brought a giant portion. Hitler asked: 'Is that the liver from one kid?' The waiter replied: 'No, from two!' At that Hitler remarked to Ada: 'The human is an evil animal of prey. Two small innocent animals were deprived of life to provide a glutton with a gourmet dish. I believe I shall become vegetarian one day.' After Geli's death he actually did convert and never tired of holding forth from time to time during meals on the brutal methods of slaughter. When Eva Braun then gave him a pleading look to not go on about it so at the meal table because it put many guests off their food listening to the discourse, this confirmed the correctness of his opinion.

On the other hand he would go into almost poetic rapture whenever he described how his own vegetarian meal had been grown. The farmer sweeping the seed fan-wise from his hand in that great gesture with his arm as he bestrode his fields; how the broadcast seed fell to earth, sprouted and grew into a green sea of waving stems turning slowly golden yellow in the sun. 'This picture alone', he believed, 'should tempt Man back to Nature and her produce, which is given to mankind in wasteful fullness.' He would always round off by saying that he did not intend to convert anybody to vegetarianism, for if he did in the end nobody would accept his invitations to dine any more.

He would often recall the meals he enjoyed most as a child. These included bread rolls with meatballs and sorrel sauce, which his mother used to make. Marion Schönmann, a native of Vienna very often the guest of Hitler and Eva Braun at the Berghof, once joked that she would make some for him. Next day wearing a chef's white outfit she caused uproar in the kitchens, set the staff in high dudgeon and created an awful mess, the result of which was meatballs as hard as iron. Hitler, who enjoyed getting the better of his female compatriot, did not miss this opportunity of berating her much-vaunted skill in cooking, and suggested she should use her recipe to defend the turreted castle she owned near Melk on the Danube. Years later he still relished retelling the story of Frau Schönmann's meatballs.

When the diners rose, he would always kiss the hand of Eva Braun first, and then that of his female partner at table. During the meal Eva Braun took little part in the conversation, at least in the earlier years. Later when her self-confidence grew she would talk if she felt so inclined. She would allow her impatience to show if at the end of the meal Hitler embarked on one of his favourite topics instead of rising. In the war years when her influence on Hitler was more certain she would even go so far as to cast looks of disapproval in his direction or ask in a loud voice what the time was. Hitler would then quickly abandon his monologue and rise from the table.

Until the war, on his walks on the Obersalzberg which led to the 'small tea-house' on the Mooslahner Kopf, Hitler would wear a ghastly khaki windcheater, far too long and several sizes too big for him, and a nondescript hat with a wide brim to protect his sensitive eyes. This hat was the curse of the photographers, for it only allowed them to get a shot of the lower half of his face. Eva Braun, very conscious of appearances, would often criticise his clothes, but he ignored her. Only if she repeated her criticism too often, and he saw it as a criticism of his taste would he let his annoyance show. When Eva once spoke disapprovingly of his hunched shoulders when walking he brushed this aside with: 'Those are the great worries of state which weigh me down!'

On these walks in wartime he preferred a black cloak. He kept to well-maintained bridle paths at the sides of the farm meadows, a walking stick in his right hand, the lead of Blondi his German Shepherd in the left. He would always go in company with the newest arrival amongst the guests. It would take a comfortable half hour to reach the tea-house, built by Professor Fick in 1937 and resembling a low, tower-like pavilion. On a rocky promontory equipped with a guard rail he would then stand enjoying the view over Berchtesgaden and Salzburg, both hands resting on the walking stick. Speer is mistaken when he says that Hitler had no feeling for the beauty of the landscape. Hitler would always wait at this promontory for his guests to catch up and then all would enjoy the view together.

Once everybody had looked their fill – far below the river Ache curled through the valley – Hitler would lead the way to the tea-house. There was a cloakroom in the porch and then one entered a room of bright marble with a large fireplace. Furnishings were deep, chintz-covered armchairs at a round table. Tall, narrow windows in the south face of the tea-house allowed a good view of the mountains; the fireplace was on the north side, above it a gold-framed mirror reflected the crystal crown lights in the ceiling and the beeswax candles in wall holders. I never saw the grate lit. As a source of warmth it was superfluous, for central heating was installed below the red marble floor tiles.

While the visits to the small tea-house on the Mooslahner Kopf formed part of the daily ritual, the tea-house on the Kehlstein was rarely visited. It was at 2,000 metres, and Hitler felt unwell in the thin air at that altitude. This little house on a mountain top was like a fairytale with which he enjoyed surprising foreign heads of state.* Hitler would often proudly relate the fascination of his visitors for the road which led to the Kehlstein, often skirting the edge of the precipice. Further on they would be impressed by the tunnel drilled into the mountain with its imposing metal lift and then the overwhelming sight over the majestic mountain world of Berchtesgaden. The construction work on the Kehlstein was Martin Bormann's masterpiece, just as the farm was also developed on his initiative.

While the guests to the small tea-house drank mostly tea or coffee, Hitler and Eva Braun preferred cocoa. The selection of cakes and pastries was very tempting, but Hitler always had apple pie, its pastry breath-thin, low in calories, with thick slices of baked apple. Later cognac and liqueurs were offered. To be a couple of kilos overweight was a serious political matter for Hitler and if it suddenly became difficult to button his jacket at the midriff and the scales confirmed an increase in weight, especially if a Party rally was in the offing, he would reject anything sugary and eat very little. He would always proclaim a diet by declaring: 'I have to eat less, I am putting on fat, I must lose it!' His iron will would bring about the hoped-for result, and then he would announce: 'So, I am back to my old weight, I have lost seven kilos in the last fourteen days!' Battling his tendency to corpulence was spurred less by vanity than his awareness of people's disapproval of well-fed orators, and most of all his fear of being ridiculed, both of which kept him on the path of moderation. Göring's corpulence on the other hand did not worry him, for he found both Göring and Dr Morell well proportioned.

---

* The Kehlstein tea-house was a gift to Hitler from the NSDAP for his fiftieth birthday. A road six and a half kilometres in length climbed 1,710 metres to a parking place at a gallery entrance to a lift. This lift rose 124 metres directly into the Kehlstein tea-house. Seidler and Zeigert, *Die Führerhauptquartiere*, Herbig, p.261. (TN)

One saw that the same fear of ridicule was the reason for his decision not to wear leather shorts, the so-called 'shorts regalia' of Bavaria, or be seen in bathing trunks. To his mind such articles of apparel were inappropriate for heads of state.

In the tea-house Hitler loved to hear amusing stories, and people who could tell them were very welcome. It would have been unthinkable to tell obscene stories or a dirty joke in his presence though – the bold comedian would receive an 'if looks could kill' look and be wise to excuse himself. The spiciest stories he tolerated were the '*Graf* Bobby' kind. For example, a nobleman had been invited to a dancer's flat where they had taken tea and afterwards taken a bath together. Now the nobleman had no peace wondering whether there had been something more on offer from the lady. Hitler would listen to stories like these with a contented smile. Often those present would score points off each other. I remember a conversation between Dr Goebbels and Dr Dietrich, the Reich press secretary. Dr Dietrich had stated that his best ideas came to him in the bath. Goebbels responded: 'Then you should bathe much more frequently, Herr Doktor Dietrich!' Sometimes in these sessions Hitler would laugh till he cried.

New arrivals at the Berghof were very welcome at the tea-house, where conversations gradually degenerated into monotonous repetitions for lack of fresh blood. Talk would become a murmur if Hitler fell asleep in an armchair, although as soon as conversation died away he would waken immediately. Hitler also showed great interest should two people get their heads together at the big round table in the tea-house, or perhaps discuss a document in an undertone, or hold an illustrated magazine in the hand and point to a particular section. Then he would want to know about it at once: 'What's new there?' Awareness of this curiosity on his part was often used to skilful effect by clever guests. In this way certain matters could be brought to his attention which were otherwise delicate to broach. The Schirachs liked to bring along American magazines.

Once, one contained illustrations of American women working in the armaments industry, in another two women boxed while standing in a sea of herrings. Hitler made fun of both but found the latter particularly objectionable.

While in the tea-house, Eva Braun would get a manservant to find out what new films had arrived from the Propaganda Ministry in Berlin. If Hitler did not require the Great Hall for a conference, after our return (usually by car, Hitler's vehicle would have an adjutant, the manservant and Blondi besides himself as passengers) she would arrange a film show before the guests retired to dress for dinner.

The procedure for dinner was similar to that at midday. Guests sat near the warm stove or on the sofas with their many cushions which surrounded the great rectangular table. A hanging lamp spread warmth and helped create a pleasant atmosphere. Everybody would be waiting for Hitler who might be talking with a conversation partner either in his room on the first floor or in the Great Hall. Hitler's talks always had priority, and it was not an infrequent occurrence that dinner would begin very late. As soon as Hitler entered, the midday ritual would be re-enacted: the manservant would appear and announce that dinner was served, and which lady Hitler was to accompany at table.

The mood at dinner was freer and the conversation less forced. The ladies would have dressed a little less formally and applied make-up to enhance their appeal. Eva Braun's younger sister, who never economised on the lipstick, often motivated Hitler into recounting the children's fable about how lipstick was manufactured in the Paris sewers. Eva Braun would hold her nose and plead in feigned despair: 'Oh please, not again!' The effect of this fable appeared to give Hitler a lot of amusement, which was why he repeated it so often.

In 1926 when Ada Klein was walking in Munich with a female friend they chanced to meet Hitler, who joined them. When a lady wearing heavy make-up passed in an open car, Hitler exclaimed: 'Now I know why so many men have stomach complaints. During kissing they eat all that stuff on women's lips!' One day he selected a very beautiful bloom from a table vase and tossed it rather insolently to a lady, his expectation being that she would put the flower in her hair or jacket. On another occasion upon seeing a woman wearing a flower he offered her another which he thought suited her better. In the earlier years Hitler took pleasure in such gallantry. Ada Klein recalled that in the so-called Eckart Room at the Braunes Haus at Easter 1933 he withdrew a small yellow chick from the table decoration, took her hand, opened it, placed the chick very tenderly inside and closed the hand again.

In the evenings one would remain seated at table a little longer. After the meal, if there was a meeting in the Great Hall a film would be shown in the bowling alley provided there was no bowling. This was rare, however, for the noise from the alley could be very distracting in the Great Hall and generally we would retire to the living room and wait for Hitler's conference to finish. Conversation had to be carried on in low tones, as mentioned, for the Great Hall was only separated from the living room by a velvet curtain. When Hitler was ready, this would be drawn aside by a waiter and Hitler would then ask: 'Shouldn't we sit at the fireside a little?'[1] That was always the prelude to an evening spent there.

The guests would descend five steps from the living room into the Great Hall, of which Hitler was particularly fond. It had a high ceiling and a floor area of almost 200 square metres. The floor was laid with a strawberry-coloured pile carpet. Three marble steps led to the armchairs around the fireplace. There was little other furniture there. Two large cabinets, some chairs near the great window, a large conference table, a globe, a grandfather clock; then a piano and some

---

1 Schroeder noted that: 'the response would usually be muted, for the sessions round the fireplace tended to go on and on, and ended, if Hitler was not in a mood for conversation, in an oppressive, brooding silence.'

small commodes. One of the large cabinets had handles carved in the shape of human heads. Certificates of citizenship and old weapons were displayed in it. In the other were old artefacts in tin behind a glass front. Magnificent Gobelin tapestries depicting hunting scenes covered apertures in the walls necessary for the film shows.

The large old masters in the Hall were changed regularly. Very often *Nana* by Anselm Feuerbach (Feuerbach's long-term lover from Rome, the wife of a cobbler), a particular favourite of Hitler, hung near the fireplace. On the long wall of the Hall was a wonderful likeness of a woman dressed in red by Bordone, red carnations in the same shade of deep red always stood on a commode nearby. The most impressive thing in the Great Hall, which had a dark brown ceiling, was undoubtedly the magnificent window, nine metres wide. It could be sunk down to show the majestic panorama of the Untersberg mountain as if in a frame.[2] The mammoth rectangular table standing in front of the window had a top of Untersberg marble and proved very useful at conferences for spreading out large maps on its surface.

Amongst the seating about the marble fireplace, a gift from Mussolini, was a black leather sofa. It was of gigantic proportions, and in relation to the size of the Hall it looked good, but was extremely uncomfortable. The square footage available for sitting on was so enormous that it was not possible to sit and lean against the back rest. At the beginning of the fireplace session one would have to sit bolt upright on the edge of the sofa, but as the evening wore on the ladies would find it more comfortable to lean against the sofa back with their legs tucked under them. The sets consisting of upholstered chairs each with a small table and suitable for small groups of guests were much more acceptable.

---

2 This large window was subdivided into ninety individual windows. Hitler, who was very proud of it, once remarked to his adjutant Wiedemann: 'Really, I built a house around a window here.'

I he fire was not lit every evening. Hitler's place was on the right side of it between two ladies (Eva Braun always at his right). He would say when it should be lit. He usually started the conversation or would intervene once a particular topic caught his interest. If he did not feel like talking, and there were evenings which palled into awkward silences, he would often burst the tension with: 'Should we listen to some music for a while?' and all would agree with enthusiasm. The music cabinet was controlled by Martin Bormann and was located at the side of the window. From the long repertoire he had drawn up the greatest favourites were the symphonies by Bruckner and Beethoven, the songs of Richard Strauss, Hugo Wolf, Brahms, Beethoven, Schubert and Schumann, and the last act from *Aida*.

Hitler was very partial to Richard Wagner's works of course. In first place for him was *Tristan and Isolde*, a work of which he once said that he would like to listen to it in the hour of his death. Hitler considered Wagner to be 'the man who re-awoke German culture from the spirit of music'. Wagner's musical language was to Hitler's ears 'like a divine manifestation'. He had seen some of Wagner's operas very frequently and nothing in the world would induce him to miss the annual Bayreuth Festival (not even the Spanish Civil War in 1936). He sponsored Bayreuth financially, and was planning to make visits to the Festival available to all sections of German society, a national pilgrimage, so to speak. The *Deutsche Arbeitsfront*, the official organisation for German workers, arranged trips to Bayreuth for workers and employees to develop enthusiasm for Wagner's works throughout all strata of society.

Hitler also enjoyed light classical music such as *The Merry Widow*, *Die Fledermaus* and *Zigeunerbaron*. A number of the male guests preferred to retire to the lounge on evenings when music was to the forefront. The frequent confrontations between Heinrich Hoffmann and Julius Schaub seemed to be provoked by music. If the argument became too loud, Hitler would send a manservant to the lounge with the request either that they should reduce the volume or return to the fireplace. These occurrences would often remind Hitler of awkward situations which tended to develop at musical presentations when his escort did not like listening to music. 'Whenever I visit the opera I have to take care that my officers do not snore. One day during *Tristan and Isolde*, Heinrich Hoffmann nearly fell over the ledge out of the box. I had to wake Schaub up to tell him to give Hoffmann a shake. Brückner was behind me snoring. It was dreadful!'

Hitler was very good at telling anecdotes like these and everybody enjoyed listening to them, even Eva Braun. If conversations were mentioned of which she disapproved this would be immediately evident and then even Hitler would notice. He would stroke her hand resting on the arm of her chair, whisper a few words and then she would disappear upstairs. This would also happen if she thought that Hitler was paying too much attention to another woman.[3]

At New Year 1938 Gretl Slezak gave me a letter to hand to Hitler privately without anybody seeing. As he was about to leave the Hall I detained him. Once all the guests had gone below to the bowling alley in the basement for drinks, he took my arm and strolled up and down with me in the Great Hall. My evening dress of roe deer-brown fluffy material with a small train, added to which my silver-fox fur cape must have looked magnificent, supported by a small tipsiness which I had got from the dinner, lent me a large slice of self-confidence and courage, for after I had handed him the letter I broke into hymns of praise about Gretl Slezak, which must have seemed close to an attempt at matchmaking. Convinced that he must share my opinion, I finished with: 'Eva is nothing for you, *mein Führer!*'

---

3 In her stenographic notes, Schroeder stated: 'If any woman was present in whom Eva feared a competitor, then she either retired very soon to her room or became so unpleasant that Hitler would notice and persuade her to withdraw "because she was tired".'

In spite of annoyance at this impertinent remark, Hitler looked at me in amusement and replied: 'But she is enough for me!' Enough? Where was 'the great love' of which so many writers have been in the know since 1945? Clearly, my attempt at matchmaking that New Year's Eve amused Hitler no end, for he made no move to leave the Hall. We had been alone together for rather too long, it seemed, for Eva Braun appeared suddenly, gave me a scowl and said in hurt tones to Hitler: 'Where have you been, we are all waiting for you!'

Hitler did not forget this episode, for a few weeks later he brought it up and said to me with a smile, 'That night you had a certain something'. That night the New Year's Eve photo was taken in the Great Hall before the fireplace. It was the last New Year's celebration at which so many guests would be present.

Another unforgettable experience in the Great Hall was Hitler's dictation of 11 May 1941. Despite innumerable attempts, a plausible explanation for the flight of his deputy Rudolf Hess to Britain eluded him. He tried out all the possible motives he could think of and tried to encapsulate them in words, but nothing seemed to fit properly. Only when he viewed the flight as the act of a madman did he seem satisfied. I had never known a dictation cause him so much trouble as this one.[4]

Hitler was a great admirer of British colonialism. In 1926 he had told his closest colleagues: 'It is not my wish that a pearl should fall from the crown of the British Empire. It would be a catastrophe for humanity.' In the prewar years when German public opinion was

---

4 On the question whether Hess flew to Britain with Hitler's knowledge or on his own initiative: one of Martin Bormann's secretaries wrote in a letter to Schroeder: 'I am of the opinion that Adolf Hitler knew nothing of the flight. Martin Bormann told me at the time ... Martin Bormann was always straight! It is unlikely that Hitler would have been so stupid as to send Hess to negotiate with a man neither knew and who was a friend of Churchill.' Hans Baur, Hitler's personal pilot, said: 'I overheard a conversation in the Reich Chancellery garden between Hitler and Göring: Hitler did not realise I was nearby when he screamed at Göring: "He has simply gone mad, he must know that by doing that he has stabbed me in the back!"'

very favourable towards the Indian independence movement, he said: 'I forbid my people to go along with this Gandhi nonsense. One does not win independence with spinning wheels, but with guns.' From several of his statements it was possible to conclude that he thought of an alliance with Britain as the most ideal solution to the problems of world politics. He considered the Royal Navy and the German Army in combination to be a power factor sufficiently strong to give world politics a new foundation. In the 1920s Hitler had begun writing a book about foreign policy.[5] In 1939, shortly after the British declaration of war, he said to Hess in my presence: 'All my work is falling apart. I have written my book for nothing.' I believe that Hess was the only person to whom he had explained the ideas developed in his manuscript, and that Hess, because of his intimate knowledge of Hitler's thinking, undertook his flight to Britain.

The Great Hall was often the venue for interesting events, visits and conversations. Hitler was very impressed by the visit of the Duke and Duchess of Windsor.[6] In the afternoon from the office window I saw Hitler with the couple on the terrace apparently pointing out to them the various mountains by name. The duchess wore a simple dark blue woollen frock of excellent cut. She looked chic and impressive with her hair centre-parted and styled in a bun. Undoubtedly she made a lasting impression on Hitler, for in the evening he said: 'She would definitely have made a good queen'. He saw in the Duke a friend of Germany and regretted that he had not fought the Establishment rather than abdicating, particularly since he could have relied upon the sympathy of the working class.

That evening at the fireside he also told us of the visit a few days before by the Indian prince and Muslim leader the Aga Khan, one of

---

5 *Hitlers Zweites Buch*, with a commentary by Gerhard L. Weinberg, Deutsche Verlags-Anstalt, Stuttgart 1961.

6 This visit took place on 20 October 1937. HRH the Duke of Windsor had abdicated as King Edward VIII on 10 December 1936.

the richest men in the world.' The conversations with the Aga Khan gave Hitler much food for thought, e.g. the opinion of his visitor that it would have been best for Europe if Martel had lost the eighth-century battle of Tours/Poitiers against the Moors, for then Europe would have become Muslim, retained its scientific knowledge and its peoples would have lived in peace with each other. The Aga Khan had given thought to the European relationship and that pleased Hitler. He found himself in agreement with many non-barbarous aspects of Islam, in particular the ban on drinking and eating the flesh of swine, and the practice of periodic fasting.

Another of the visits by prominent statesmen to the Berghof which Hitler was fond of describing was that by Lloyd George[8] in 1936. He had been impressed by the geographical situation of the Berghof, by the house itself, its furnishings and above all the view from the gigantic window over the mountains. German measures to curb unemployment, reduce working hours and introduce state health insurance, as well as other social advances, also impressed him. Dr Ley had acquainted Lloyd George before his visit to the Berghof with the work of the *Arbeitsfront*, the official workers' organisation.

On the other hand the visit of Knut Hamsun[9] to the Berghof left a bad taste in the mouth. This happened in June 1943. During a meal, Baldur von Schirach had mentioned Hamsun's visit to the Journalists' Congress in Vienna and urged Hitler to invite the Norwegian to the Berghof. After initial reluctance Hitler agreed and Knut Hamsun came. During the conversation between Hamsun and Hitler, Dara Christian and I heard a heated exchange – we were

7 This visit took place on 20 October 1937. The Aga Khan III (b. 2.11.1877 Karachi, d. 11.6.1957 Geneva) was the forty-first imam of the Ismaeli sect.

8 This visit took place on 4 September 1936.

9 Knut Hamsun (b. 4.8.1859 Lom, Norway, d. 19.2.1952 Grimstad). Novelist; 1920 Nobel Prize winner for literature; during the Second World War Nazi sympathiser, member of Norwegian Quisling Party; after the war convicted of collaboration and fined.

in the lounge, which was separated from the Great Hall only by a curtain. Holding our breath we crept closer. Hamsun had had the gall to take Hitler to task over the measures introduced by Gauleiter Terboven in Norway, urging in emotional tones that Terboven be recalled. Maybe because he was rather deaf, or possibly because Hitler would tolerate no contradiction, we heard Hitler shout at him: 'Be silent! You know nothing about it!'

Hitler had said precisely the same thing on Good Friday 1943 to Henriette Schirach at the fireplace, she told me in 1978. I remember that evening Eva Braun had sat at Hitler's right before she went upstairs, and to the left of Henriette. I had also noticed that, while the other guests were talking, an argument developed between Henriette and Hitler, the subject of which was an occurrence in Amsterdam a few days previously. She had been awoken at night by an unusually loud disturbance and had watched from a hotel window as some weeping women were ordered forward across a bridge and disappeared into the night. From her friends she learned next day that this had been a deportation of Jewish women. She promised to bring the matter to the attention of Hitler, which she was now doing. Hitler answered her in a very brusque manner: 'Be silent, Frau von Schirach, you understand nothing about it. You are sentimental. What does it matter to you what happens to female Jews? Every days tens of thousands of my most valuable men fall while the inferior survive. In that way the balance in Europe is being undermined,' and here he moved his cupped hands up and down like a pair of scales. 'And what will become of Europe in one hundred, in one thousand years?' In a tone which made it evident that he considered the matter closed, he is said to have declared: 'I am committed by duty to my people alone, to nobody else!'

The guests noticed that Hitler had now become morose, and there was visible relief when a waiter appeared suggesting that he might refill the glasses. Another great sigh of relief went up when just after midnight Dr Goebbels arrived, but it was misplaced, for Goebbels launched at once into a diatribe against Baldur von Schirach, accusing him of fostering Austrian policies in Vienna. Hitler said that it had been 'a mistake to send Schirach to Vienna, and also a mistake to have annexed the Viennese into the Greater German Reich.' When Schirach pointed out that 'the Viennese are all for you, *mein Führer*', Hitler retorted, 'I am not in the least interested, I reject them.' At this Schirach declared that under the circumstances he was resigning his post, but Hitler waved this aside by saying: 'That is not your decision. You will stay where you are.'

Next morning there was a deathly stillness over the Berghof. However this had nothing to do with the departure of the Schirachs, who had driven off in the early hours without so much as a by-your-leave: on Martin Bormann's orders it was always quiet across the entire Berg every morning because Hitler spent most of the night studying reports and other documents and slept in more or less until noon. All house guests in the floor above his had to pay heed. One had to tiptoe around the bed and not bathe until midday. All guests were also required to make no noise on the terrace, where Eva Braun liked to spend time amongst her friends in a deckchair until Hitler appeared.

Frau Schneider[10] was her friend of longest standing. Of the other women, one or another of the doctors' and adjutants' wives would be in favour with Eva Braun from time to time, and would be invited to Portofino with her, this being a place she adored. All the others would then be wary and maintain a reserve towards the reigning favourite. It was often an odd bunch up there on the Berg.

From 1944, enemy aircraft began to overfly Berchtesgaden. The sirens would howl frequently and the smoke batteries would

---

10 Herta Schneider née Ostermeier (b. 4.4.1913 Nuremberg) knew Eva Braun from their primary schooldays. Eva Braun was a frequent visitor at the Ostermeier's because her parents were not interested in her. In 1936, Herta married, and from then until 1945 spent long periods at Obersalzberg with her children. On 28.4.1945 she left for Garmisch-Partenkirchen with Margarete Fegelein, Eva Braun's sister.

conceal the region. Hitler was expecting a concentrated attack on Obersalzberg, as he did on his FHQ. In 1943 bunkers were built, ready by Christmas. They saved my life in 1945. Within a few steps of the back door of the house there was an iron door from where sixty-five steps led down to the bunker complex.

Chapter 15

The Order to Leave Berlin:
My Leave-taking of Hitler

FTER THE FÜHRER-BUNKER IN the Reich Chancellery park
had been reinforced, Hitler withdrew his FHQ to Berlin
in January 1945. The bunker had been intended as a
temporary refuge during air attacks, but after the upper rooms
of the Radziwill Palace, particularly the library, had been made
uninhabitable by incendiaries, Hitler spent most of his time with
his staff in the bunker.[1] It extended below ground into the Reich
Chancellery park, where there was an emergency exit in the form of
a small concrete turret. There were several stairways from the main
building down into the bunker.

In the Radziwill Palace, the Adjutancy Wing, including the
Staircase Room, was undamaged, and so at the beginning of 1945 we
secretaries would take our meals during the day with Hitler behind
drawn drapes with the lights on while outside the spring sun shone
down on the gutted Hotel Kaiserhof and the Propaganda Ministry.

---

1 The *Vorbunker* (built 1936) and Hitler's bunker (built 1943) lay below the
Reich Chancellery palace in the Wilhelm-Strasse and extended below the Reich
Chancellery park. Access was by a stairway from the Reich Chancellery palace
and a 105-metre-long corridor known as the 'Kannenberg Corridor' because of
the provisions stored there, or from a tower-like entrance in the park. An alleged
corridor into the Propaganda Ministry suggested in many sketches never existed.

The evening meal was served in the Führer-bunker in Hitler's small, sparsely furnished room. Already narrow, it was equipped with a small writing desk, a small sofa, a table and three chairs. To move across the room required a repositioning of the chairs. The room was cold and unpleasant. On either side was a door, one leading to his bathroom, the other into a cramped bedroom. The study was dominated by a portrait of Frederick the Great[2] which hung over the writing desk. With his large, powerful eyes the old ruler glared down at Hitler. The oppressive narrowness of the room and the overall general mood in the bunker had a depressing effect.

At six in the morning, when Hitler received us after the nightly situation conference, he would usually be lying exhausted on the little sofa. His physical decline made daily advances despite his desperate attempts to hold himself together. He always managed to rise to greet us though, sinking back after a while, his manservant raising his feet for him. He was almost permanently emotional, and his talk was increasingly the monotonous repetition of the same stories. At lunch, dinner and the nightly tea sessions (i.e. in the early hours of the morning) the same again. Thus almost every day he would tell us: 'This beast Blondi woke me again this morning. She came to my bed wagging her tail and when I asked her: 'Do you have to do your business?' she dropped her tail and crept back to her corner. She is a sly animal.' Or: 'Look, my hand is improving. It is not trembling so much, I can almost hold it out firmly.'

The things he talked about became gradually more flat and uninteresting. He no longer discussed the Church, racial problems, economic and political questions, about being Nordic and German, Ancient Greece or the rise and fall of the Roman Empire. He, who had always been so passionately interested in all matters of

---

2 This was the portrait by Anton Graff. Hitler's attitude at the end can be summarized precisely by a letter from King Frederick to Podewils on 27.4.1745, exactly 200 years before: 'I shall either hold out or, if not, I desire that everything shall be destroyed and the Prussian name be buried with me.'

science, zoology, botany and human development spoke out in the latter months only on dog-training, nutrition and the stupidity and degeneration of the world.

The morning tea session usually went on for two hours. Afterwards Hitler would rise and drag himself to the dog's box. Blondi had had puppies in March, and from the litter Hitler had selected a male puppy to raise and train himself. He would remove this animal from the box, sit in his room with the puppy in his lap, stroking it incessantly while muttering its name, Wolf. After a while he would return the puppy to its mother and take his leave of us to rest. This was latterly around 0800. It would not leave him much time for sleep, for the sirens would generally start up at about 1100. On the approach of enemy bombers he would always get up, for he feared that a bomb falling diagonally could penetrate and collapse the bunker wall. Since the bunker was below the water table, there was a danger that in such a case the water would rush in. Accordingly when enemy bombers were arriving he would dress fully and even shave. During an air raid alarm he would never remain alone in his room.

Dinner, usually between 2100 and 2200, was customarily an extended affair. The approach of enemy aircraft would often be announced during this period, when the wire and police network would be switched on. The radio channel broadcast a monotonous bleeping when not passing reports about the bombers. We used to sit listening to the bombs exploding, and there was never a day when the government district was spared. In the heavy air raid of 3 February 1945 fifty-eight HE bombs fell around the Reich Chancellery. Every time a bomb exploded in the vicinity, the bunker, lying in ground water, would tremble perceptibly. If the lights flickered, Hitler would say: 'That was near. That bomb could have hit us!'

After the All-clear, he would at once request a damage report, and listen to it calmly without interrupting. The nightly situation conference would not begin until long after midnight, and would

175

often last until dawn. Then the tea session would follow, he would play with the dogs and sleep a few hours until the next aerial intrusion, which would take us to lunch. Afterwards he would call the afternoon situation conference, and the whole game would begin again.

On Hitler's fifty-sixth birthday on 20 April 1945, Berlin was surrounded, and the first Russian tanks reached the outskirts. We could hear the thunder of the field guns from the Reich Chancellery. The chorus of congratulations from the personal staff and the military that morning was very restrained in comparison to earlier years, whereas that of the Allies was much more impressive. The series of rolling air raids lasted from early morning until 0200 next day. We no longer left the bunker. According to the service roster, Johanna Wolf and I had to keep the boss company until lunch. The mood was very gloomy as we ate.

That evening during the bombing raid just before 2200 Johanna and I were summoned by Hitler. He received us in his room looking tired, pale and listless. The situation over the last four days had changed considerably, he told us. On 16 April at lunch in the Staircase Room when I asked him whether we would remain in Berlin he had replied almost involuntarily: 'Of course we shall remain in Berlin. You need have no fear!' I told him that I had no fears since I had come to terms with dying. However I could not imagine how Germany could carry on when our forces were being sandwiched ever more firmly between the Americans and the Russians. 'Remain calm', he went on in annoyance, 'Berlin will remain German, we just have to gain time!' Even in his last address to the Gauleiters on 24 February 1945 in Berlin he had informed them of his unshakeable conviction that 'we must gain time!'

Now the tune had changed. 'Over the last four days the situation has changed to such an extent that I find myself forced to disperse my staff. As you are the longest serving, you will go first. In an hour a car leaves for Munich. You may take two trunks, Reichsleiter

Bormann will give you further instructions.' Since I had no family, I requested permission to stay in Berlin. This would allow my junior colleague to leave instead. Her mother lived in Munich. He would not accept this.

> No, later I will found a resistance movement,[3] and for that I need you both. You are the most valuable people to me. If it comes to the worst, the young will always come through. Frau Christian (Dara) will in any case get away and if another of the younger girls fails to make it, that is Fate!

He did not take his leave of us as he usually did with a kiss to the hand, but gave us a handshake instead, probably his way of indicating that he would hear no further appeals and that the matter was closed. He must have noted our subdued mood for he added, perhaps in an attempt to comfort us: 'We shall meet again, I am coming down in a few days!' This order to abandon Berlin on 20 April 1945 was not what I had expected for myself, since I had already decided to use the cyanide capsule which Skorzeny had sold me for a bottle of whisky. Trevor Roper, the British historian, pretended to know my movements better than I did, for in the German language version of his book, *Hitlers Letzte Tage*[4] he wrote: 'Two of Hitler's secretaries, Fräulein Wolf and Fräulein Schroeder . . . fled on 22 April . . .'

I had always abhorred sudden and unexpected enforced journeys. This latest order by Hitler awoke in me far greater feelings of reluctance than ever before, and left me in a state of confusion. As if stunned I departed Hitler's room to begin packing along with my colleague Wolf. None of my possessions was in storage. I had left several trunks in the west and east in 1944, and had them forwarded to me in Berlin at the beginning of 1945 before the Allied

---

3 Schroeder confirmed that Hitler said this. What it meant remains a mystery.
4 3rd edition, Ullstein, 1965.

advance, on the basis of Hitler's assurance that my things would be safest there.

On the way to the Voss-Strasse bunker, where we secretaries had a room for sleeping and storage, I saw armaments minister Speer in the telephone exchange. I told him of Hitler's order and asked him then about Dr Brandt, whose fate concerned me greatly. Hitler had sentenced him to death for defeatism and he was being held prisoner in a Berlin villa. Speer told me: 'We will spring him!'

The vestibule of the Voss-Strasse bunker was crowded with civilians from Voss-Strasse sheltering from the air raid. The room allocated to us was originally built as a transmitter room. I was very unhappy about the room, for the ceiling and walls were sound-proofed and suppressed the tones of conversation. It was a dead room, oppressively quiet like a tomb.

The packing seemed senseless. Suddenly the telephone rang. It was Hitler. In a weak voice he said: 'Children, the hole is closed up (we were to have driven through the Czech Protectorate). The car cannot go through and you will have to fly early tomorrow.' He rang again after midnight: 'Children, make ready, hurry, the machine will take off as soon as it is warmed up.' His voice sounded flat, and he broke off halfway through the conversation. I called out, but although he had not hung up he made no reply. These were the only telephone calls from him I ever received in my twelve years of service . . .

A short while later, around 0230, we struggled through the crowded corridors of the Reich Chancellery bunker on Voss-Strasse. It sounded like a beehive. Everybody stared at us and our two cases with curiosity. I felt strange and passed the anxious bystanders full of shame. In the courtyard of the Radziwill Palace a lorry stood ready. Johanna Wolf and I handed over our cases. Johanna had an unpleasant feeling about her luggage and after it had been stowed she had second thoughts about parting with it. I had not fully realised the chaotic situation, and I told her there would be no problem. As ir luuur transpired, we went to Tempelhof airport and our luggage to Staaken.

In the courtyard of the Radziwill Palace chaos reigned. All vestiges of order for the departures had vanished. Unknown drivers from the *SS-Leibstandarte* waited with their vehicles for their scheduled passengers. As no light could be shown, it was very difficult to find one's way around. When we finally located our vehicle, its driver did not know Berlin, and he had no orders to take us to Tempelhof or Staaken. Eventually he got us to Tempelhof, how he managed to get round the red tape I have no idea. It was a macabre drive through the night past burning houses, smouldering heaps of rubble, ruins and smoke, and *Volkssturm* men hastily erecting street barricades. In the middle distance we could hear the thunder of Soviet artillery.

At Tempelhof airport nobody had knowledge of the Ju 52 of which Hitler's Luftwaffe adjutant Oberst von Below had spoken. The airport commander advised us to try to board a Junkers transport bound for Salzburg whose arrival had just been notified from northern Germany. After some negotiations we succeeded in this. Without luggage, only a travel bag and knapsack, packed at the last minute on Schaub's orders and which contained round tins of 'Shoko-Dallmann',[5] the aircraft took off in rain and snow. After an exciting flight over burning villages and towns we touched down at Salzburg in the early morning. One can imagine our fright when through the cotton-wool ear plugs we heard sounds similar to shooting and the machine seemed to lose height quickly. We sat speechless in the aircraft between soldiers seated on green ammunition cases. I do not remember a single word being spoken. We were as if paralysed as we landed. The silence was suddenly oppressive.

While on the bus for Obersalzberg a few hours later I reflected on how lucky we were to have come out of this flight alive. It was

---

5 'Shoko-Dallmann' were vitamin tablets with caffeine covered in chocolate and marketed in round tins.

actually a double miracle that we had survived. The Ju 52[6] which took off from Staaken, and on which we were booked, crashed at Börnersdorf near Dresden. One of the two female bodies burnt to a crisp was identified as me because my trunk was stored in the cargo hold. The victims were interred by the Wehrmacht. I did not learn of this until several years later. The crew had allocated our two unclaimed seats to two other women, and it was their remains which were wrongly identified after the crash. German soldiers in the Börnersdorf vicarage removed some of the items from my trunk, and left the remainder for the Soviets. This was at any rate what I was told by the priest, who was unable to reveal any details at all about my alleged burial and said I should contact the authorities in East Berlin. The identity of the woman who took my place aboard the aircraft and was buried under my name was researched for many years but remained a mystery.[7]

---

6 Actually a Ju 352 of the *Führer-Staffel*, piloted by Major Friedrich Gundelfinger.

7 Hitler's favourite manservant Wilhelm Arndt was one of the passengers aboard this flight. The official list of the dead was: Major Gundelfinger, pilot; Basler, radio operator; Arndt; Budka; Becker; Fiebers; Schleef; an unknown male and two women; E. Krüger and Christine Schroeder. 'The two women were carbonised and identified from their clothing.' The unknown male may have been a member of the SS-Begleitkommando who 'left on a flight to Upper Bavaria with a manservant and two secretaries...' Else Krüger was not the other woman identified. She was Martin Bormann's secretary and remained at the Reich Chancellery until her escape from Berlin on 1 May 1945.

Chapter 16

The End at the Berghof

U PON OUR ARRIVAL AT the Berghof we found some guests already there. Eva Braun's sister was very pregnant. Their mother, Frau Franziska Braun, and Herta Schneider, Eva's long-term friend, were also present. They had no idea of the catastrophic situation in Berlin and asked when the Führer would be coming down. They saw us as the vanguard, for besides Hitler's naval adjutant Jesko von Puttkamer some of the *SS-Begleitkommando* had moved into quarters at the Berghof, proof that Hitler had at least given some thought to coming to the alpine redoubt.

There were frequent air raid alarms, when Obersalzberg would be hidden under a smoke screen. The enemy aircraft passed overhead without bombing. Two days later, on 24 April 1945, Hitler's personal physician Dr Morell arrived. He was very distressed and bitter: the Führer distrusted him, he said, and had sent him packing. It had hit him hard. After a short stay he took his leave saying he was going to Bad Reichenhall. Even Frau Kannenberg turned up in order to join her husband at Thumsee.

Here I must mention something about Dr Morell. Dr Karl Brandt was often incorrectly described as the Führer's personal physician. Dr Brandt and the deputies he had suggested, Dr Haase and Dr von Hasselbach, were only *Begleitärzte*, that is, they were available to perform emergency surgery on Hitler if so required during his travels. The personal physician (*Leibarzt*) was Dr Theodor Morell. Dr Morell had a luxury practice on the Kurfürstendamm in Berlin, most of his patients being from the artistic world. He originated from Hesse, was of average height, corpulent and wore a good-humoured expression. Hair sprouted from his ears and cuffs. On his thick fingers he wore exotic rings obtained during overseas voyages, on which he had also picked up some foreign eating habits. For example he would not peel an orange but bite into it until the juice squirted out. He was also vain. If a photographer reached for his camera, Morell was suddenly at Hitler's side. The Foreign Ministry Protocol Section, which was responsible for the award of foreign decorations, rightly feared that Morell was wearing medals to which he was not entitled, and this could compromise Hitler. Moreover, Morell was said to be a profiteer. Another quite special objection to him was the foul-smelling delousing powder he had patented and which he spread in large quantities around his barrack hut at FHQ.

How had he been appointed Hitler's personal physician? In 1936 when Hitler's chronic gastro-intestinal disorder would not respond to treatment, Heinrich Hoffmann had recommended a wonderful doctor of his personal knowledge, and he succeeded in overwhelming Hitler's aversion to having an unknown physician treat him. When Dr Morell brought about a decisive improvement in the complaint with the Mutaflor drug (used nowadays for ulcerative colitis), and which renewed the colonic bacteria, and also rid Hitler of the eczema on his legs, Morell won Hitler's total confidence. Hitler named him his *Leibarzt* and later made him a professor.

As soon as Hitler reported any discomfort, Morell would be on the spot with his injections. Any cold, even amongst Hitler's close staff, was suppressed before it developed. Hitler had 'no time to be ill' he repeated over and over, and Morell based his treatment on that dictum. He began with harmless glucose, vitamin and hormone injections. Then he went over to 'Vitamultin', a wonder-drug he had produced in his own pharmaceutical laboratory, available in

ꞮꞮꞮꞮꞮꞮꞮꞮꞮꞮ · ꞺꞺꞺ ꞮꞺꞮꞮꞮ ꞺꞮꞮꞮꞮꞮꞮ Ɪ Ɪ ꞮꞮꞮꞮ ꞮꞮꞮꞮꞮ, Hitler ꞮꞮꞮ ꞮꞮꞮ ꞮꞮꞮꞮꞮꞮꞮly
dependent on this drug until one day it no longer had the desired
effect and Morell had to look for something stronger. My assumption
seems confirmed by an article appearing in edition 7/1980 of *Spiegel*
magazine under the title *Hitler – An der Nadel*. This was based on
the book by Leonard L. and Renate Heston, *The Medical Casebook
of Hitler*, which concerned itself with the same question. Morell's
files were made available to the US psychiatrists and the drug
'Vitamultin', containing the stimulants pervitin and caffeine, was
described as 'an especially effective preparation because caffeine
enhances the effect of pervitin'.

In the autumn of 1944 when Dara and I took tea alone with
Hitler, we found him in a strikingly relaxed mood. The waiter had
placed his painful leg on the sofa for him, and now he was stretched
out comfortably. During a murmured conversation he suddenly
threw open his arms and spoke ecstatically of 'how lovely it is when
two people find themselves in love'. Dara and I were astonished, for
we had never seen this mood before, Hitler given so mysteriously to
the joys of love.

Afterwards we sought out Dr Morell in his hut and asked why the
boss was behaving so strangely. Morell looked at us over his glasses
with a sly smile: 'So you've noticed? Yes, I am giving him hormone
injections from bulls' testicles, that should pep him up!' In March
1980, Robert Scholz, who had worked on Rosenberg's staff, told me
that Morell had asked Rosenberg to get him some bulls' testicles.

That Hitler was dependent on stimulants prescribed by Morell
is proven by several reports. After the attempt of 20 July 1944, Dr
Erwin Giesing, who had been called in to treat Hitler's damaged
ear drum, made it known that Morell was treating Hitler with
ill-considered medications. One morning Dr Giesing discovered
on Hitler's breakfast tray a small bottle of anti-flatulence pills
containing two powerful poisons. When he asked the servant
Linge how many the Führer took daily, he was told 'Up to sixteen'.

Appalled at Morell's negligence, he had Dr Brandt, who as head of the Health Department was no longer constantly at FHQ, come at once to Wolfsschanze. Dr Brandt and Dr Hasselbach explained to Hitler that the trembling of his left hand and gradual loss of vision were the result of the poisons in the anti-flatulence pills and that it was irresponsible of Dr Morell to have made them freely available to be eaten like sweets.[1] Hitler would hear no evil spoken against Dr Morell, upon whom he was now so dependent that he ignored the advice of Brandt and Hasselbach. Hitler thought that their only intention was to get rid of Morell and, since they knew that he, Hitler, could not live without Morell, they must be aiming indirectly to get rid of him too.

The extent to which he believed this became clear to me at a luncheon at the Reich Chancellery in March 1945. From now on Hitler did not want Brandt and Hasselbach at FHQ. His distrust of Dr Brandt grew when he heard reports allegedly made by Brandt as to the hopelessness of the war. The fact that Dr Brandt had sent his wife Anni from Berlin to Liebenzell, and not to the Berghof, a day before the Americans arrived at Liebenzell, earned him the death sentence.

On 16 March 1945 Johanna Wolf and I were scheduled to provide Hitler with company at the table for lunch. As always the table was carefully laid, the lamp standard switched on and the curtains drawn, hiding the ruins of the Hotel Kaiserhof and the Propaganda Ministry. We sat waiting in the Staircase Room far longer than usual. Finally, probably around 0230, the servant Linge opened the door and announced: 'The chief is coming.' Hitler followed him in with

---

1 In her notes, Schroeder recorded: 'In the autumn of 1944 the boss took "anti-flatulence tablets" containing two strong poisons including belladonna. I remember Dr Giesing saying that all the health problems Hitler suffered came from taking these poisons on a regular basis. Hitler complained about his serious loss of vision . . . I remember how often he used to scratch himself.'

THE END AT THE BERGHOF

⌐ worried from his dining room about nnnh illy and gave vent to
his anger as soon as we had sat down:

> I am very annoyed with Albrecht.[2] Eva is right in disliking him.
> As soon as I do not see to everything myself, nothing gets done. I
> expressly ordered that the new winding entrances to the bunker in
> Voss-Strasse should have iron underpinning. I asked Albrecht if it
> had been done. He said yes. Now I have just seen that the entrances
> have only been given a concrete foundation, which is senseless. I
> really cannot rely on anybody any more. It makes me ill. If I did not
> have Morell I would not be able to look after everything myself, and
> then I would be in a complete mess. And those idiots Brandt and
> Hasselbach wanted to get rid of Morell! What would have become
> of them the gentlemen failed to ask themselves. If anything happens
> to me Germany is lost, for I have no successor!

This talk of no successor was not new. After Hess went to Britain in
1941, Göring was the official successor, but Hitler did not think he
was capable. I once argued with him when he said there was nobody
who could be his successor. He replied that Hess had gone mad,
Göring had lost the sympathy of the people, and the Party did not
want Himmler. When I told him that Himmler was the name being
mentioned by many people, he began to get annoyed. Himmler
was a person with absolutely no feeling for music. To my objection
that that was not so important nowadays, for the arts could supply
competent people, he retorted that it was not so simple to do that or
he would already have done it. From that I deduced that in Hitler's

---

2 Alwin-Broder Albrecht (b. 18.9.1903 St Peter/Freisland). 27.6.1938–30.6.1939 as
Korvettenkapitän deputised for Jesko von Puttkamer as Hitler's liaison officer to
the German navy; 30.6.1939 following an altercation between Raeder and Hitler
discharged from Wehrmacht service but retained the right to wear naval uniform;
1.7.1939 appointed personal adjutant to Hitler in rank of NSKK Oberführer,
where he had responsibility amongst other things for building work at the Reich
Chancellery; 1.5.1945 disappeared without trace.

opinion none of the proposed candidates would be considered as his successor. At the suggestion of Himmler he became angry and asked what had possessed me to say such a thing. It hurt his vanity that those of us who knew Himmler and himself should place Himmler on a par with him. He left offended, saying: 'Keep on racking your brains for who should be my successor.' On the subject of Morell, Hitler also stated that 'without Morell he would be all out of joint and lost', but towards the end of the war he did eventually become suspicious of Morell, and feared being poisoned by him. On 22 April 1945, Dr Morell was expelled from Berlin.

During my internment at Ludwigsburg Camp Dr Brandt arranged a brief meeting with me. He told me that the Americans had put him into a cell with Morell. He had told Morell: 'You swine!' which signified that he held Morell responsible for having ruined Hitler's health. This would certainly not have been done on purpose. What was Morell to do when, as time went by, medicaments lost their potency on Hitler, who then demanded that Morell kept him able to work? Ultimately there was probably nothing else he could do but give in to Hitler's wishes. Whether Morell took into account the possible side-effects is not known . . .

Albert Bormann, Martin Bormann's brother, had meanwhile arrived at Obersalzberg from Berlin and was living in the Berchtesgadener Hof with his very pregnant wife. On the morning of 23 April 1945 he was summoned to Göring's property above the Berghof. Afterwards Albert Bormann dictated to me the content of this conversation. Göring had asked him where the records of the situation conferences were kept. 'They must be destroyed immediately', he said, 'or the German people will discover that for the last two years they have been led by a madman!' Albert Bormann told me to type a string of dots in place of this sentence. He believed that Göring was intent on being Hitler's successor.

That same evening the Berghof was suddenly surrounded by armed SS. Nobody was permitted to leave the house. My first thought was that Himmler had staged a coup The men of the *SS-Begleitkommando* stood at the inner doors of the Berghof vestibule with machineguns at the ready and magazine pouches on their belts. Amongst them, with Stoic calm, was Konteradmiral von Puttkamer, a thick cigar clamped between his teeth. Nobody could explain why the Berghof had been surrounded. Some hours later after many unsuccessful telephone enquiries, an orderly managed to discover from the SS barracks higher up that Göring had been arrested. Radio communication to Berlin was no longer possible.

Wednesday 25 April 1945 was a sunny spring day with a cloudless sky. There were still some patches of snow lying around, but it was not cold. I had booked an appointment for 1000 with Bernhardt hairdressers in the Platterhof hotel. There was an acute danger of air attack but I decided to ignore it and stay in bed. In recent days aircraft had overflown the Berghof but not bombed. Towards 0930 the early warning alarm sounded. Straight away the sirens howled and at once American bombers* appeared over the Hohe Göll mountain and dropped bombs. One exploded nearby. I grabbed my handbag and coat and ran into Johanna Wolf's room, telling her to get to cover quickly. Without waiting I ran down the steps of the old building, or rather I flew down under the air pressure, to the bunker entrance only a few metres across the courtyard where sixty steps led down into the refuge. The second bomb fell at the side of the old house where our rooms were located and destroyed the stairway. Probably nobody had seriously considered that the Berghof would ever be attacked, and thus all were taken by surprise and many tumbled into the bunker only half dressed.

A half hour later the second wave arrived. The major attack on the Berghof began. The bombs rained down, many directly on the bunker. The explosions echoed eerily against the rocky mountainside. At each hit I ducked involuntarily. The technical installations

---

* The planes were actually from the RAF, 617 Squadron. (TN)

of the bunker, so highly praised as secure, stopped working. The lighting and ventilation failed, and water began to enter the bunker by way of the steps. We feared that Frau Fegelein, who was within a week or so of giving birth, would miscarry. The chaos and fear were indescribable.

We left the bunker eventually at about 1430, slowly plodding up the sixty steps into the daylight. A picture of appalling destruction greeted us. The Berghof had been badly damaged. The walls still stood (only one side had been burst open) but the metal roof hung in ribbons. Doors and windows had disappeared. Inside the house the floor was thickly covered with debris and much of the furniture had been demolished. All the ancillary buildings had been destroyed, the paths scrambled to rubble, trees felled at the root. Nothing green remained, the scene was a crater landscape.[3]

Since there was nothing habitable, Greta Fegelein and Herta Schneider moved into Eva Braun's bunker, Johanna Wolf and I into Hitler's. A few days later Herta and Greta, after spending the intervening period packing, left by lorry and car from Hitler's ready-vehicle park on the Berg for Garmisch, where Herta lived. They had filled many trunks with Eva Braun's clothing and left them at Schloss Fischhorn near Zell am See where there was an SS post. A short while before, Eva Braun had written to her sister: 'We await hourly the end. We do not intend to fall alive into the hands of the enemy,' and she concluded with the hope that Greta 'should have no worries, she would see her husband again.' Here Eva was either mistaken, or she wished to put her sister's mind at rest.

A day or so later Johanna Wolf went by car to Miesbach to ask friends if they would put us up temporarily. Two men from the

---

3 The first wave of bombers which came in over the Hohe Göll took out the flak and smoke batteries, the second wave dropped no less than 1,232 tons of bombs. The bunkers and underground galleries, up to a hundred metres down, were largely undamaged, and of the 3,500 potential victims in the area at the time, only six were killed. Seidler and Zeigert, *Die Führerhauptquartiere*, Herbig, p.270.

SS *Hauptmann* Willhelm Weiße and his known at the Berghof mentioned the possibility of getting false papers for us, also possible lodgings. Meanwhile Schaub arrived and without a word set about clearing Hitler's safe in the Führer-study. On the terrace of the Berghof he put a few cans of petrol to work burning letters, files, memoranda, books, etc. He only allowed a lad[4] from FHQ to help him; everybody else he deliberately ignored. He exchanged no pleasantries with us, no message from the boss, nothing of what was happening. Schaub's bonfire below a leaden sky made a miserable impression.

When Schaub disappeared into the ruins of the Berghof for a brief while, I had a closer look at what he was burning. A shoebox filled with Geli Raubal's correspondence caught my eye. Unfortunately I took only a single letter from the carefully assembled batch with male handwriting. It was however conclusive and set out clearly and distinctly the situation in which Geli had found herself. I also took a bundle of Hitler's architectural plans, which I hid from Schaub and retained. A short distance away from the bonfire, where the compacted snow had heaped up against the terrace wall, was an A4-size binder burnt at the edges similar to an old-fashioned accounts ledger. It had a white label affixed to the cover with the typed title 'Idea for and construction of the Greater German Reich'. Unfortunately I left this where it was.

Albert Bormann lived with his wife, who had given birth during the bombing raid, in the Berchtesgadener Hof, as did Schaub. They only came up to the Berghof to organise food and alcohol. Schaub also brought a friend, Hilde Marzelewski, a dancer from the Berlin 'Metropol'. On 29 April it was announced in a radio broadcast that

---

4 This 'lad' was actually thirty-year old SS-Untersturmführer Heinrich Doose (b. 1.7.1912 Kiel, d. 16.1.1952 Piding). From 1937 with the *SS-Begleitkommando* and Schaub's driver; had previously been the driver for generals Burgdorf and Maisel and was present at the suicide of Rommel; on 21.4.1945 flew from Berlin to Ainring and brought Schaub from Hitler's flat in Munich to the Berghof for the work of destruction; afterwards took Schaub's family to Kitzbühl/Tirol; 2.6.1945 arrested by CIC at Berchtesgaden; 7.4.1948 released from internment.

Hitler would not leave Berlin. At last it was clear to me that all was lost. Albert Bormann told the men of the *SS-Begleitkommando*, 'Do not lose courage, it is not the end.' I asked myself what else it could possibly be.

When Hitler's death was announced on 1 May 1945 the change occurred in a manner scarcely to be described. Chaos broke out on the Obersalzberg. People from Berchtesgaden stormed the farm and cleared it, dragging off animals and breaking open stockpiles of potatoes. From the Bechsteinhaus, the former guest house for state visitors, and Speer's house, the native population removed not only the articles which were easily transportable but also all the furniture. Nothing was left in the Platterhof hotel hairdresser's shop.

In the cavernous Berghof bunkers where we were living strange women appeared, possibly friends of the Kripo officers, and made off with full containers. The police officers so previously devoted to law and order, the house staff and SS men of the *Begleitkommando*, all were suddenly transformed and unrecognisable. After clearing the Berghof kitchen of rubble, house administrator Mittelstrasser made off with a loaded lorry. His wife followed him a few days later after extensive packing. They were not heard from again. The cook Blüthgen, a previously demure young girl, had risen to absolute power. Previously clumsy and dim, she matured overnight. Negus, the Scotch terrier so adored by Eva Braun but loathed by everybody else because he growled at everybody and nibbled at their boots, slunk unnoticed and abandoned through the ruins. He had not been badly treated before, but now he was just another stray.

Negus was symbolic of the change that had come over the place; I felt alone and abandoned too, incapable of deciding my next move. The Pension Posthof at Hintersee near Berchtesgaden had long been reserved for employees and members of the adjutancy and Führer-household in Berlin. Food and drink were sent there for them. Albert Bormann had arranged rooms for Johanna Wolf and myself in this pension. He kept insisting that I should come at once, but I preferred to wait for Johanna firm, Qui, the Annelii will began to close in he was suddenly of the opinion 'that it was not good for everybody to be concentrated in one place. It would be better if everybody took it upon themselves to find their own accommodation.' But where? I had neither the means to take off, nor anywhere to go after so many years cut off from the world in Hitler's circle. So I stayed at the Berghof, living in the bunker.

The Berghof staff wanted to ship out the furniture and I contacted Albert Bormann at the Berchtesgadener Hof to obtain his agreement.[5] I also mentioned to him the intention of the Kripo (*Kriminalpolizei*) people to blow up the bunker rooms where Hitler's private art collection was stored. Boxes of hand grenades were already placed at the bunker entrance. I considered it madness to destroy these valuable paintings. Albert Bormann gave me instructions and authority to remove them and give everybody a note of what I had removed. Meanwhile the Kripo officials had begun destroying everything they could lay their hands on in the bunkers. In Eva Braun's bunker I surprised them smashing her valuable porcelain. These bore her insignia, painted by Sophie Stork, a monogram in the form of a four-leafed clover designed by Dr Karl Brandt. When I expressed my horror, they told me that 'everything had to be destroyed which indicated the existence of Eva Braun'. What remained of her wardrobe, hats, dresses, shoes, etc., everything in fact which indicated a woman's presence, was burnt on the terrace. Photo and film albums of Eva Braun with Hitler were senselessly cremated. The Kripo officials even ripped out the fly-leaf of any book with her name on it. It was pure madness, but apparently Schaub had the dead Hitler's orders to go through with it. Even the valuable silverware was to be destroyed, but here at least

---

5 In her notes Schroeder wrote: 'I obtained his permission that the girls should have some of the furniture. He had no idea what to do about the paintings. I was to give everybody a note of what I was taking and remove them myself.'

somebody saw sense and on 5 May an SS lorry arrived to cart away the silver, the carpets, tapestries and paintings.

It came about thus. That same evening Fegelein's adjutant Hannes Göhler[6] suddenly appeared. I told him the story and expressed my disquiet. I mentioned that they were going to destroy all the paintings. He shared my opinion that it would be unforgivable and called up the lorry next morning to remove the paintings etc. to Fischhorn. I collected the most valuable pieces of artwork, Eva's silver cutlery and sculptures and so forth in the bunker rooms and got the *SS-Begleitkommando* men to load them on the lorry. There were some very large paintings, including a Bordone and a Tintoretto, which were difficult to carry down the snowy southern slope now that the stairway to the road was unusable. The SS men were not slow to explain all the difficulties involved – so much for discipline! The lorry eventually arrived at Altaussee near Salzburg. Dr Emmerich Pöchmüller, during the Second World War director-general of the Austrian salt mines and charged with the safekeeping of art treasures, said some years later in a conversation with Henriette von Schirach: 'At the last moment just before the Americans arrived, they sent me a part of Hitler's private collection from the Obersalzberg!' Amongst the invaluable treasures salted away at Altaussee since 1944 were those which Hitler had scheduled for the planned museum at Linz, mainly paintings by nineteenth-century German artists, but also very important works by Dutch, Italian and French painters, together with furniture, sculptures and artistic handicrafts.

Hitler considered Greece and Rome to have been the cradle of culture. It was there that the concepts of cosmos, spirit, nature and science had first found expression. He frequently made known his satisfaction that through his travels to Rome and Florence it had been possible for him to admire the immortal masterpieces which he had only known in the past from photographs. He rejected Italian

---

6 Johannes Göhler, SS-Sturmbannführer from 21.12.1944.

modernism. He found it most lively related to Impressionism and Expressionism. This 'artless art' – his own term – was in his opinion the work of the Jews. They had made a great hoo-ha about this garbage so as to bump up the price while keeping for themselves only old masters. He did not think much of most contemporary German artists although he did frequently buy their works, even those he did not like, in order to give them some encouragement. 'Our modern artists', he said, 'can never give the same attention to detail, nor have the patience, as those of the great art epochs.' Here he meant the Antique and Romantic epochs: he rejected the Renaissance because it was too closely associated with the cult of Christianity.

Art dealers knew that Hitler was not interested in anything up to and including the fourteenth century. He left Göring to look out for Early and Late Gothic. All paintings obtained by Hitler through art dealers were paid for above board. The money came from the so-called Postage Stamp Fund devised by post minister Ohnesorge. Every stamp bearing Hitler's image brought him a small royalty, especially special stamps with his head commemorating a Nuremberg rally, art exhibitions, the annexations of Austria and the Sudetenland, and his birthdays. The journal of art purchases was kept by Schaub under lock and key although I made the entries in it.

Hitler's plans with regard to building art galleries were far-reaching. Every town should have a small picture gallery. Linz would have the finest one. Hitler's passion for Linz was extraordinary. He had also planned a huge museum for the city, with a hall for each individual century. The paintings would not be crowded together as they are at the Louvre – 'touching each other', as he said – and the individual halls would have furniture of the period. The Linz museum was one of his favourite conversation pieces at evening tea.

Hitler had a true passion for architecture. He had read a great deal of specialist literature and knew all epochs in great detail. He had little feeling for the Romanesque style and rejected Gothic out of hand because it was contaminated with Christian mysticism. His admiration was focused on the Baroque and its creations in Dresden and Würzburg. It is superfluous to mention his enthusiasm for the new German style, for he himself had been the force behind it, although the true creator of the neo-Greek Classic style had been Professor Troost. After the architect's death, Hitler laid a wreath on his grave at each anniversary.

Hitler's knowledge of architecture was astounding. He knew by heart the measurements and ground plans of all important buildings in the world. In his opinion the architecture of Paris and Budapest towered over all other capital cities. During the war he said more than once: 'that it would be his happiest day when he could cast off his uniform and devote himself to matters of art'. He had worked out a gigantic programme for the reconstruction of cities destroyed by war and for artistic monuments. He took pride in his order:

> ... that every historic building is to be photographed in colour inside and out: and it is to be done so thoroughly that future architects and artists will have exact files to work from, for the culturally irreplaceable heritage of earlier times must be rebuilt, and rebuilt so true to the original as only people can. And colour photographs make that possible!

In his enthusiasm for his own ideas he co-opted architects for talks. He would sketch out for them what he had in mind. I have seen architects and engineers of renown staggered by his ability and imagination. Even in the war he could always find time to debate architecture and art. Hitler's plans for postwar Berlin and Hamburg were simply immense. Whenever he declared: 'I will make Berlin into the finest city in the world!' he would straighten up, and his voice and gestures dispelled all doubts. The idea of rebuilding Germany lent Hitler new, unexpected vitality even when he was spent physically. If he returned from a taxing situation conference exhausted, he would quickly find reserves of energy if a technical person invited him to look over new building plans and models. In February 1945 Professor Hermann Giesler brought the great model of Linz to the Reich Chancellery cellars. Hitler would often stand before this model and tell people (I remember particularly Dr Ley and Kaltenbrunner) how he would rebuild Linz. He also planned for the city a round porcelain hall, all in white and gold.

The two SS men from the Berlin *Hauptamt* brought false identity papers for Johanna Wolf and myself. Upon receipt I destroyed everything bearing my true name. It was not much, for I had lost my papers with the trunk in the Börnersdorf air crash. I even threw out my leather jewellery box with my initials 'C.S.' so unthinking had I become. I waited daily for Johanna Wolf, but for understandable reasons she failed to return. The next time I saw her was in internment, but they always kept us separated there. The house staff gradually left the bunker one after another. The *SS-Begleitkommando* wanted to drive to Linz to link up with Sepp Dietrich who was carrying on the war more or less by himself. They made spasmodic attempts to obtain fuel for the journey and ammunition. Since I was still undecided as to my future they urged me to join them. But what should I do amongst fighting troops? I could not contact anybody for help or advice, even the telephone lines to Hintersee were down. No vehicles were available and it had started to snow again. A thick layer of snow had settled over the damaged road. It required real athleticism to reach the road over the ruined stairway. Some odd types I had never seen before, probably attached to the police squad, had camped in the bunker, boozing and smoking. Any trace of discipline had long gone.

When news came through that the American armoured spearhead was already at Chiemsee, the only possibility open to me to get away from the Berghof was to go with the lorry taking the paintings to Schiffhorn in Austria. I turned down the offer by August Körbers of the *SS-Begleitkommando* to join his men in their attempt to find the German troops still resisting. I cast a despairing last look at the ruin of the Berghof. Ertl, an old police officer, must have noticed my misery, for he attempted to console me as I climbed into the lorry. During the drive I realised that the time for weighing up the possibilities was now past. I had to decide either to keep going for Austria or get out at Hintersee. As I was still hoping for advice from Schaub and Albert Bormann, and I knew they were staying at Pension Post, I decided for the latter. Upon my arrival I found them both celebrating their escape with champagne. Hitler's dentist, Professor Blaschke, was with them, a slim man, scrupulous, quiet and pleasant. He was a reformer and if not actually anti-alcohol then at least a strict moderate. With a look of disgust he pointed to the bottle of champagne on the table and said: 'That is responsible for much!' He was deflated as I was, for he had not reckoned it would end like this.

Seeing that Schaub and Albert Bormann were only interested in their own futures and on getting away from Hintersee at the earliest opportunity, I remonstrated furiously: 'It is a scandal for you to look after yourselves and leave us to our fate.' This hurt Albert Bormann and upset him very much, for he was a soft and sensitive man. He said only that he could not carry on his life with his surname. Schaub and he then disappeared quickly, leaving me alone. Augst, the employee in Albert Bormann's Chancellery responsible for arranging lodgings in the Pension Post, and who in earlier timers had been very friendly and forthcoming, now made it plain that he was extremely displeased to see me and said: 'What, now you are coming along too? There are no more single rooms, all that has stopped!'

Here too the sudden change in attitude and tone. Along with Frau von Puttkamer, wife of the naval adjutant, her children and mother, Frau Dönitz, wife of Admiral Dönitz, with her sister Frau Linge, wife of Hitler's manservant, and children, a remarkable community had developed. It also included Schaub's female friend Hilde Marzelewski, a dancer from the Berlin 'Metropol' and Erich Kempka's ex-wife, whom he had divorced on Hitler's orders for her having been a prostitute before the marriage. Kempka had rented for her an apartment on the Würmtenheim and subsequently remained in touch with her, and in due course she had filtered down to Pension Post at Hintersee. She was responsible for causing some very unpleasant scenes there.

My stay became daily more unpleasant. Although the hotelier had been paid to place the establishment at our disposal and supply food, alcohol and cigarettes, the food suddenly vanished. No explanation was forthcoming although the hotelier had definitely had it in his possession. Food grew increasingly scarce and none was on sale at Hintersee. Our daily fare was mushy peas. Meanwhile the Americans had arrived at Berchtesgaden and the town hall had been evacuated to house a company of US troops. At Hintersee we all crowded together in the smaller annexe. There was always an excited situation whenever one of the *SS-Begleitkommando* leaders appeared from hiding in the mountain refuges. They were a thorn in the side of the new hotelier, who made it unmistakeably plain every day that he wanted us all gone. The atmosphere became daily more threatening and worrisome.

We had heard that Gaullists and black French troops were looting and robbing in the Berchtesgaden area. One day two armed Gaullists burst into our room. They rummaged around, opened all drawers without a word and finally decided on two small paintings I had brought from the Berghof and hung on the wall. They also relieved our baggage of two small radios, but failed to look under the bed where I had stowed the trunks I packed at the Berghof, thus leaving something for the Americans to loot later. Next morning, 22 May 1945 towards 0700, there was a knock on my door. A CIC man said he was looking for Albert Bormann and Fräulein Fusser. The former was hiding out in the Berchtesgaden area under the name Roth. This they knew. Then he asked: 'And who are you?' Undoubtedly the hotelier had already told him. It gave me a nasty feeling of apprehension.[7]

---

7 From the CIC report it would appear that the informant was another guest. The person also informed the Americans about Erich Kempka, who was then arrested

That same afternoon another CIC officer came for me. When his female assistant went through my handbag, removing all the contents, I became enraged, at which the officer told me: 'You will have to get used to that kind of thing.' After my first interrogation by Mr Albrecht,[8] this officer told me in good German: 'You are a wanted person. But at least you talk naturally, whereas the Gauleiters and ministers captured to date speak in newspaper phraseology. I shall consider whether to spare you or tell the fourteen journalists in the next room about you.' That day he still felt sympathy for me, but after a few days journalists from the periodicals *Time* and *Life* showed up, amongst them the well-known Jack Fleischner. Following the interrogations I made plans for the future with Ilse Lindhoff, with whom I shared a room (she had been secretary to Hauptmann Wiedemann, Hitler's former adjutant, and had married one of the *SS-Begleitkommando* officers). If we were to be persuaded into 'collaborating' I wanted to find a room for us both in Berchtesgaden to get away from the awful conditions at Hintersee. At that time it was not permitted to stray further than six kilometres. Ilse suggested we could buy a horse and cart and head for Lüneburg Heath where her in-laws lived. It was a nice plan, but nothing came of it.

On 28 May 1945 I was bundled into a jeep by two American soldiers together with my two cases and an Erica typewriter. At the CIC offices in Berchtesgaden some of the former FHQ stenotyists were transcribing my shorthand notebooks. The material was innocuous, short letters accompanying a gift of bacon from Hitler to his sisters. He had advised them: 'under no circumstances to eat the bacon raw!' I realised that years of internment might now lie ahead.

---

at Hintersee on 18 June 1945.

8 Lt Erich Albrecht was a German who had once worked at the Reich Ministry of Economics. He had emigrated to the United States as a Mormon.

Appendix

The following is an extract from the interrogation protocol of **Fräulein Schroeder** held at Berchtesgaden on 22 May 1945 and conducted by **Erich Albrecht**, an officer of the US Counter-Intelligence Corps. (The original version can be seen on microfilm at the University of Pennsylvania, Charles Patterson Van Pelt Library, 46M-11FU, US Army 101st Airborne Division.)

Mr Albrecht: When did your employment with Hitler begin?

Schroeder: I was available permanently for him from 1933. Previous to that I worked for him when needed. Fräulein Wolf was with him from 1929. A Fräulein Daranowski came additionally in 1938.

Mr Albrecht: In the last years of the war what was an average workday?

Schroeder: We had no set hours. We were always on call. Hitler was very much a night person and generally did not start work until the evening. Basically we sat up all night. It was really the opposite of normal. At the end in Berlin we would get to bed around eight in the morning. We would start off with the situation conferences which were held at night. After the night conference Hitler would always take tea with his intimate circle. This was composed of his female secretaries, Frau Christian, Fräulein Wolf, Frau Junge then a doctor, either Dr Morell or another one – at the end Dr Morell did not attend because his health was not up to it – plus a personal adjutant, usually Gruppenführer Albert Bormann. Hitler used these sessions to relax. Politics was not discussed at tea. Therefore Hitler never invited officers with whom he had to work, for otherwise the conversation would always come round to military business. He wanted to get his mind off the battle maps. He often used to say that 'in his mind's eye he could only see maps'. Earlier on, tea used to finish sometime between five and seven in the morning. Then he would go to bed if he didn't have reports to read. Hitler would usually get up at eleven. He did not sleep much. He would take breakfast, then Herr Schaub would come with the air raid reports and inform him which officers had been told to attend the conferences.

Mr Albrecht: At these conferences would Hitler make decisions about air defence?

Schroeder: In the presence of Herr Schaub he would probably just grumble. Hitler never gave Schaub instructions because he was not part of the military. Hitler was not satisfied

199

with the handling of air defence. He had the feeling that it was not being done properly, that we had the means, but it was not being used.

Mr Albrecht: Hitler would not give Schaub orders?

Schroeder: No, there would have been no point. Schaub was an old factotum and Hitler did not esteem him greatly. He used to say: 'I wouldn't have Schaub if there was another chief adjutant.'

Mr Albrecht: When did Hitler deal with his personal correspondence? Did he dictate his letters personally?

Schroeder: Only letters of thanks or congratulations. Towards the end he didn't dictate letters.

Mr Albrecht: What was your main job as secretary?

Schroeder: Early on Hitler used to dictate his big speeches for me to type directly into the machine.

Mr Albrecht: Did he edit them afterwards?

Schroeder: He used to correct them himself a lot.

Mr Albrecht: Did anyone else go over them?

Schroeder: No.

Mr Albrecht: Even Goebbels had no influence on the contents?

Schroeder: No, he just provided statistics if they were called for. Hitler composed all his own speeches. He had a very good style and would keep putting finishing touches to them to the last moment.

Mr Albrecht: Did Hitler dictate orders personally to the front troops?

Schroeder: No, that was mostly done by the Wehrmacht.

Mr Albrecht: Apart from letters of thanks and so on did Hitler have personal correspondence with friends?

Schroeder: No, he always emphasised that that was his great strength, even in the early days, to have written no letters: if they had fallen into the wrong hands they could have been exploited.

Mr Albrecht: You were present at mealtimes?

Schroeder: Towards the end only at lunch and the teas at night.

Mr Albrecht: What things were discussed at lunch?

Schroeder: They were not of a political nature. People talked about architecture, theatre, music, the German language, about things to be done in the future, about his plans.

Mr Albrecht: Was rebuilding the cities discussed?

Schroeder: Yes.

Mr Albrecht: Whose job would that have been?

Schroeder: Professor Frick had already started on it. Professor Giesler was to complete it. In the end Speer would have taken it over because it was his province.

Mr Albrecht: There was no general rebuilding plan?

Schroeder: No. Medical matters were also talked about at lunch. Professor Morell was very interested in hormone research. This subject also interested Hitler. He thought there was still a lot to be done in this field. Hitler was also interested in nutrition.

Mr Albrecht: Racial questions belonged in the political arena?

Schroeder: Occasionally the subject was touched upon. I never gave it much thought because the theory has a lot of holes in it. Many women have deceived their husbands. I often told Hitler that.

Mr Albrecht: Could one debate freely with Hitler?

Schroeder: Yes, up to a point. I knew where my limits lay.

Mr Albrecht: Was Fräulein (Eva) Braun present at these mealtimes?

Schroeder: Fräulein Braun was only in Berlin towards the end. She attended occasionally.

Mr Albrecht: Did Hitler look on her as his wife?

Schroeder: He treated her that way.

Mr Albrecht: He looked on her as such?

Schroeder: Yes, I said so.

Mr Albrecht: There were no children?

Schroeder: No. Some years ago I read something about that in an American paper. A lot of what was said is untrue. Leni Riefenstahl was mentioned once. There is a kind of woman who does not refute rumours like that. Leni Riefenstahl was that kind of woman, she used it for her own purposes.

Mr Albrecht: What type of relationship was there between Hitler and Renate Müller?

Schroeder: There was none. Hitler thought she was a good actress because she looked the part of the perfect German maiden. But he had no personal relationship with Renate Müller. Towards the end Hitler would not spend even half an hour at the meal table. Usually Reichsleiter Bormann would report after the meal. Lunch was often taken around four or five in the afternoon.

Mr Albrecht: Did Hitler have no personal correspondence?

Schroeder: No, on principle. He wrote a short letter to his sister when he sent her some bacon he had received as a gift from Spain. He had no sense of family. He admitted it himself. Hitler had two sisters. His full sister was Paula Hitler who lived in Vienna. His half-sister Angela Hitler, widow of Raubal, married Professor Hammitzsch in Dresden.

Mr Albrecht: What was the reason for his having such a poor family relationship?

Schroeder: Well, first of all he didn't have any real siblings. His father married three times. The father grew up an orphan. He worked his own way up. He learned the craft of shoemaker in Austria then went to school in the city. In the end he ran a Customs office and got himself a property.

Mr Albrecht: Did Hitler talk about his childhood?

Schroeder: I made lots of notes about that. I left them in my luggage at the Reich Chancellery in Berlin. I took more interest in his life than his family. Supper was around nine or ten. When we were at FHQ, the secretaries attended, in Berlin only Fräulein Braun did. Fräulein Braun is not very healthy, she is very delicate.

Mr Albrecht: Was she ill?

Schroeder: Not actually ill, but very delicate and tired. The Berlin climate did not suit her.

Mr Albrecht: At the nightly tea was Hitler a lively talker?

Schroeder: Yes.

Mr Albrecht: When was the last tea?

Schroeder: On the night of 19 April 1945.

Mr Albrecht: Was Hitler very depressed in the final days?

Schroeder: The final days were from the beginning of April, I would say.

Mr Albrecht: In September 1944 he was laid up a long while in bed!

Schroeder: That was as a result of the attempt on his life on 20 July 1944. All the officers present suffered severe concussion and ear injuries. Hitler was the only one not confined to bed. At that time I used to dine with him alone. He was very depressed in the days leading up to 20 July 1944. He had a premonition, he felt that an attempt was being planned on his life. He even told me once and in these words: 'I note there is something afoot.' On the day before he did not feel all that good. When I was dining with him alone he said: 'Nothing must happen to me now, for then there would be nobody there to take over the leadership.'

Mr Albrecht: Whom was Hitler considering as his successor?

Schroeder: Not Göring or Himmler. After Hess went, Göring was automatically next. But Hitler didn't think he was capable. Once I argued with him when he told me he had no successor. He said that the first one, Hess, had gone mad. The second, Göring, had lost the confidence of the people, and the Party did not want the third, Himmler. When I told him that Himmler was being mentioned a lot amongst the people he got very upset. He said that Himmler had no ear for music. When I protested that in these times it was not so important, able people could be drafted in to handle the area of the arts, Hitler would not have it. He said it was not so easy to get capable people, otherwise he would have done so. From that I inferred that in Hitler's view none of those envisaged could be considered his successor

Mr Albrecht: Which other people came under consideration?

Schroeder: Nobody. He got very indignant at my assertion that Himmler's name was being bandied a lot amongst the common people. He said – something out of character for him – 'whatever possessed you to say something like that?' It hurt his pride that we who knew him and Himmler should put him on a par with Himmler. He went out that midday offended and said: 'Keep people busy thinking about who my successor should be.' On 20 July 1944 I did not expect to be invited to dine after the attempt. To my surprise I was sent for at 1500 hours. I was amazed at how fresh and lively Hitler looked when he came up to me. He told me how his manservants had reacted to the attempt. Linge had raged, Arndt had wept. Then he said, 'Believe me, this is the turning point for Germany, now it will be all downhill again: I am pleased that the filthy swine have unmasked themselves.' On 20 July 1944 I told him that he could not possibly receive the Duce. He replied: 'On the contrary, I must receive him, for what would the world press write if I didn't?' Shortly after lunch he left the camp to greet Mussolini. Finally at the end of September 1944 Hitler had to confine himself to bed on account of the bomb plot of 20 July 1944.

Index